Long Trail to the Promised Land

By Michael L. Billingsley

A15 Publishing
5219 Monticello Avenue #5037
Williamsburg, VA 23188-9998
www.A15publishing.com

ISBN 978-1-970155-16-7

FIRST PRINTING

Dedication

To the women in my life who preserved the ideas and materials for this story, I am very grateful. My grandmother, Florence Edith Stenger Waugh, My great-aunt, Cassie Bell Stenger, and my mother, Patricia Ann Waugh Billingsley. These ladies were born and raised in Council Grove, Kansas, as the second and third generation descendants of Jacob and Charlotte Stenger, an immigrant German couple. They endured the hardships of Army life in Texas and New Mexico before and during the American Civil War, eventually finding their "Promised Land" in a small town in eastern Kansas on the Santa Fe Trail.

Thanks also for the infinite patience of my wonderful wife, Diane, who suffered through several years of my fits and starts in writing this story. Thanks also to my good friends, Bill and Nancy, whose rich historical perspective and similar family background, further inspired my writing.

Also, special thanks to my classmate John and other authors and who kindly reviewed my text and offered much valuable advice.

Michael L. Billingsley

Forward

I suppose I was a little unusual growing up, in that I was more interested in our ancestral genealogy than anyone else in my family. I was raised in part by a grandmother of German descent, who didn't speak German, but used a lot of terms and idioms that I later found to be derived from German customs. I had heard stories about my German ancestors since I was a small child. When I was in my twenties, parts of an old diary were found in my great aunt's attic trunk, written in German before the mid 1850's, changing to English before the American Civil War. The broken English portions were more easily read, and some of the German writing had been translated. The tales were mostly entries of travel and daily life on the plains and trails of west Texas, New Mexico, Colorado, and Kansas. A number of family letters and accounts, along with scarce military records were also used to reconstruct these events.

My mother and grandmother were born and raised in Council Grove, Kansas, where my great-great grandfather, a German immigrant, who, after spending several years in the U.S. Army in Texas and New Mexico, adopted a Santa Fe Trail landmark as his permanent home. Council Grove was his base for more than twenty years as a soldier, wagon outfitter, teamster, and wagon train guide on the Santa Fe Trail. Council Grove was the "last chance" outfitting and supply base on the long journey to Santa Fe from Independence or Westport Landing (part of present-day Kansas City), the Missouri River points of departure to New Mexico, Oregon, and California.

The family of Jacob and Charlotte Stenger were among those pioneers who helped build America, living much of their lives, "where the rubber meets the road," but more accurately, "where the wagon wheel meets the rut." This is their story, not unique, but instructional for those who may be unfamiliar with the hard lives and sacrifices endured by our not so ancient forbearers. This picture of life on the prairies and deserts of the southwest in the second half of the nineteenth century is not meant to be completely accurate historically, nor a definitive history of my maternal ancestors. It is simply the story of their journey, the daily risks of life on the frontier, the tedium of a slower pace of life, the heartbreak and joy of family life, separation and reunion. Where coincidence and documentation allow, their experiences are woven into the stories of a few of the famous people they encountered. Many of the characters are of necessity fictitious, but some are well-known pioneers and personalities who braved the often-perilous journey on the southwestern trails, or otherwise helped transform New Mexico from a remote Mexican province into a territorial outpost in the westward expansion of America to the Pacific Ocean. Theirs was an important contribution in fulfilling the dream of "Manifest Destiny," a Continental United States of America.

CONTENTS

Chapter I. San Antonio, 1855

Jacob Stenger looked into the bedroom where his wife, Charlotte, was struggling through childbirth. Jacob was nearly beside himself, so excited about the birth of his first child. He thought about the wonder of life about to be brought into the world. Charlotte had been his nurse and comforter in the past. Now he wanted desperately to comfort his young wife in her painful moments. He could barely keep himself from rushing to her side as she moaned and cried out. Frau Schmidt quickly pushed Jacob back into the parlor where he had been nervously pacing. He nearly fell over Gretchen, the German midwife, who was scurrying back and forth from the kitchen after boiling water and preparing clean towels and sheets. She scowled at Jacob, but kept her balance and disappeared into the birthing room. Jacob apologized to Gretchen and continued his pacing. His thoughts drifted back to the circumstances that had brought them to America.

Barely a year before, Charlotte Hagemeister took the chance of her life, crossing many principalities of Germany in the dead of winter, from Detmold to Bremerhaven, and booking passage to America, in order to be reunited with her beloved Jacob. What a horrible Atlantic winter crossing it had been, barely surviving those five weeks of icy storms at sea, frigid and incessantly seasick. Then, banned from entry through the port of New York, with "no more Germans" allowed to enter through the eastern ports that year, she had endured the long trip around Florida to be reunited with Jacob. The port of Galveston, in the new State of Texas, was the first anchorage willing to process the new wave of German and middle-European immigrants.

The immigrants came for many reasons. First, there was political oppression and the threat of war, then poverty and loss of their ancestral property which accompanied the turmoil of the late 1840s in central Europe. There were countless dislocations as a result of the many small revolutions that had followed the loss of the balance of power among the great and small nations of Central Europe. The Austrian Chancellor, Cardinal Metternich, was gone, along with thirty years of peace he had orchestrated after the defeat of Napoleon. Now Prussia and her allies, and Austria and her ally Bavaria, were struggling for regional dominance. For Jacob and Charlotte, it was more personal. Jacob Stenger, a proud young Bavarian soldier, had been wounded in a skirmish with a Prussian patrol in northern Bavaria. His bravery, displayed in the encounter, had been rewarded with the honor of serving in the Guard Corps of Crown Prince Leopold (Maximilian II). The prince soon became King of Bavaria when his Father, King Ludwig, abdicated under political pressure. Jacob was honored at first, but soon developed a desire to leave military life while recovering from his wounds. After much soul searching, he thought he had found his calling as a priest, and he entered seminary in Augsburg, not far from the Bavarian village of Wemding, where he was born, and Eichstatt, where he had attended secondary school, the Gymnasium.

About a year into his training for the priesthood, Jacob had a life changing encounter, meeting Charlotte Hagemeister, a nurse at the Kaserne Kranken Haus, the military hospital in Augsburg. As a military veteran he was eligible for treatment of lingering problems for his old leg injury. The musket-ball wound in his right thigh had not been serious enough for amputation, but he periodically needed removal of migrating metal shards and a few bone fragments working their way to the surface. After minor surgeries, he would have a few days of dressing changes at the hospital. The bandaging was usually done by one the Schwesters, or sisters, the nuns trained as nurses. His favorite nurse was Charlotte, very pretty and charming, and so gentle

2

and kind. Charlotte was not a native Bavarian, but born and raised in the small town of Detmold in the North Rhine-Westphalia region. They were immediately attracted to each other, but both were sworn to lives of chastity by their religious vows. After many months they found themselves hopelessly in love, and decided to renounce their vows and spend the rest of their lives together. They knew they would be scorned by the church, with their families offering little comfort for their decision. They had few options for a happy future in Germany, and decided they should move as far away as possible.

Jacob's pacing in the front room of the house in the German section of San Antonio was reaching a quick tempo, when the wailing of a newborn penetrated his thoughts. He was instantly overwhelmed with excitement, followed by concern for Charlotte. He stood at the door of the birthing room, nervously waiting for the German midwife to come out with the news.

"Gott Sei Dank!" declared the tough little woman as she cracked the door. "It's a boy! Mother and child are fine, Jacob!"

What a glorious thing, Jacob thought to himself, dumbstruck with joy and relief. Jacob was ecstatic at the good news, enjoying for the moment the backslapping from his new friend Paul, a previous German immigrant several years older than Jacob. After a few minutes, Frieda Schmidt opened the door, inviting Jacob to see his wife and new son. Jacob stood frozen for a few seconds as he looked down on his beautiful Charlotte and the newborn at her breast.

Finally, Charlotte said, "Jacob, isn't he wonderful?"

"Oh, yes! You are both so beautiful!" Jacob replied, tears welling up in his eyes.

"What shall we call him, Jacob?" Charlotte asked.

"No, Charlotte, remember that we decided to name him after your poor late father, Wilhelm," Jacob reminded her.

The moment was almost too much for Charlotte, having received the news of her father's passing only six months ago, the letter from her mother only recently arriving two months ago.

"Alright, Jacob, Wilhelm it will be, but he is born an American, and we will call him William." Jacob gently embraced his wife and child for a few minutes, but was invited to wait in the parlor for a while, to allow the midwife to attend to mother and child.

Jacob returned to the company of his fiend, Paul, who had broken out a bottle of Schnapps and two small glasses. Paul Schmidt, originally from Bremen, had been in the Republic of Texas, now a new American State, for nearly a decade. Paul had settled in the growing German quarter of San Antonio. He owned and operated the largest blacksmithing and wagon business in town. Paul had moved to Texas when a German prince, Karl of Somals-Braunfels, had purchased land north of San Antonio and led the first wave of German settlers to the area many years ago under the charter of the Adelsverein, the society for the protection of Germans in Texas. Paul Schmidt had gone to sea as a young man on a merchant ship and had been to Philadelphia on more than one occasion. There he had met other Germans, some from families who had come to America generations before, and was infected with their enthusiasm for this new land and this experiment in freedom, so different from the class system of Europe. Paul had joined thousands of German-speaking people seeking new opportunities in the Texas Republic, now part of the United States.

Jacob and Charlotte had been reunited with Paul's help at the Port of Galveston and a couple of days later reembarked for Indianola, on Matagorda Bay, a day's sailing distance southwest along the Texas coast. From this tiny inlet, many German immigrants began the journey into south central Texas, bound for San Antonio and the Hill Country to the north. Nearly exhausted from her grueling sea voyage, Charlotte was ecstatic to be with Jacob again after more than three years separation. On the trip down the Texas coast to Indianola, there was a lot of catching up to do that their monthly letters had not been able to provide. Jacob had arranged a cabin for himself and Charlotte as a married couple. Paul would take the wagon along the coast to Indianola, and meet them at the docks.

After supper that evening in Galveston, the couple bid good night and boarded the ship for Indianola, due to depart at first light in the morning. They went to their cabin, and made love for hours, making up for lost time after three years of separation.

Charlotte recounted the details of the voyage across the Atlantic.

"Jacob, as you know from my letters, I left my nursing position in Augsburg over six months ago and returned to my parents' home near Cologne. I wanted to spend as much time as possible with my family before coming to America. My parents were getting older, and it was very hard to say goodbye to them and my sisters. They were disappointed to see me go, but gave their blessings. I made my way to Bremerhaven, and with the help of a family friend, booked a cabin on a steamship to New York. The ship was large and fortunately proved to be reliable, even though the weather was horrid. It was brutally cold for much of the Atlantic crossing, and we encountered storms nearly every week, taking nearly five weeks from Bremerhaven. I got over my seasickness after the first week, but some others were ill for the whole voyage. There were even three deaths onboard. When we got to New York, finally, the authorities would not let us go ashore. They have blocked Germans and some other Central Europeans from entering this year. I had planned to take a coastal steamer around Florida anyway, but I felt sorry for some of the other passengers who were forced to sail to Virginia or the Carolinas to enter the country. Some of them had to take wagons overland to get back to New England or Pennsylvania. Anyway, the trip around the eastern coast to here was a lot better. We were allowed to send a letter ahead before leaving New York, so that you would know the day of my arrival. The journey seemed endless, until I saw you standing on the dock. I almost fainted from relief and joy. I love you so much, darling."

Jacob answered, "Charlotte, I love you more than you could ever know. I have been faithful to you always, and I have seen things and been places that I could never have imagined. This is a beautiful land, but so different in many ways from Europe. The dominant culture is English for the most part, but mixed with Spanish and Native American, "Indian" influences. Fortunately, there are a lot of German settlers around San Antonio where we will be living."

Jacob went into detail about his Army experiences, so that she would understand how he ended up in Texas. Charlotte was interested, but it was a lot of information to absorb, and she was tired of traveling. But now she was with her wonderful Jacob again, and she was safe with her soldier, now an American soldier. She had plenty of time to learn to story about how it all came to be. At the moment, sleep was what she needed, safe in Jacob's arms.

Jacob, unable to sleep, mused about how he had arrived in New York in the summer of 1851. Finding no work, and without English language skills, he enlisted in the Army. The Regiment of Mounted Riflemen, based at Jefferson Barracks in St. Louis, on the Mississippi River, was recruiting soldiers, largely European immigrants at the time. The Mounted Rifles had been formed in 1846 to support the opening of the Oregon Trail from Independence, Missouri to the Pacific coast. Their mission had been interrupted by the War with Mexico, where the regiment served gallantly. Returning to St. Louis after that war, the regiment was later sent on a 2,500-mile march to the West Coast, establishing lines of communication to Fort Vancouver and northern California. After basic training at Jefferson Barracks, Jacob was assigned, along with most of his regiment, to various Texas frontier forts, to provide protection against Indian raids on the military supply road from San Antonio to El Paso, Texas. Jacob was at first assigned to a small trail post, west of the Pecos River, which later became Fort Davis. His company was primarily responsible for maintaining the water point and horse and mule replacement stop. They performed some escort and patrol duties for travelers and local settlers in the area, along the raiding routes of the Apache and Comanche tribes from the north and west. Realizing that he could not bring a wife to this remote and desolate post, Jacob soon requested a transfer to San Antonio. There was an opening at the 8th Military District Quartermaster Depot for a German-speaking soldier to help with the procurement of food and forage supplies. The Hill Country north of San Antonio was heavily populated with German settlers, and German speaking soldiers were extremely helpful in dealing with the farmers who sold produce, grain, hay, and livestock to the Army. By mid-1853, Jacob was detailed to duty as a clerk at the Alamo-based quartermaster depot. At that point finally, he could send for Charlotte. Now there was a chance to start their life over in the New World. It had taken six months to arrange her travel, and another three months of travel to Bremerhaven, the voyage across the north Atlantic and finally to Texas.

The couple were met two days later at Indianola on Matagorda Bay by Paul, who had driven the wagon from Houston. Paul Schmidt, Jacob's part-time employer, picked up Jacob and Charlotte and her belongings for the trip to San Antonio. Paul had hired Jacob to help with teams of mules and horses and blacksmithing duties. He made trips to Indianola, a four-day trek to the coast, at least four or five times a year to pick up iron stock and other supplies for his wagon and blacksmithing business. The materials were usually shipped from the East Coast or New Orleans.

Paul and Jacob had first met when Jacob went looking for a part-time job in San Antonio to earn enough money to bring Charlotte to America. The two men had taken to each other right away. Their accents and customs differed a bit, Jacob thinking Paul to be a Dutchman at first, with his low country intonations. Paul had quickly realized the concern, explaining his Jutland-Friesian accent, the coastal dialect of northern Germany. It was certainly different from the High German speech of Hanover and Bavaria. In a way, this dialectic difference would help Jacob perfect his transition to English, the speech product of countless English generations of immigrant Germanic Angles, Jutes, Danes, and Saxons. English was mainly Germanic, with a large measure of Latin and French thrown in.

Charlotte knew about Paul from Jacob's letters, but was still puzzled about the accent. "Paul are you originally from Holland?" she asked.

Paul laughed, explaining, "My German is known as Plattdeutsch, more on the Dutch side, compared to your high German accent, used in the middle and southern sections of the homeland."

Charlotte apologized, not wanting to ask any more embarrassing questions. Paul, sensing her embarrassment, continued,

"Don't worry, Charlotte, we will all have to spend more time practicing our English, and maybe a little Spanish." She smiled at him, acknowledging that the point was well taken.

Paul, short-handed in his San Antonio blacksmithing business, had immediately offered Jacob a part-time job. Jacob had some experience with teams and wagons during his military service in Bavaria. He had always enjoyed working with horses and mules and knew firsthand that no army could prevail without the superior mobility these loyal and dependable animals provided in support of cavalry operations, artillery transport, and supply train operations. Jacob was extremely grateful for the part time job and the small spare bedroom offered to them by Paul and Frieda Schmidt.

Charlotte liked Frieda from their first meeting after arriving at the Schmidt's modest house in the growing German section of San Antonio. The Schmidts had no children and Frieda confessed that she had never been able to conceive. She was very happy in her marriage with Paul, and she had cultivated an active social life in their adopted new home in Texas. She was active in their church and enjoyed during charitable work, especially providing meals for poor families in town. She asked Charlotte about her background as a nurse, and was very interested in how she and Jacob had met and how they had decided to so radically change the course of their lives. Frieda told Charlotte that she completely understood the difficult decisions involved and how wonderful her commitment was to Jacob.

During their first year together, Jacob and Charlotte were happier than ever. Jacob's job at the Alamo was a blessing. He kept normal office hours except for occasional depot inspections or inventory checks. Once a month, he had to attend mounted drill or weapons training. Most Saturdays and a few evenings were spent at Paul's shop. Charlotte helped Frieda Schmidt with her cooking and household chores, and they were becoming good friends. Charlotte's English was getting much better. The Stengers were introduced to other German families by the Schmidts, and their social life was growing. Now they were starting a family and wouldn't be too much longer until they needed a home of their own. They never told Paul or Frieda that they had not yet formally married. It was just assumed that they had been married in Germany. Anxious to avoid scandal, Jacob and Charlotte would be secretly married a year later. The secret was soon found out after the time when William was born. The busybodies in the German community would begin to probe the circumstances that brought Jacob and Charlotte to America and the timing of the birth, which was later found to be out of wedlock. Charlotte's life would soon become much more difficult, as she would now be looked down on by the local society.

Chapter II. The Hill Country, 1856

Jacob could not have known at the time, but this new start in the wagon business would become the foundation of the next twenty-five years of his life in this strange new land where he now found himself and his new family. Texas would be the point of departure for adventures and challenges they could not yet begin to imagine. About three weeks after the birth of William, Jacob accompanied Paul on a two-day trip to visit the farms of several German immigrants a few hours north of San Antonio. They were driving along brisk pace on the way to deliver some hardware and to purchase locally grown produce, which Jacob was authorized to purchase for the Army.

As they neared New Braunfels, the unofficial capital of this heavily Germanic area, Paul suddenly offered Jacob a permanent job. Jacob listened with great interest.

"Jacob, I need more help with the blacksmithing and wagon business. My business is growing rapidly, and I need someone else besides Herman, my chief blacksmith, to be able to expand and grow. I would really like you to go full time and become my partner." Jacob listened intently as Paul laid out his plans. Paul had built up a thriving business which encompassed much of San Antonio, and extended into the growing German villages of the Hill Country. First, New Braunfels was established near Comal Springs, followed by Fredericksburg on the Pedernales River, and then Kerrville. A host of other little German communities would follow, including Boerne, Luchenbach, Comfort, Castell, and Hilda. These farming communities had settled over the past decade or so usually including other Central European immigrants. The Texas Hill Country was well suited for German settlement. A number of aquifers were supported by multiple honeycombed subterranean caverns in the area, carved out by the elements eons before. A variety of vegetation and trees flourished there, and climate was varied enough to support many crops, even vineyards. German town names dominated the area, but activities were integrated with Anglo-American communities as far north as Austin and Johnson City.

Jacob thought about the surprising offer for a few minutes, and finally answered, "Paul, I am very flattered, and it is a generous offer. Two things, however; first, I am obligated to finish my Army enlistment which ends next summer, and second, I am concerned about Charlotte's happiness. You and Frieda have been wonderful to us. I can never thank you enough. The local German ladies, however, have not been very kind to Charlotte. As you know, we never married until after William was born, and they have not been understanding about all of that. As we were formerly Catholic, and most of the local Germans are evangelical, it has been especially hard for Charlotte to be treated with respect. I am going to have to work on this with Charlotte. I would really like to be your partner, but her happiness has to come first."

After a few minutes, Paul reassured Jacob that he fully understood the predicament, and whatever Jacob decided would be fine with him. Jacob finally said, "I will do my best to make this work, and I will keep this confidential and let you know as soon as possible."

The wagon rolled into the main square of New Braunfels, and Jacob enjoyed reading all the signs written in German over the local shops. He jumped down from the wagon just long enough to buy a German language newspaper to take back to San Antonio for Charlotte to read. He quickly noted a disturbing headline about State's rights and run-away slaves back east. He didn't like the whole idea of the plantation system. Paul agreed Jacob that nothing good would come of this system of human bondage, and that there was likely a lot of trouble to come from this. Paul made a delivery of some iron hardware to a local general store, and they had a quick lunch at the Comal Springs Inn. The bratwurst and beer were excellent, but they needed to get back on the road in order to visit a few farms on the way to Bourne, Comfort, and Luckenbach, and then on to Fredericksburg for the night before heading back to San Antonio. This route took them through shallow valleys and up and down hilly country which appeared to be arid. Underneath this sandy soil, however, subterranean caverns supplied water flowing through honeycombed aquifers, carved out by the elements, eons before. The hardy German farmers who lived here were able to grow an amazing variety of vegetables, from gourds and melons to cabbage, potatoes, corn, wheat, millet, and garden vegetables to apples, pears, and other orchard fruits. Jacob filled the wagon to the top of the sideboards, and also purchased a half a dozen milk cows. The bulk of the produce was bound for the quartermaster section at the Alamo. At one farm, Paul and Jacob helped repair a broken wheel and wagon tongue for Ludwig Neustadt, a farmer originally from the Rhineland near the Mosel River. Using a few wagon parts and tools they carried under the wagon seat the repair took only a little over an hour, to the amazement and delight of the old man.

The two friends thoroughly enjoyed these twice monthly trips to the Hill Country, and they provided a valuable service to the German community living north of San Antonio. These were hard working independent settlers for the most part, who were in many ways more disciplined than their neighbors of Anglo descent. Their farming practices were intensive and generally more efficient than many of the American settlers who had come to Texas from the east coast and the southeast states. Many of them had borrowed from the sharecropper and chattel servitude methods of colonial plantation farming. In particular, the Germans were not keen on the use of slave labor, a southern tradition developed over generations. Their distaste for indentured servitude, especially slavery, would have serious ramifications for Germans in the years to come.

San Antonio lay immediately to the south with more than two hundred years of Hispanic culture and was the trading center for the region. Most of the German immigrants were farmers, along with a few ex-patriot intellectuals displaced by political and social upheaval in Europe. The German communities in San Antonio and New Braunfels were easy places to visit with the large contingent of

Germans, many of whom had been there for a decade. In New Braunfels, German was the dominant language, including the newspaper, but outside trade with the English and Spanish speakers made it necessary for the Germans to learn these languages, at least enough to carry on simple trade. Paul Schmidt spoke English very well and his Spanish was reasonably good, which allowed him to operate a small freight business in the Hill Country and within fifty or so miles of San Antonio, delivering new wagons, mules, livery, hardware, and farm equipment. Jacob was able to join him occasionally when his military duties allowed.

Jacob was happy to be living here, in a thriving community with plenty of work. He wanted to leave the Army and go full time with Paul, but things weren't as easy for Charlotte. It didn't take long for the town gossips to spread the word about William's birth prior to marriage. Charlotte would become more and more isolated, and scorned, as time went on. Her only real friend was Frieda Schmidt. Charlotte would soon long for a more anonymous life.

By 1856, beginning their third year together in the new land, Jacob and Charlotte were just settling down in their adopted German community in Texas. William, a few months before, had begun to take his first toddling steps. The wagon and livery business was good, and Paul was very generous in teaching the craft of wagon and mule team outfitting to Jacob. Paul and his wife Frieda couldn't have been nicer to the Stengers, but the German community was less accepting. Charlotte became increasingly unwilling to socialize within their community.

"Jacob, I just can't go to these social gatherings anymore, all the women look at me scornfully, or ignore me. Nobody wants to be seen talking to me," she would complain.

"Darling, you must be patient," he would answer. "Some people will always be mean, usually because they want to feel superior." As the weeks and months went on, Jacob began to realize that he would not be able to resolve his wife's unhappiness with her social situation, and he began to look for opportunities to relieve her suffering.

Jacob was beginning to wonder if he was right to pursue his dreams of success and happiness here in San Antonio. Not only was his wife unhappy, but he had also begun to notice that things were changing in Texas. Many of the German settlers were becoming uncomfortable with the increasing talk of Texas joining the southeastern states in rebellion over southern state's rights, especially regarding the institution of slavery. The whole concept of slavery was unpopular with the Germans, many of whom had left Europe in the first place to escape the old feudalistic system of indentured servitude for the promise of freedom and opportunity. Slavery just didn't sit right with most of them. German farmers believed in hard work and individual ownership of their land. In recent years, the Missouri Compromise and the Dread Scott Decision had seemed to ensure the southern states would be able to continue indefinitely their hideous system of unpaid forced labor. As the split between North and South became more and more likely, many Germans in Texas raised their voices in support of the Union. Jacob had enough experience and foresight that he could be fairly certain which way Texas would turn, if forced to choose sides. When Jacob had first come to San Antonio, he was introduced to a few of the concepts that had led to the founding of his new homeland. He already knew that America was founded on sound principles of human rights and individual freedoms, and he was familiar with the Declaration of Independence. What he didn't know much about were the ideas that had led to and helped form the U.S. Constitution and the Bill of Rights.

When Jacob arrived in San Antonio, Captain Johnson, the commander of the 8th Army Depot, had recognized that this soldier was an intelligent and educated man. When Jacob told his commanding officer that he would like to know more about the founding of this country, Johnson offered him access to his small library which he kept in his office at the Alamo. Jacob borrowed some of the commander's American History books, including a copy of the Federalist Papers and a couple of other books about the Constitutional Convention. He spent a fair amount of his off-duty time reading about those deliberations. Jacob knew enough European history that he quickly recognized what a departure these ideas were from all previous western philosophies of government. He felt at the time that these ideas had been a great departure from previous ideas about government and human rights. The experience of reading these materials had cemented his beliefs that he had definitely made the right decision about coming to America, and how human beings should be treated.

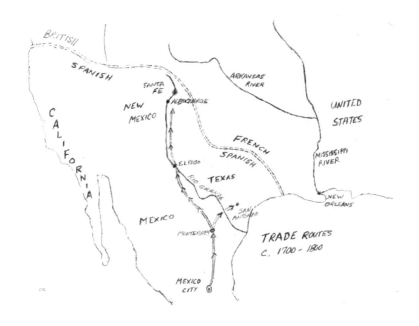

BRITISH

SPANISH

SANTA FE

NEW MEXICO

ALBUQUERQUE

ARKANSAS RIVER

UNITED STATES

C A L I F O R N I A

FRENCH SPANISH

EL PASO

RIO GRANDE

TEXAS

MISSISSIPPI RIVER

NEW ORLEANS

MEXICO

SAN ANTONIO

MONTERREY

TRADE ROUTES
c. 1700 - 1800

MEXICO CITY

Chapter III. The Trade Routes (El Camino Real)

The War with Mexico in 1846-48 had changed everything for the Southwest. Suddenly, over two hundred years of exclusive Spanish and Mexican control of the region was coming to an abrupt end. Conflicting claims to Texas and other border areas, eventually led to unavoidable conflict. The Mexican government did not recognize the legitimacy of the Republic of Texas, formed after the 1836 revolution. The new president of Mexico, General Santa Ana, was still angry over his losses to the "Texians" a decade earlier. Texas was seen as territory to be retaken. In addition, there were trade and tariff disputes between the U. S. and Mexico, and debts owed to the Americans dating back to the Mexican Revolution of 1821. There were other considerations, including Mexico's desire to maintain exclusive control over access to the gold and silver mines of the southwest and mountain west territories of New Mexico and California. The Americans, conversely, wanted California, which they saw threatened by British claims in the northwest, and needed overland access through New Mexico. New Mexico had long been an important asset of the Spanish Empire, and more recently, the Mexican Republic. By 1846, John C. Fremont had entered California, and had begun to foment a Texas-style revolution to establish an independent republic. At the same time, the U.S. had outlined a treaty with Britain, taking over the Oregon Territory. Mexico had reason to be concerned about American expansion. The U.S. government had even offered to buy upper California and Santa Fe from Mexico, but were rejected. Eventually, boundary disputes and a Mexican attack on U.S. troops near Brownsville, Texas, led to declarations of war.

There had been a well-established trade route, El Camino Real (The Royal Road), from Chihuahua to Santa Fe since the early 1600s. New Mexico and Santa Fe, as outposts of the Spanish northern territory, were nearly totally dependent on Mexico for supplies, especially manufactured goods. The supply trains originally came only once every year of two from Mexico City, more than 1,600 miles to the south. Chihuahua was only 700 miles to the south, which allowed more frequent resupply visits. The merchants of Chihuahua were also able to take textiles, hides, and silver back from New Mexico, and make handsome profits. Not until the Santa Fe Trail was established starting in the 1820s from Missouri, were there any trading alternatives for New Mexico. Even then, Chihuahua merchants were able to influence the Mexican government to keep American traders at bay through high tariffs and harassment. When the War with Mexico came, General Kearney's Army marched down the Santa Fe Trail into New Mexico to neutralize Mexican forces and to establish invasion routes into the interior of Mexico and west to southern California. Arriving U.S. forces found little or no resistance in New Mexico. At the same time, General Fremont in California was able to overwhelm the Mexican forces quickly, eliminating the need for Kearney to move to the west. The main fighting of the war had already shifted to the south and into the heart of Mexico, eventually leading to the American victory near Mexico City. The parties eventually signed the Treaty of Guadalupe Hidalgo, ceding both New Mexico and California to the United States. After the Mexican War ended, the Americans established the new U.S. territories of New Mexico and California. To protect these conquered possessions and the new borders, a number of Army posts and forts were built in west Texas and throughout New Mexico and the Southwest. Protection was also needed against certain Indian tribes hostile to the increasing number of white settlers moving west. Mail and coach passengers required additional security as new overland routes from Texas to California were opened. This westward thrust required teams and wagons hauling material, supplies, and people to build and maintain new outposts and waystations along the route.

As a young student in Germany, Jacob had developed a love of history and the cultural clashes and fusions that changed nations and even continents. He pondered both ancient and more recent events, trying to gain perspective. Jacob was fascinated by the interactions of different cultures and political systems, especially as his newly adopted country continued to expand westward. He was convinced that the United States would eventually control the center of this great continent from Atlantic to Pacific. At the same time, it promised to be a mighty struggle, producing both winners and losers, not leaving any group unchanged. The greatest impact would likely be on the original inhabitants, the Native American tribes.

Despite the great job offer from Paul, to stay in south central Texas, with a promising future in the wagon and freight business, Jacob's greatest concern was about his wife's unhappiness. Charlotte was looked down upon by many neighbors and felt like a social pariah.

"Maybe we should have stayed in Germany!" Charlotte complained to Jacob. "It couldn't be any worse there. At least we had some family who might eventually accept what happened to us."

Jacob could only say, "Maybe you are right, Charlotte dear, but we are here now and there is no going back. I will find a way for you to have some peace and privacy. We will find a place where no one will know or care about our past."

Suddenly, everything seemed to come together for Jacob. He reflected on the revulsion that he and many other immigrants had over the issue of slavery in this "bastion of independence" called Texas. It was something he didn't have much time to think about at first, but he came to realize that slavery could not be justified in this new land of freedom and opportunity. Jacob began to look for opportunities outside of the German community. One day on his way to work, he noticed some new signs posted along the streets of the Mercado, the Mexican market square. The signs read, "Drivers and teams wanted to haul freight to New Mexico! Military and civilian contracts available! Inquire at Quartermaster Section, 8th Military District HQ, The Alamo." What had the boss come up with now? Jacob decided to investigate. He got in line outside the contract office and waited his turn.

16

Captain Johnson looked up at the dusty soldier standing in front of his desk at the Quartermaster Office. "What can I do for you, Private?" he asked.

Jacob had stood in the line of teamsters for half an hour. "Sir, I wanted to see what jobs you might have hauling freight to New Mexico. I'm thinking about leaving the Army when my enlistment is up this summer."

The depot officer hesitated for a few seconds, "Well, we've just filled all the teams authorized from here to Fort Bliss and Fort Fillmore. But, last I heard, the Army needs a few teams for transport of stores up the Rio Grande to Fort Craig and the northern areas including Albuquerque, Santa Fe, and Fort Union." Captain Johnson called for Jacob's military file and read it over for a few minutes.

"I've seen orders that your home unit, Company C of the Regiment of Mounted Riflemen is being reassigned from Fort Davis to Fort Stanton, a new post in southeastern New Mexico. I can cut you orders as a wagon driver to get you to Fort Craig. Since the northern part of the territory is supplied from Missouri, you might be able to get freight work on the Santa Fe Trail."

Jacob had heard of the Trail when he was at Jefferson Barracks in St. Louis, but he had no real idea of exactly where it was or the distances involved. It sounded like an awfully long way to go. "How far is it to Santa Fe?" Jacob asked.

"I haven't been there myself," Johnson replied, "but I'm told it is more than 800 miles from here, and nearly 900 miles from Santa Fe to Independence, Missouri, and Fort Leavenworth, where the supplies are picked up by wagon. They are sent up the Missouri River by steamboat from St. Louis."

Jacob thought about it for a minute, but the line behind him was getting restless, and he might not get another chance. "Where do I sign up, Captain?"

Captain Johnson smiled and directed him to fill out some papers for the clerk. "There is a train of wagons scheduled to leave here in two weeks for El Paso with supplies for the forts along the way, and as far as Fort Fillmore. You must provide your own wagon and team of four mules able to haul at least three thousand pounds of freight. Your daily rations and fodder will be provided by the Army, along with replacement mules as needed. When you leave here, you will be under the control of the train commander and the quartermasters at your destinations, dropping off your last cargo at

Fort Fillmore. From there, you are on your own as far as Fort Craig. Some of the Apache and Comanche tribes have been raiding the wagon trains for the past few months, so you will need to be in a wagon train traveling with a military escort, especially anywhere north of Fort Fillmore. By the way, I would consider re-enlisting if I were you. The pay isn't as good as being a civilian contract hauler, but your family would be able to utilize military subsistence, and quarters."

Jacob thanked the Captain, picked up his authorization papers from the clerk, and left the Alamo, driving his rig slowly back to Paul's house.

Jacob spent a restless night in bed, not telling Charlotte of his decision until morning. He was apprehensive about his decision, knowing how fierce the Indian raids in the Hill Country had been last year. The Comanche and their Mexican suppliers, the bandits known as the Comancheros, had a long-standing blood feud with the "Texians" over encroachment on their lands. A chain of forts from Fort Smith, Arkansas, to Fort Stockton, Texas, had been established over the past decade as outposts providing a modicum of safety for settlements to the south of Indian Territory, the lands north of the Red River. Beyond west central Texas, there was additional danger from hostile Indian attack, especially Apache raiders from the mountains of southeastern New Mexico, and the Davis Mountains of west Texas. Jacob had some experience with the Apache from his early days at Fort Davis. Traveling through that country with his family was going to be a huge step beyond the safety of San Antonio, and he would be giving up a promising future as a partner with Paul Schmidt. He feared that Charlotte would have a very hard time adjusting to such a great change. They had been together for only two years, but Jacob had managed to save over half of his earnings from his part time blacksmith and livery work. His generous friend, Paul, had given him a wagon and team of his own from the outset. Jacob had also acquired his own horse, and two milking cows for the baby. He knew that he could make this change financially, but what effect would it have on Charlotte?

"New Mexico?! Missouri?!" Charlotte cried out after hearing the plan. "Where in the world did you come up with this idea? You don't know anyone there. Where will we live? What about the children? You know that I am expecting again! The new baby will be here in only six or seven months, Jacob!"

18

"I know that Charlotte," Jacob retorted, "but this is what you wanted, a chance to get away from these old biddies here, who will not give you any peace. Oh, I know that it won't be easy! But, we can get to Santa Fe in six or seven weeks. I can find you and William a place to live while I go to Fort Leavenworth with the military supply trains. I will be back by the end of summer, before the new baby arrives. There are good people and good doctors at the military posts. It will be safe for you, and no one will know anything about our past or our personal secrets. Charlotte began to sob quietly for a minute or two. Jacob moved to comfort her in his arms.

"Jacob, I am scared," pleaded Charlotte, "but we have been through great difficulties before, and you have never let me down. I trust that you will do what is right for our family." Jacob hated to leave this place where so many of his fellow German immigrants had come to settle and thrive, but was convinced deep down that his wife's peace of mind and self-esteem were more important than the convenient life they had found in Texas. Big changes were coming to Texas, more than he wished to face. He remembered too well the angst in his native Bavaria when the unrest and revolution came. He had grown up in an atmosphere of upheaval and uncertainty. Trouble was coming to the South, and Texas could not avoid becoming involved. There was already secession talk brewing in Austin and eastern Texas. The Anglos were talking about forming militias and southern loyalty groups. Most of the Germans in the Hill Country held anti-slavery beliefs. What would happen if they didn't support the cause? Jacob knew how rough things could get when people started choosing sides. Had Bavaria not suffered for joining the Austrian Confederation? No, the time to go was now! It might be impossible to avoid getting caught up in it if he stayed here. After a few nights of discussing all of this with Charlotte, his mind was set. They had to get settled at the other end of the journey before winter. The choice to go west was clear. They would leave San Antonio in mid-June and take the job with the Army supply trains.

Chapter IV. Westward!

The supply train commander rode up the street to Alamo Square and into the milling crowd of teamsters. He rode into the middle of the men surrounding him on foot, reinforced the orders for the supply convoy, and reviewed the important instructions and rules required of all the drivers for a successful trip of over six hundred miles through the southwest Texas chaparral and mountain deserts. The gathered company were well aware of the hazards of heat, scarcity of water, and the possibility of Indian attacks. They would use the lower route of the San Antonio - El Paso road. The lower road as far as Fort Lancaster was relatively safe from Indian attack, but not totally. Beyond that area, wagon trains required military escorts through areas where the traditional Apache and Comanche north-south raiding routes crossed the military roads. A whole chain of U.S. Army and Texas Ranger forts and outposts had been established after the war with Mexico, to protect settlers and the southern military supply routes to El Paso and New Mexico. In addition, protection was increasingly required for civilian traffic moving west to the new territories of New Mexico and California.

Captain Patrick Murphy sidled his mount among the bustling group of men and raised his hand to quiet them. Murphy was a tough

Irishman, born and raised in South Boston. He had fought his way through two campaigns in the Mexican War as an enlisted man, and was decorated for gallantry in action at Cerro Gordo, when his unit was attached to Captain Robert E. Lee's Engineers. The end of the war found him with a battlefield commission and a decision to stay in the Army. Patrick loved the Southwest and never returned home. He was a good soldier, well respected by all he served with. He was competent, fair, and expected absolute obedience from his soldiers and anyone else he was responsible for. Murphy had been a convoy commander for the past two years, moving supplies west from San Antonio, the western most supply terminal at the time. The roads from San Antonio were only marginally improved over the years since the war, and fraught with hazards, including unforgiving topography, drought, and frequent Indian raids.

"Listen up men!" shouted Captain Murphy. "At sunrise tomorrow we begin the six-hundred-mile journey to El Paso, then Fort Bliss at Franklin, and on to Fort Fillmore in New Mexico Territory. We have over fifty teams hauling military supplies, and half a dozen ration and fodder wagons to feed us on the trip. All the wagons have been inspected by the train master, Sergeant Debowsky, and you all have received your deficiency lists. The quartermaster will be coming by this afternoon with axes, shovels, spare axles and wheels, and other essential parts and tools where they are needed. Any final repairs or refits must be completed before dark tonight. The garrison blacksmith will be available for any shoeing or livery repairs needed. After we leave San Antonio, there are no major repair facilities until El Paso. Every wagon is required to carry two full barrels of water and keep them filled every chance you get. There is no water point after we cross the Pecos River until we get to Fort Davis. If your animals come up lame, there are limited replacement mules at Fort Lancaster and Fort Davis. The livestock must be kept watered and fed. We have enough rations for 35 days, not counting game taken along the way; so, don't be wasteful. Each musket or rifle should have a minimum of two hundred and fifty rounds. Check your ball, cap, and cartridge stocks now. The trip is over six hundred miles, and we need to make close to twenty miles a day. There are some slow areas around the Devils River, and the Pecos, where we have to make multiple crossings due to the narrow canyons. It will sometimes be necessary to do twenty-five or thirty miles a day elsewhere to keep on schedule. When we stop at night, or encounter hostiles, keep close to the wagon ahead of you, so the train master can get you circled up tight. Unhitch your animals and stake and graze them inside the circle of wagons so they won't get stampeded. The border areas, around Fort Clark and Bracketville have been quiet recently. No Lipan Apache or Kickapoo raiders from Mexico have crossed the Rio Grande so far this year. After we cross the Pecos, we may encounter Comanche raiding parties, but we don't expect large numbers. Finally, starting tonight, no whiskey will be tolerated on this trip. You must keep your wits about you at all times. Now, get your final preparations done, and bed down early. Get up at first bugle call and be ready to move out at sunrise. Sergeant Debowsky will lead the train. I will be ahead with the Mexican and Indian guides and half of the mounted escort. The other half of the troop will pull up the rear of the train, led by Lt. Lambert. There is no turning back after Fort Inge, as no return military escort is available beyond that point. We will move west to Fort Clark, turn north through the Devils River Gorge, the hardest part of the road for the wagons, and northwest up to Fort Lancaster on the Pecos. Again, from there to Fort Davis, there is no water point. Without water, your animals are unlikely to survive. Any driver who doesn't obey strict water discipline will be subject to court martial. We will halt the train for one day at Fort Davis to recover and make repairs, and replace animals as needed. From there the wagons will move southwest through the mountains to the Rio Grande following the lower road up to El Paso. Half the wagons are bound for Fort Bliss, and there will be a two-day layover before the train moves on to Fort Fillmore. Any questions? If not, be formed up and ready to move out at second bugle call."

Jacob strode back to his sector of the assembly area around the Alamo headquarters. His wagon was number thirty-two in line. Little William was playing with a stick in the dirt, close to his mother, on the side away from the road traffic. The blonde healthy one year old was now a toddler, with a constant babble of German baby talk and an occasional English word or two. Charlotte knew her English wasn't that good yet, but that was due to a lack of contact with Anglos, which would no longer be the case. There were a few other German women in the area, but they would become scarce as they moved further west. Only three other families were in the train. Charlotte was cooking the mid-day meal of bacon, beans, pan-fried potatoes, and pan bread. It was already hot in the early June sun, the only shade from an awning she had fashioned from the spare wagon canvas, poles, and rope. Jacob went over his inspection list. The past two years in Paul's blacksmith business, the Hill Country travel, and a couple of supply trips to Indianola with Paul had prepared him well for wagon readiness. He had repaired many wagons with broken wheels and axles. He had already included two extra wheels, an axle-spindle skein and nut, and a large timber lashed under the wagon for a major axle repair or emergency travois. He had a sack of tools and extra grease. Jacob even brought some harness and rein leather, and extra buckles. His team was sound and strong, and he had a reliable Appaloosa mount. The family could not bring much furniture as there was little room to spare after the three thousand pounds of boxed government supplies were loaded. They did manage a sturdy rocking chair and a small folding table and a straw mattress. Cooking gear included a small swinging pot for suspension over campfires and a cast iron skillet and cooking utensils. The Army provided rations including a small barrel of flour, a bucket of cooking lard, a small barrel of potatoes, two slabs of salted bacon, and a case of hardtack crackers. A milk cow was allowed in tow since they had a small child. Jacob had sold his other cow to another family with small children. A bucket of salt was handed out for cooking and preservation of any wild game taken along the trail, such as wild pigs or deer. Jacob was a crack shot with his new .44 caliber Colt repeating carbine with revolving cylinder action. It was similar to his pistol, holding paper, ball, and powder filled cartridges in its six-cylinder magazine. Shots were ignited by percussion caps set on the vent nipples at the rear of the cylinders. These two weapons allowed Jacob to get off a dozen shots before reloading. With the rifled carbine, he had dropped many a deer at up to two hundred yards distance. He had learned to wear a long, cuffed gauntlet on his left hand to protect it from powder blow-by from the front of the cylinders, a problem only encountered with revolving carbines and rifles, where the left hand was held forward of the revolving magazine. It was very important when loading the paper cartridges to make sure there was no loose powder left on the front of the cylinder block, otherwise a chain fire reaction might ignite all the cartridges in the cylinders waiting to be fired, spraying the lead bullets forward into the left arm and hand. The Army had issued a few of these revolving carbines to mounted troops, but the chain fire accidents delayed general issue of the weapons. A decade would pass, including a civil war, before the Army would solve this problem with tubular magazines in the stock, and later weapons sequentially feeding the new copper and brass jacketed cartridges into a lever action chambering mechanism.

Charlotte managed to bring a few herbs and peppers along, mostly to flavor the meat. There wasn't enough room or a way to bring or preserve vegetables or poultry or eggs. A few jars of cooked and preserved fruits and vegetables were allowed. The military trains were on a strict timetable and could not be slowed by any long encampments on the way. Jacob knew that Charlotte was nervous. He tried to keep the conversation light as they ate the noon meal. She was quiet and reflective, without complaint, as she fed William and prepared a napping place for him behind the seat of the wagon. He fell asleep in a few minutes, despite the heat, as she fanned him gently.

"I know you are anxious about the trip, Charlotte," Jacob offered, trying to calm her fears. "The Captain says we will be in New Mexico within a month, with any luck at all."

Charlotte remained silent for a moment or two before answering. "Jacob, darling, I am alright. I am getting over my morning sickness and feel pretty good right now. I know this new life will be hard, but a least we can be free from the scorn of these hypocrites in San Antonio. I just want to raise my children without being looked down on."

Jacob was amazed at the strength of his wife. "Don't worry, Schatze, no one will ever look down on you again!"

Daylight and the first bugle call came earlier than Jacob would have liked. He had been up past midnight helping some of the other teamsters with last minute repairs of wagons and harness gear. Charlotte started the breakfast fire while young William continued to sleep soundly, despite the ruckus of the early morning preparations for movement. Jacob was finishing his first cup of coffee when Sergeant Debowsky trotted by, yelling at some of the teamsters to finish packing up and to start lining up in the assigned order, forming the trains. Jacob like the discipline imposed on the usually rowdy teamsters. It seemed abrasive to some of the men, but he knew how import it was to have that discipline, especially if the convoy came under attack. Charlotte was cleaning up after a small hasty breakfast. Jacob shoveled dirt on the campfire and spread the ashes. They hitched the mules and mounted the wagon. William fussed a little, but went back to sleep. Jacob pulled the wagon out of the camping area and up the street, pulling in behind wagon number thirty-one, his horse and cow in tow at the back of the wagon. The dawn light was nearly full now as the first glint of sunlight started to show on the nearby houses and onto the Alamo itself. Right on cue, the bugle later sounded assembly as a few of the slower teams and wagons were marshaled into position, Sergeant Debowsky barking at them in the harshest terms. The sergeant galloped from the rear of the train to the lead wagon, as the train groaned forward past the Mercado, teamsters whistling and cajoling the mules through the narrow streets. Slapping of reins and snapping of whips filled the dusty air.

The first hundred miles out of San Antonio were relatively uneventful, save for a few wheel tightening adjustments, and the first day loss of one renegade lead mule. The mule, spooked by a rattle snake, bolted his team and nearly turned the wagon over, breaking his leg in the process. He was shot and replaced two days later at Fort Inge, a small post southwest of Uvalde, at the western edge of the Edwards Plateau. The train overnighted there, choosing not to fight through a driving rainstorm. That evening Jacob visited a few of his fellow enlistees from their Jefferson Barracks days. He told them he would probably see them again in New Mexico. A day later they reached Fort Clark and Bracketville, the end of the first leg of the trip.

Fort Clark was built in 1852 to reinforce the U.S. border at San Felipe Springs, a major crossing of the Rio Grande from Mexico. American troops contended with Mexican forces for this area in the early days of the Mexican War. It bordered the traditional Indian raiding routes of the Comanche, Apache, and Kickapoo. Fortunately, this sector had been fairly quiet over the past two years as Fort Clark, and Fort Lancaster to the north, provided a partial deterrent to raiding parties using this north-south corridor.

The train was moving well at this point, covering up to 35 miles a day. The leg of the military road encountered several small to medium stream crossings, the approaches having been gradually improved since the Mexican War. After dropping off two wagon loads of supplies at Fort Clark, the train redistributed some of the load to the two empty wagons and continued west and northwest following the Rio Grande. They then turned north toward the Rio San Pedro, better known to the Americans as the Devil's River. The first crossing was made several miles above its confluence with the Rio Grande to take advantage the easier terrain on the west bank of this short but twisting river. Access to the western bluffs of the valley was less steep from the west side of the river, than from the east side further north. Once the top of the escarpment was reached, it was a straight shot north and east of the Hope Hills to Camp Hudson, a newly establish Army sub-post on the west bank of the river. This route was preferred to the more tortuous and narrow canyons of the lower river valley, reducing the number of fords, and shortening the journey by at least one day. The three-day trip was quiet, and the advance party had found abundant game, bringing a dozen or more deer and antelope into camp each night. Only one Apache hunting party had been seen, and they kept their distance from the scouts and pony-soldiers. No hostile intent was evident, and no shots had been fired. The campfires roared as the welcome venison and other game was roasted and consumed by all, along with beans and pan bread. The river and one other stream had been crossed in the last couple of days, and the animals were allowed to drink their fill to prevent heat exhaustion during the hot days to follow.

Camp Hudson was near a bend in Devil's River, and the train stopped for half a day to replace a few exhausted mules and Army mounts. The wagons were inspected, and a few wheels repaired or re-greased. The river was low this time of year, and the trains followed it north for about forty miles with only two crossings, a much easier route than the Pecos River Valley to the west. The water barrels would be topped off before turning northwest to Fort Lancaster, further north on the Pecos, where an improved fording site would take them west toward Fort Davis. The eighty-five mile stretch from the headwaters of Devil's River to Fort Lancaster was a three-day open country trek across open prairie and chaparral, a hot and dusty wasteland. A short swing northeast on the third day led into the eastern approaches to Fort Lancaster on the Pecos. There would be a day of bivouac and rest, and a chance for the dragoon escort to saddle fresh mounts. In addition to the horses, a few dozen mules were replaced from injured or ailing wagon teams. After delivering two more wagon loads of provisions to the post commander, Captain Granger, the nearly mile-long train circled up near the river and settled in for the night. They were virtually halfway to El Paso, and right on schedule on this first night of July. The first half of the trip had been hot and tiring, but with minimal losses. One wagon was lost when an axle broke in mid-stream, turning the wagon over in the water. Most of the cargo was saved and redistributed to other wagons including two spare wagons that had left supplies at Fort Clark. There had also been a brief hostile action between the advance scouts of the dragoon escort and a small band of Comanche encountered coming out of Devil's River Canyon. The Indians were driven off, with two braves shot from their mustangs, but one of the scouts had taken an arrow to his thigh and his horse was killed by an arrow through the throat. The scout had lost a fair amount of blood, but the surgeon at Fort Lancaster would be able to remove the arrowhead from his leg. He was expected to survive, barring complications. The news of the hostile action did not make Charlotte happy. As she prepared the evening meal, Jacob could see tears on her face. He put his arm around her shoulders.

"Jacob, I am frightened!" she sobbed.

Jacob squeezed her a little tighter. "Charlotte, it was only a few Indians, probably a hunting party." Little William clung to his mother's skirts, unsettled by her crying. She drew him near, hugging and kissing his head.

"Charlotte, it will be alright," Jacob assured her, "This is a large train, and we have a squadron of dragoons to protect us. Sergeant Debowsky told me today, that after we move on from here, the few wagons with families and children will be drawn inside of the wagon circle at night. I will be sleeping with my carbine ready at my side, and no harm will come to you or our son." Charlotte stopped crying, but remained silent as they finished their supper. She took William into the wagon and prepared their bedding. Jacob stayed by the fire for another hour as the coals died down. He would sleep on the ground under the wagon tonight on a palette of blankets with his long canvas duster for a cover. Watching the bright stars this night, he struggled to remember the names of the zodiac figures he had learned as a boy, then quickly fell asleep, exhausted.

Dawn came early on these June days, and Jacob had already been up for an hour, just finishing his second cup of coffee. Charlotte had heard her husband rustling about and was up quickly to fix breakfast. She milked the cow, but there wasn't any to spare, only what was needed for William. Milk cows were not well suited to this kind of movement, unable to graze at will, and not getting as much water as needed to maintain good milk production. No matter, William was doing well enough on bacon and biscuits, and she was grateful. It was a cool morning for this time of year, and the coffee was especially welcome. Charlotte knew that the next few days of the journey to Fort Davis would be stressful and potentially dangerous. They would have to get by with the water they could carry from the

Pecos River. Besides, she had heard Jacob and the other men speculating about encountering hostile Indians. She almost broke down when two other small children in the train came down with fever, although the Army doctor at Fort Lancaster had checked them over and said that, without a cough or skin eruptions, it was likely not too serious. Time would tell, she thought, time would tell.

As dawn began to break, orders were barked throughout the encampment, the animals hitched up, and sleeping and cooking gear quickly stowed. The wagons were lined up to the west, awaiting the usual ride-by by Sergeant Debowsky. The advanced party was already three miles ahead of the train when the sergeant bellowed out, "Wagons ho!" The departure was uneventful, and the train creaked forward at a crawl. The lead wagon was instructed to maintain a three-mile per hour pace, faster in the morning hours than the two miles per hour dictated by the one-hundred-degree heat expected by early afternoon. The major part of the day's travel had to be completed by the two o'clock rest period, when the train would circle up for the afternoon meal and two hours for rest and watering of the animals. Hay feeding was only allowed during the night stops, usually around sundown. The first day and the second morning went well as the train followed the Pecos Valley north before turning west into the Ojo Escondido, a dry valley which climbed gradually through the surrounding bluffs up to the high West Texas Plain, a desert plateau. The train stopped at the top of the valley, as the mules were showing signs of heat exhaustion during the climb, and Sergeant Debowsky thought it would be best to take the midday break. After the noon meal, three riders from the advanced party came galloping into camp, heading toward the sergeant.

"Sarge!" the Corporal called out, gasping for breath, "We ran into a sizable band of Comanche warriors about ten miles west near Leon Springs, you know, that old dried-up watering hole that turned alkaline. Sarge, two of our Indian scouts were surprised and killed. The rest of us formed a skirmish line and held off two charges, must have been more that seventy of them. Captain Murphy told us to ride like hell back to the train and warn you!"

"Where the hell are the rest of the men?" Sergeant Debowsky demanded.

"I guess we are about ten minutes ahead of the rest, Sarge."

Debowsky reacted quickly, sending a runner for Lt. Lambert, the second in command, who was just finishing his meal. Lambert arrived less than two minutes later. As Debowsky briefed Lambert, some of the advanced party were straggling back to the train. Four wounded men were riding double, hanging onto the riders in front of them. Two horses were missing and two riderless horses were bleeding from arrow wounds. Following Captain Murphy's orders, Sergeant Debowsky had circled the wagons prior to the rest period. The train was able to quickly prepare for attacks if necessary. Debowsky and the Lieutenant rode around the wagons, barking orders. A flurry of activity ensued, with men rushing about, gathering their teams and livestock into the wagon circle, staking and tethering the animals. Men began unloading and taking cover behind ammunition boxes placed under the wagons. The small number of women and children were hustled into two wagons inside the circle, guarded by four men. Just then, Captain Murphy and his troopers galloped into the center of the wagon circle. Charlotte Stenger had already started sorting out the wounded and was tending to their injuries. Captain Murphy quickly counted heads and found that his group of twenty had two missing, four wounded, and they were four horses short. Murphy then turned to the area where the wounded were being treated. Charlotte was assessing injuries and could see that the wounds were not particularly serious except for one corporal with a gunshot wound to his right shoulder. She handed off William to one of the other women, and her nurses training and instincts took over. The soldier with the shoulder wound was bleeding steadily. Charlotte tore the hem of her petticoat, folding a portion into a compress, and put heavy pressure on the wound to stop the bleeding. As it subsided, she tore off another cotton strip and began to wrap the shoulder and chest to secure the dressings. As the bleeding finally ceased, she doused the bandage with some whiskey from a box in her wagon. She turned her attention to the others. Two had superficial grazing leg wounds that had already stopped bleeding, and one had a bullet wound to his hand. The pinky finger had been cleanly severed and was gone. She washed these wounds with whiskey and dressed them with cotton wraps. Sergeant Debowsky suddenly appeared with a medical chest he had retrieved from the Captain's wagon. Charlotte called him an angel and opened the chest, relieved to find a large amount of clean bandaging materials, and a few instruments and scissors.

While all the medical attention was taking place, Charlotte had barely noticed the gunfire all around her. Within five minutes of the return of the advanced party, the Comanche war party were starting to circle the outside of the wagon train. Most of the dragoons and other soldiers were joining the drivers under the wagons and getting into firing positions. The circling Indians were slinging their left leg over a makeshift saddle hook and hugging their mount low on the neck, firing from under the horse's neck, on the side of the horse away from the wagons. Minimizing their exposure, protected by the body of the horse, these amazing horsemen were known for their skill of firing from awkward positions even at a full gallop.

Despite suffering some immediate casualties, most of the drivers and soldiers were able to maintain cover under the wagons,

behind their crates and saddles. The Comanche seemed to have the upper hand at first. Captain Murphy, however, was an experienced fighter and had been in similar situations before. Within minutes he had his non-commissioned officers shouting at the men under the wagons to shoot the horses. Painted ponies began to stumble and fall, with disastrous consequences for themselves and their riders. After a few minutes, the withering fire from the soldiers' carbines, and the deadly accurate fire from the breech loading Sharps rifles of the teamsters, forced the attackers to break contact. Captain Murphy quickly ordered a cease-fire, "Save your ammo men, they may make another run!" The remainder of the raiding party, now estimated to be less than half of the original number, withdrew to the south about a quarter of a mile from the wagons, just out of shooting range. A group of men attended a fire in one of the wagons, started by a fire arrow. It was controlled with only the loss of the canvas top.

The second attack never came. The Comanche gathered their wounded, left their dead, and were seen half an hour later trotting off toward the west, using the late afternoon sun to mask their movement.

The encounter had proved too much for the war party chief. He probably realized that he was up against a smart, tough wagon train commander who could more than match his arrows and single shot rifles and muskets. The blue coats with their newer rapid-fire weapons were able to overcome the superior mobility and tactics of the raiding party. The chief realized that he could not challenge this particular wagon train again, or risk losing most of his warriors. Just to be sure it wasn't a trick, Captain Murphy sent out a few of his Indian scouts to make sure the Comanche chief wasn't planning another ambush somewhere down the road. The scouts followed the tracks of the retreating warriors until dark. Their trail was last seen heading due north, through the sagebrush and chaparral, presumably toward home.

With the train apparently secure, Jacob crawled out from his firing position under a wagon, assessing the situation. The Captain and Sergeant Debowsky were mounted and checking on casualties and cargo. Other than some minor canvas damage from fire arrows, no wagons or supplies were lost. Jacob quickly found his wife and child safe. William was huddled with another teamster's wife who had gathered the children, hiding them in a wagon inside the circle. At the improvised dressing station, he soon found Charlotte, two other women, and a soldier caring for the wounded, now more than a dozen in all. A couple of soldiers with abdomen and chest wounds were writhing and delirious, not expected to survive. She gave them laudanum from the Army medical chest and what whiskey she could find to ease their suffering as their blanket litters were loaded into one of the spare empty wagons. The remainder of the day was spent collecting and preparing the dead, two teamsters and three troopers. Their bodies would be taken along in a spare wagon. Charlotte and the others continued their heroic medical attention of the wounded, who now totaled eleven, most with minor limb wounds, but two or three had more serious wounds, which would require amputations. One soldier had been shot in the side of his abdomen, through and through. The bleeding had been stopped with compression bandages, and apparently no vital organs had been hit. His fate would not be known for a few days. He would need a surgeon's attention when they reached Fort Davis. Three dragoon horses and five mules had also been found with gunshot or arrow wounds, lame and hobbling, and were shot. The train had enough spare animals to haul the wagons to Fort Davis.

The soldiers and civilians slept warily that evening, without further incident. After a cold breakfast of leftovers, no campfires allowed, they broke camp at 4 a.m. and headed west. The group was shaken, but Captain Murphy had spent a good part of the evening going from wagon to wagon, reassuring the teamsters and the few families that they could make Fort Davis in two and a half days. He had wisely ordered Lt. Lambert to take two wagons, with three empty water barrels each, back down the arroyo to the Pecos River during the night. They were accompanied by a small, mounted patrol and returned to the train with their precious liquid cargo just before dawn. The Captain had made this trek many times, and he knew that the next two days would be among the hottest and driest of the trip. The train would have to make the longest part of each day, the first fourteen to sixteen miles, before noon. From noon to five in the afternoon, the summer heat would be overwhelming for man and beast. Experienced desert travelers knew that the risk of heat stroke for humans and animals was highest during those hours. The time was best spent resting, making as much shade as possible from spare wagon canvas, and watering the draft animals. This day was good as could be hoped for, except for the loss of one of the two expectant casualties. Charlotte hailed one of the dragoons who was headed to the front of the train.

"Trooper, Corporal Gerald McElroy died around mid-morning, most likely from internal bleeding, due to his gunshot wound to the lower abdomen," she yelled to him. "Captain Murphy knew McElroy from the from the Mexican War! Please let the Captain know!" Both men grew up in the Boston area, and had fought together with Colonel Robert E. Lee at Cerro Gordo. Murphy was disheartened and saddened by the news. He insisted on burial at the Fort Davis cemetery, and would personally send a letter to McElroy's family. As the sun started to lower in the west, the supply train moved on, making another ten miles before dusk. The train stopped for the night at an abandoned ranch, which had been burned out by Comanche raiders. There were some corrals for the livestock, but no other comforts. That might, Cut. Murphy would write a proper letter to the deceased soldiers' families back home. He no sooner finished the letters, than Charlotte Stenger came to report the death of the other badly wounded soldier, Private Jimmy Mason, a recent addition to the command, from Virginia. The Captain would have to wait until they reached Fort Fillmore to find out his next of kin and a forwarding address. These were not the first letters, nor the last, that Patrick Murphy would have to write to the families of his fallen men. This was a fact of Army life on the frontier, but it was never easy. There were other seriously wounded men on this train, and Murphy prayed that he could a least deliver them to the surgeon at Fort Davis, for a chance of survival. Charlotte returned to her wagon after one last check on the less severely wounded. It was late in the evening, and she was nearly spent. William had already been bedded down by Jacob, and it was a relief for her to see his peaceful sleeping face. After the horrors of the past two days, it was almost more than she could take. Jacob embraced her, as they watched their son resting so quietly.

She began to sob softly. "Jacob, why are we doing this? It is so hard to see these men die - if I could only have done more for them."

Jacob held her tight. "We will be at Fort Davis tomorrow night, Charlotte. You have done all you could to help these men. Their wounds were just too severe. There is an Army doctor and an infirmary at Fort Davis. The wounded will get the proper medical care they need, and you have most likely saved the lives of the others with your wonderful nursing skills." He held her until she stopped sobbing, and tucked her in next to William, gently rubbing her back until she slowly fell asleep, exhausted. Jacob made himself a cup of coffee, trying to relax next to the campfire while eating Charlotte's unfinished supper. What a couple of days, He mused. How lucky they had been, turning away such a fierce and large raiding party. Earlier in the evening, he had overheard Captain Murphy and Sergeant Debowsky discussing the incident, while Murphy made out his after-action report. They were experienced professional soldiers, doing their duty as expected. Many of the younger soldiers and most of the teamsters and family members were still rattled and emotionally fatigued. Jacob had enough military experience to appreciate the calm demeanor of the career soldiers, even though he knew that they probably experienced the same fear as the others. The difference was that they had been through enough fighting in the past, to channel their fear into disciplined action when needed, and to later reflect that they would more than likely have to go through similar circumstances again and again. This was the life of a soldier, a life of service, putting the interest and safety of others ahead of his own. Jacob felt honored to be associated with such people. He pulled his blanket around himself with his head on his saddle, and watched the fire burn down until he fell asleep.

The morning came early. Jacob stirred before first light, dozed for a few minutes and arose. He woke up Charlotte gently, trying not to startle William. A hot breakfast of biscuits and gravy was made from leftovers from the evening venison drippings. The rest of the wagons were carrying out similar predawn tasks as the sentries were changed. The wagon train came to life with harnessing and saddling of animals, and the morning fires were put out. It had been a quiet night except for an occasional coyote howling. The moon had been nearly full, a discouragement to any would-be Indian infiltrators. Before dawn the wagon train was well on its way, following the advance scouting party, which had a half hour lead. The desert night was cooler than expected, a fact the commander appreciated. He could push the train a little harder in the morning, assuring its arrival at Fort Davis before nightfall.

They would follow an unnamed dry riverbed most of the way. This stream originated as Limpia Creek in the southeast part of the mountains just north of Fort Davis. In the eastern three fourths of its course, the riverbed was usually dry, except for the occasional desert cloud burst. After it passed Fort Davis, it was dry for most of the year. Wells dug into the river bottom near the fort supplied most of the available water for the post. This water was hauled to the cisterns at the post in barrels on wagons. There was usually just enough to support the few hundred men and animals of six companies of the 8th Infantry Regiment stationed there. A few thousand gallons could be stored in cisterns, usually only filled during infrequent rainstorms. Although not abundant, this source of water made Fort Davis the only reliable source of water between the Pecos and Rio Grande, less than 100 miles to the west of the fort. It was a critical location allowing wagon trains and coaches to cross the nearly one hundred and fifty miles of desert between the two rivers. The fort backed up against the Davis Mountains, the remains of ancient volcanic upheavals which had weathered away over eons of time, revealing crystalline rock columns and unusual formations.

The afternoon stop was delayed until nearly three o'clock, due to the slightly cooler air in the morning. The wagon train used up almost all of the remaining water it carried, but they only had to travel fifteen miles in the late afternoon and early evening, making it to Fort Davis by eight thirty in the evening.

The first order of business was to deliver the wounded to the post infirmary. Some were very weak by now, and the post surgeon, Dr. Matthews, conducted a hasty triage. Most of the wounded were stable and alert requiring only wound care and dressing changes. The soldier with the shoulder wound appeared to be doing well, with no sign of sepsis. His wound would be debrided later by the surgeon. The other soldier with the abdominal wound, had a large swelling on his right side with purulent drainage from the exit wound. He was no longer able to keep water down and had a fever. His prognosis was not good. The Army surgeon, though well-schooled and experienced in surgery as a veteran of the Mexican War, knew that this was most likely peritonitis, carrying a grim prognosis. He gently explored the wound with a probe, and placed a gauze drain, but knew that with a fever, this type of contaminated abdominal wound was almost uniformly fatal, especially in the field. There were no proper facilities to care for this unfortunate young man. A medical corpsman was instructed to give the soldier sips of laudanum, a mixture of wine and opium, to dull the pain and suffering. Most of the evening until well after midnight was devoted to evaluation and treatment of the less severely wounded.

Meanwhile, the wagon train was formed up in a defensive posture just south of the post headquarters building near the corral area. The mules and horses were furnished with hay and water, and the post mess facilities were opened up to feed the hungry teamsters and soldiers. Guards were posted and the exhausted travelers bedded down for the night. Captain Murphy reported to the post commander, Lieutenant Colonel Seawell, for a debriefing of recent events and to make arrangements to deliver four wagon loads of supplies to the post quartermaster. This was a fairly large installation for its location, with nearly four hundred troops who had to be resupplied frequently.

The next morning a burial detail was assembled, and the dead soldiers and teamsters were given a brief service at the post cemetery before interment. Wooden crosses were placed, inscribed with their name, rank, and unit for the soldiers, and birth and death years. All available troops, the teamsters, and family members attended a short prayer and hymn service, followed by a rifle salute. There was certainly a degree of sadness, but most of those present were just happy to be alive after the ordeal. Many realized that this experience was just part of life on the frontier, unpredictable and likely to be short.

After the noon meal and a short rest period, Sergeant Debowsky returned to the business of getting the train ready for the final leg of the trip to the Rio Grande Valley, where the train would follow the river up to El Paso del Norte, and Franklin, the site of Fort Bliss. There were fewer than ten days to go now, and Debowsky was anxious to get home. He inspected each wagon, ordering a few repairs by the post blacksmith. Only one wagon was found to be damaged heavily and unfit to complete the trip. One of the wagons to be left at Fort Davis was unloaded, and the cargo from the damaged wagon transferred to it. Fifteen mules and six horses were determined to be lame and unable to continue. They were replaced with new animals from the post corrals.

During the past three weeks on the trail, Sergeant Debowsky had recognized that Jacob was a good teamster and knew a good deal about maintenance and repairs. He seemed to be very calm in the way he worked with the drivers around him. They responded well to Jacob's help and his natural leadership ability. Over coffee one night on the trail, the sergeant had asked Jacob about his past military experience.

"Pvt. Stenger, would you mind telling me why you came to America, and how you ended up in the Army?"

Jacob thought it over for a minute and replied, "You see, I had been a soldier in the Bavarian Army, and was wounded in a border patrol skirmish. My leg wound took a long time to heal and would require many visits to the hospital in Augsburg. I was discharged because of my wounds, and I entered into seminary to be a priest. I still had to have periodic minor surgeries for over a year. I fell in love with a nurse at the hospital, a nun. Things became too awkward for us to remain in Germany. We decided to run away to America and get married. I had to go first, to get a job and a place for Charlotte, who would come when I was ready. When I got to New York, I met a few Germans who were helpful, but I was unable to get a job at that time, and my English wasn't very good. I ran into an Army recruiter who talked me into enlisting with the Mounted Rifle Regiment in St. Louis. It sounded like a good thing to do, St. Louis had a lot of German immigrants, and after a few months, I would be able to send for Charlotte. I had no idea the Mounted Rifles would be redeployed to Texas, as they had recently come back from opening the way to California. Anyway, I was sent here to Fort Davis, with no chance to have Charlotte join me. After a year at Fort Davis, I asked for a transfer to San Antonio and was later detailed as a clerk at 8th Military District Quartermaster in San Antonio. I was finally able to send for Charlotte, and we made our home in San Antonio with help from Paul Schmidt, my part time employer."

Jacob didn't go into detail, but told the sergeant that circumstances made it necessary for them to leave San Antonio due to Charlotte's unhappiness there. Debowsky nodded in understanding, and assured Jacob that he didn't need to go into personal details. He allowed that he thought Jacob to be a good and honorable man, and that was all he needed to know. Jacob thanked him for the remark and told him that his enlistment was up in a few weeks, and that he intended to eventually become a civilian wagon master after his time in the Army. Debowsky encouraged Jacob to stay in the Army, and that night at Fort Davis, recommended him for reenlistment. Jacob was invited to the post headquarters to talk to the officers, and an hour later signed up for a second five-year hitch, being sworn in with some other soldiers from the regiment by the post commander, Lieutenant Colonel Seawell. Jacob decided that he needed the stability of the Army to support his family, in this time of uncertainty, in a new environment with too many unknowns. He needed stability and security for his family until he could establish himself in New Mexico, find out more about the Santa Fe Trail, and how to reach his eventual goal.

That evening, Jacob made his rounds of the barracks, visiting with a few soldiers he had known since his Jefferson Barracks days. Sadly, three of them had been lost in action against the Apache since he had moved to San Antonio. He would spend some time with the survivors in the next few years, as he found out that night that the Regiment of Mounted Riflemen was being reassigned to the Department of New Mexico. He and some others from Fort Davis would be going to a new post, Fort Stanton, near the Pecos River. The Mounted Riflemen would be spread out far and wide all over New Mexico, but they would maintain close ties for years to come. Jacob could not avoid randomly running into old Army pals wherever his travels would take him.

Sergeant Debowsky needed some help. The Captain was anxious to move out early in the morning, and the teamsters were starting to get nervous after the events of the past week. The battle with the Comanche raiders was still taking its toll, and the whole train was on the verge of exhaustion. Jacob was recruited to help with getting the other teamsters ready for the last stretch of the journey. He and the sergeant visited each teamster that afternoon, making sure they were ready, and reassuring them that the worst of the trip was over. The terrain would be easier from here, three days over the desert to Sierra Blanca, then down to the Rio Grande Valley and water. From there it was an easy three days along the river to El Paso and Fort Bliss. A dragoon patrol from San Eleazario had just come in that morning and reported no hostile Indian sightings along the route for the last three days. That same patrol would accompany the train back to Fort Bliss, reinforcing the regular escort troops. At dawn, the mule train was formed up and ready as Captain Murphy and the scouts led the way southwest into the Marfa Basin and turned northwest between the Sierra Vieja and the Davis Mountains. Following the desert floor in a northwesterly direction for 80 miles below the Eagle Mountains to the west, the train arrived at Indian Hot Springs below Sierra Blanca Peak. The trip was uneventful over the three days, except for the heat which was well over 100 degrees by two o'clock in the afternoon. By starting at dawn each day, the train was able to cover the ground in three days. Best speed was made in the cool morning hours when at least 20-25 miles could be pushed from the teams. After the rest stop in the afternoon, another 10-15 miles were finished before dark. Scouts would reconnoiter for a good overnight spot and start a small brush fire before dusk, to guide the mule train into a night camp area, usually along a deep dry-wash or ravine. This limited the approaches of any unfriendly Apache who might be in the area. No large number of Indians were seen during the three days as the train passed through these high desert basins. By mid-morning of the fourth day, the advanced party had spotted Three Mile Mountain behind Indian Hot Springs and had sent a rider back to the train. Although these seven well known natural artesian wells yielded plenty of water, it was highly mineralized and non-potable. Even so, it could be very useful for bathing and washing away the trail dust. Captain Murphy decided to rest here until morning. The wagons had preserved enough drinking water, and they would be on the Rio Grande the following night, finding enough fresh water there to make the final two-day push onto Franklin and Fort Bliss.

Charlotte was looking very tired again and needed the extra rest. After the camp was secured around the hot springs, she took William down to the nearest pool and gave him a good bath. She had to let the towels cool first to prevent scalding, as the water was over 100 degrees. After an early supper that evening, while Jacob put William to bed, Charlotte returned to the springs and waded into a shallow pool where a couple of other women were bathing. They held up sheets for each other for privacy and took turns bathing and washing their garments and changing into clean clothes. It was to all a welcome relief to feel at least a little bit clean, and so relaxing to feel the warmth of the water on their skin. The desert air cooled rapidly after the sun disappeared over the western horizon. Charlotte yearned to leisurely soak in a real bathtub, but this was a blessing for the time being, and the end of the long trip across western Texas was only a few days away. She was also very thankful that their young boy was well, despite the intensely hot days in the desert. Remarkably, none of the few children in the trains company had developed any fevers or other illness up to this point.

Jacob sat on a small barrel next to the wagon and lit his clay pipe with a wood splinter lit from the dying coals of the cooking fire. He was tired from the last three days in the heat, but grateful that they had not encountered hostiles. He had watered and fed his team after encampment and found them to be in good condition. A few animals from other teams had suffered from the heat and would not be able to take the yoke for the rest of the trip. Sergeant Debowsky had wisely taken fifteen additional mules from the corrals at Fort Davis, roped and in tow behind some of the wagons. He checked each team and replaced eleven mules, two so sick or lame that they had to be shot and left on the trail. Sometimes it was difficult to destroy these loyal hard-working animals, but it would have been worse to drag them along to suffer and die a day or two later anyway. The wagons were holding up fairly well, although Jacob had to repair one wagon with a broken rear axle. After removing the freight, wagon jacks raised the rear of the wagon, and the broken axle beam removed from the large U-bolt axle fasteners. Jacob used the spare beam he carried under his own wagon, fashioning a new axle beam with saw and adz, and wedged the iron spindle skeins over the ends of the axle, pinning the iron sleeves to the wooden axle on the inside of the journals. Finally, he reinstalled the axle incorporating the reach, or coupler beam, with the U-bolt hangers connecting to the bolster blocks of the wagon. The wheel hubs were re-greased and mounted over the axle skeins and were secured with large washers and cotters. Jacob's experience in the wagon works allowed him to finish the job in a little over two hours, less than half the time it would have taken an average teamster.

After a well-deserved overnight rest, the supply train was on the road at sunrise. The road to the Rio Grande followed a westward course from the hot springs, past Three Mile Mountain, skirting the north end of the Malone Mountains. From there they passed between the numerous dry washes on a gentle grade down to El Chemical, a small Mexican border village. The Mexicans had been farming both sides of the river for many decades as the bottom was quite fertile. In this area the Rio Grande was slowly shifting to the south, but the local farmers continued working both sides, even though the Mexican War had established the river as the international boundary. No trouble had been seen here with the Mexican authorities in recent years, but the border dispute would go on long into the future. The locals caused no problems with travelers through the area, as long as their crops were not disturbed. Captain Murphy was sensitive to the interest of the local farmers, and wisely moved the caravan upriver to make camp where there would be no harm to the corn crops in the area. The mule train had made over 35 miles by then and it was nearly sundown as the teamsters pulled the wagons into a large semi-circular encampment. The escort checked the area for another five miles up-stream to make sure there were no Mexican Army patrols nearby. They returned in a little over an hour having encountered no threatening soldiers or Apache bands. With a good fresh water supply now available, the supply train could relax their water restrictions. That evening, both man and beast drank their fill. After securing their position for the night and attending to their animals, the supper fires began to spark up. That night, pickets were posted a quarter mile out on the likely approaches to the camp, and all seemed quiet. A few Mexican families waded across the river, which was low at this time of year. Seasonal thunderstorms were yet to come in the fall. Some of the villagers carried large baskets of corn and vegetables and wanted to trade for any manufactured goods, tools, or calico cloth. The military train didn't carry much in the way of textiles, but some of the teamsters were willing to trade hand tools for some of the fresh produce. This was a real luxury after a month in the desert wastes. Many of the wagons also carried flour and coffee which were also in short supply with these villagers. Captain Murphy and some the other

40

soldiers and teamsters spoke enough Spanish to get through the deal making, and the Mexicans were invited to stay and talk over coffee around the campfires. The Captain was always interested to hear any news of Indian raiders or Mexican Army patrols. The locals were saying that things had been real quiet in this area for week. The Apache from the mountains of southeastern New Mexico were not on the warpath, and they had not been around the valley for over a month. There were reports of a couple of stagecoach attacks up north in the Guadalupe Mountains the week before, but no large war parties had been seen. Captain Murphy knew that it was always good policy to treat the local farmers well to encourage them to share this kind of information. The mood among the teamsters was good, with only couple of days left to Fort Bliss. Murphy knew from experience not to relax too much. Complacency was the biggest enemy. One was never too safe in Apache country. Fortunately, this wagon train would encounter no more hostiles on the way to El Paso.

FT. BLISS 1854

Chapter V. El Paso

Early the next morning after breakfast, the train was moving forward toward El Paso, following the old Spanish mission trail established by Don Juan de Onate, the Mexican born conquistador and first Spanish governor of New Mexico, more than two hundred and fifty years earlier. El Paso del Norte would be established as the southern-most outpost of the Spanish provinces which would become New Mexico. The crossing of the Rio Grande at this point was a natural demarcation between the Mexican province of Chihuahua and the northern territories east of California, collectively called New Mexico, extending north well into the Rocky Mountains. The Rio Grande valley was seen as an oasis and a blessing to the Spaniards who had to first cross the great Sonoran Desert, parched and exhausted. The river was seen as a natural boundary at this point, which then turned north, leading to the heart of an agricultural society established centuries before by Pueblo Indians, who had slowly converted from hunter-gatherer tribes to settled farmers. There were also great legends about cities of gold and great wealth in these lands. Although the fabled golden cities of Cibola and El Dorado were never found, enough mineral wealth was discovered to entice the Spanish to explore and exploit the land. Onate and his successors had built several mission churches in this area over the years, to civilize and convert the Indians, and to establish military outposts, or presidios, to protect travelers and residents. The military road to Fort Bliss passed by the mission of San Eleazario, where the train camped the next night, and past the missions of Socorro and Ysleta on the final stretch into Franklin, Texas, and Fort Bliss. After the War with Mexico, Franklin became El Paso, Texas, and the city, El Paso del Norte, south of the river, would be renamed Juarez City.

Spirits were high at the end of the second day on the mission trail as the train approached Franklin and Fort Bliss, located nearby at Magoffinsville. The month on the trail from San Antonio to El Paso had been long, hot, and dry; not to mention the encounter with the Comanche war party. But, all in all, the teamsters were happy to be near the end of the trip. They would stay at Fort Bliss for a couple of days to deliver their cargo, before taking a few wagon loads of supplies on to Fort Fillmore, one day further north in New Mexico Territory. Most of the civilian teamsters would not be making the return trip to San Antonio, as they had signed up for this trip as Jacob had, to make it to the West and opportunity. Some would continue on to California, and a few would continue to drive wagons for the Army on this route. A few, like Jacob, would eventually settle along the trails leading west to New Mexico, California, or Oregon. Many would start their journey from Westport Landing, or Fort Leavenworth, the Missouri River bases, and the last major outfitting centers for the long caravans heading westward.

Fort Bliss, the post established in 1848 across the river from the Mexican town of El Paso del Norte, was originally part of Smith's

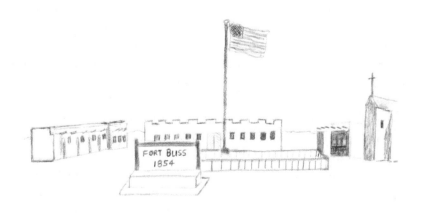

Ranch and Franklin, which later became downtown El Paso, Texas.

Because of frequent flooding, Fort Bliss was later moved and re-established at Magoffinsville in 1854. The War Department felt that a military post was necessary in the area, not only as a presence to intimidate Mexican ambitions, but also to help protect American travelers and settlers from hostile Apache and other Indian tribes in the region. A number of forts were built in the Rio Grande Valley after the Mexican War, to provide safe passage along military supply routes from south central Texas, and along the Santa Fe trail on the northern route to New Mexico from the United States by way of Missouri. The settlements around El Paso were growing rapidly in this period as the area became an important link to the Southwest and California. As the train pulled into Fort Bliss late in the afternoon, Jacob turned and smiled at Charlotte. "What are you thinking about, Frau Stenger?"

"A bath, a real bath!" she sighed, noting the numerous copper wash boilers heating up over fires near some of the houses. "They must have some real tubs, somewhere in this place." A month on the trail was long enough without a bath, not counting the brief blessed evening at the Indian Hot Springs. There were women and children here, lots of them. Charlotte would waste no time in getting acquainted with some of them, at least enough to get a nice soak in a tub. The fort was a welcome site, and almost the end of the line for this supply train, with Fort Fillmore only another day or so north. Captain Murphy marshaled the forty-plus wagons of the train into the depot area, where twenty wagons were scheduled to unload their cargo of ammunition, quartermaster supplies, barrels of flour and sundry items. Five wagon loads of hay and oats were directed to the mule barns nearby. The remaining fifteen wagon loads, bound for Fort Fillmore, were assembled separately near the corrals about 100 yards away, and guards were posted. All the teams of mules and the horses were unhitched after delivering their freight, and the animals were taken to the corrals, inspected for injuries by the post veterinarian and his men, replacing a few mules and horses found to be lame or at risk. The dragoon escort was quartered in the barracks closest to the corrals and barns. The teamsters were camped nearby, looking forward to a few days rest and replenishment after an arduous month on the trail. A few would travel on in two days to Fort Fillmore, along with the escort troops, which included elements from the Regiment of Mounted Riflemen being reassigned to various posts, camps, and stations in New Mexico. After an early supper in the mess facilities, the few families from the train were introduced to the families of some of the non-commissioned officers assigned to Fort Bliss. The wives of these NCO's knew what these women and children had just been through, as most of them had come here in much the same way. In fact, the hot water boilers were being set up to provide baths for the families on the train. They would also be offered a bed for a night or two. Charlotte and William were escorted to the quarters of the ranking non-commissioned officer at Fort Bliss, Sergeant Major Hans Schultz, and his wife Lisa. They were both Pennsylvanians of German descent and could carry on a rudimentary conversation in German with Charlotte. Lisa invited them inside the small white frame house and offered tea and cookies. She had just received some fresh milk from one of the cows kept in a barn at the corral area and poured some in a small cup for William. After an hour of relating the events of the past month to Lisa, Charlotte asked if she could bathe her child and put him down for the night. Lisa got some hot water from a copper boiler on a fire in the back of the house, mixing it with water from a barrel on the back porch, and pouring it into a dish tub big enough for William to sit in. After a little fussing, the one-year-old relaxed, and happily splashed the water while the two women scrubbed him clean. He appeared to be as healthy as could be expected after such a long journey. A minor diaper rash was dusted with some talcum powder, and he was diapered and dressed in a cotton nightgown. Charlotte took him to the guest room and rocked him to sleep in a cradle that Lisa had used for her now-grown children. During this time, Lisa prepared a bath for Charlotte in a large bathing tub kept in a room off of the porch. While Charlotte was relaxing in the warm water, Lisa took her clothes outside, washed them, and hung them out to dry for the next day. She took one of her own cotton nightgowns from a small dresser, along with two clean towels, and went into help Charlotte with washing her hair. Just as she finished washing her hair, Charlotte let out a short moan.

"What is the matter?" asked Lisa.

"I just had a pain in my lower abdomen," Charlotte answered. "Oh, God!" Charlotte cried out. "Now it is a really bad cramp, getting worse."

Lisa asked Charlotte when she had her last period. Charlotte explained that she was almost four months pregnant.

"Have you had any problems like this lately?" asked Lisa.

"No, nothing since I got over my morning sickness about five weeks ago," Charlotte answered. She suddenly grabbed her belly as another cramp seized her. About this time both women saw the appearance of dark red blood in the tub water.

"Oh, my God!" cried Charlotte. Lisa helped her stand up, and a small amount of blood appeared, with some solid tissue falling into the bathtub.

"Oh Lord, Charlotte," Lisa gasped, "You are having a miscarriage." Charlotte slumped down into the tub again, sobbing. Lisa quickly laid out a large towel on the wooden floor, and helped Charlotte out of the tub. She wrapped a cloth between her legs and helped her lie down on the towel, covering her with another bath sheet. Charlotte was sobbing uncontrollably by now. Lisa tried to calm her, assuring her that she would be alright. Lisa covered her with a blanket, as she was shivering by this time.

"Charlotte, it will be alright," Lisa said. "Just stay as you are. I am going to build a fire in the fireplace in your room. The sun is down, and we need to keep you warm. I will be back here in ten minutes, just lie still."

After a very long ten minutes for Charlotte, Lisa returned with a couple of diapers, checked Charlotte and removed the small towel, replacing it with the diapers.

"Charlotte, you are going to be fine," Lisa comforted her. "The bleeding has subsided. I am going to put this cotton nightgown on you and help you to bed. William is asleep and doing well. I will watch him for you tonight. You need to rest and sleep. In the morning, I will send for the post surgeon, Doctor Stanley. He will make sure that you are alright and not having any complications. You have lost your unborn baby, and the stress of the journey may have been too much. You are young and should certainly be able to have more children. The doctor needs to examine you to be sure, but if it had to happen, better now than later in your term."

Charlotte could say nothing, being full of shock and grief. She just kept sobbing. Lisa dressed her and helped her to bed in the guest room. Charlotte could only think of Jacob, and how he might react to this devastating news. The fire was warming the room now, and her shivering began to subside. She cried herself to sleep.

The sweet aroma of grilled hotcakes were the first thing Charlotte noticed when she awoke. She suddenly remembered the night before, wishing it was only a bad dream. She was not in any pain now, but felt fullness in her abdomen. A quick check of her bed clothes revealed a small dark patch of blood underneath her, but no active bleeding. She called out for Lisa, who opened the door a few seconds later.

"How do you feel dear?" Lisa asked.

"Alright, I think," replied Charlotte. "What time is it?"

"Almost eight in the morning," Lisa answered. "Dr. Stanley will be here in an hour, and I have sent for Jacob. My husband talked to him last night. He was upset about losing the baby, at first, but was mostly concerned about you. The Sergeant Major told him it would be better to let you sleep. Your husband will be here to see you soon."

Just then, there was a knock on the bedroom door, and Jacob and Hans were standing outside. "Just a few minutes, Jacob," cautioned Lisa. "The doctor is on his way to examine your wife, and I have to get her cleaned up and ready. Why don't you men go into the kitchen and have some of those griddle cakes I just made." Jacob thanked her and briefly went to Charlotte's bedside and sat on the edge of the bed and hugged her.

"I am so terribly sorry, Liebchen. I know this is a huge disappointment for you, and also for me. I am just glad that you are doing well, and that you had a kind lady to be with you last night."

Charlotte buried her face in Jacob's chest and sobbed. "I will be fine, she said. "Would you please bring William to me?"

"Of course," said Jacob. He left the room for a minute and returned with their son. William stretched his arms out to his mama, and she held him tight to her.

"Please take care of him until the doctor comes," Charlotte said to Jacob.

"Of course I will, darling." Jacob took William into breakfast with him, while Lisa brought in warm water, fresh towels, and a clean gown for Charlotte. After she had helped bathe and dress her, there was a knock at the front door. The Sergeant Major escorted Dr. Stanley to the guest room.

"The doctor is here to see Charlotte," he announced.

Dr. Stanley introduced himself and expressed his regrets about the miscarriage. "It was certainly fortunate that you had Mrs. Schultz to take care of you last night. She has had a lot of experience with pregnancies here at Fort Bliss, and is qualified to be a midwife, I would venture." Charlotte gave half a smile. "Let me go look at what she saved from last night, before I examine you to make sure you are safe to travel in a few days."

After he had examined the fetal remains, and examined Charlotte, the surgeon explained to her that the baby could not have been carried to term. It had probably been non-viable for the better part of a week. After explaining what she had been through in the previous month, Charlotte began to sob softly. The doctor told her that the stress had been too much for her and it was better that the baby was lost when it was. This didn't make Charlotte feel better, but later she would reflect that this result was a lot better than leaving a widower and an orphan behind. Dr. Stanley told her that she should stay at bed rest for at least another three days before traveling on to Fort Fillmore.

When Jacob realized that they could not go on with the rest of the supply train the next day, he was very concerned. Sergeant Major Schultz reassured him that they could travel with a troop of dragoons being reassigned to Fort Craig the following week. Jacob could take his wagon to Fort Craig where he would obtain orders to be stationed at Fort Stanton. Jacob could pull casual duty at the corrals at Fort Bliss in the meantime. The week at Fort Bliss went quickly. Charlotte was more than ready to be up and about in three days and was able to take care of William then. She was extremely thankful for the care given to her and her son by Lisa Schultz. Lisa shrugged it off, joking that she was born to be a mother hen. It made her life out here in the desolate west a little more tolerable when she was able to be of help to people. There were a lot of comings and goings from this place, from both east and west, and among the local population. El Paso had been a crossroads for a long time. A lot of the local Mexican women worked as domestic help for the Army wives, which provided at least some relief from the drudgery of cooking and cleaning and laundry. She also enjoyed the cultural differences and interactions with the Spanish speaking natives. In a couple of years, her husband would be able to retire with a small pension, and they would probably return to Pennsylvania where they had a large extended family.

Chapter VI. Welcome to New Mexico

Fort Craig was just over 100 miles north of Fort Fillmore, or about four to five days by wagon, depending on the weather. After leaving Fort Bliss in El Paso and delivering the last major load of supplies at Fort Fillmore, Jacob and five other wagon teams traveled north with a detachment of the 1st Dragoons who headed for a new assignment at Fort Defiance in Navajo territory in the northwest. They had followed the El Camino Real along the long dry mountain desert passage known as the Jornada del Muerto. The group camped the first night at the ruins of Fort Thorn, a small post built near a swampy part of the river, and later abandoned due to the risks of malaria. Heavy mosquito infestation caused the groups to move upwind from the marsh. Charlotte didn't get much sleep that night, fighting to keep the pesky insects off of William. The party broke camp early, happy to leave the mosquitos. They followed the river road north toward Fort Craig, successor to Fort Thorn. It was built farther north at the next large bend in the Rio Grande, in order to protect the southern approaches to the supply depot at Albuquerque. The river basin was much less swampy in this area, and closer to the town of Socorro, thirty miles to the north. Later in the day, a strong thunderstorm came out of the mountains to the west of the river, lasting about an hour.

Charlotte and William retreated under the canvas in the middle of the wagon, while those outside and on horseback were drenched. "Welcome to New Mexico!" shouted the lieutenant in charge of the dragoons, as he galloped by. Just over an hour later, everyone cheered as the sun came out again. The thunder-boomers moved east, accompanied by some strong gusty winds. By the time the group stopped to camp for the night a few hours later, everyone had dried out for the most part. Sagebrush clippings were used to kindle some driftwood and piñon pine branches for the evening campfires. The dragoons had surprised a small group of antelope in the brush, and they made a tasty addition of wild meat to the usual supper of beans and biscuits. The next afternoon, as the detachment neared Fort Craig, they crossed the river from the east to the west bank at the ford nearest the post, entering the fort at the main gate on the western side. Fort Craig, unlike most frontier posts, had become one of the largest and best protected installations west of the Mississippi, with its thick adobe walls and formidable moat enclosing the entire facility. Fort Craig was critical for the defense of the northern New Mexico command and supply infrastructure, and the Santa Fe Trail. Since the War with Mexico, the most important supply route to the U.S. Army in New Mexico was the trail from the Missouri River bases, delivering supplies to Fort Union in the northeast part of the territory. The headquarters for the Army Department of New Mexico was in Santa Fe, with a smaller depot in Albuquerque. After the threat from Mexico ended in the late 1840s, the mission of department changed to preventing attacks by, and punitive measures against hostile Indian tribes in the territory, primarily Navajo and Apache. Fort Craig, despite its strength and size, had problems with a crowded garrison making it hard on military families. Outside of the commander's quarters, many families had to share space. The lower ranks had two or three families in a small set of quarters. It became evident to Charlotte after the first week, that she would not be able to tolerate the conditions very long. When Jacob came back from his first escort assignment to Fort Stanton, she let him know this in no uncertain terms.

"Jacob, this is terrible. This is no way for women and children to live. William and I have a small bedroom in the quarters of a corporal's wife and two other children. There is a small cooking area under the porch, which we share, and the outhouses are a two-minute walk away. It is hard enough trying to toilet train a two-year-old in the best of circumstances, let alone after a long walk in the dark. These quarters for the lower ranks' families are very cramped, built almost as lean-to structures against the wall of the fortress. When it rains, the log and mud roof leaks like a sieve. How can we live like this?"

Jacob was very frustrated. "Liebchen, I know this is very difficult, but I can't do much about it right now. I will find a way to make it better. No families are allowed at Fort Stanton, the Apaches are very hostile around there. I am scheduled to do some escort missions to Fort Union to bring supplies back to Fort Stanton. You know I am always looking for a situation which will be better for my family. I will be going on an escort to Fort Union soon, and hopefully I can find something better for you there."

Chapter VII. Escort Duty

Jacob's unit, the Regiment of Mounted Riflemen, was scattered all over New Mexico in the 1850s at large and small posts. Five of the companies were assigned to Fort Stanton to help control of the aggressive Mescalero Apaches of southeastern New Mexico. The Mescalero Apache were a southern branch of Athabaskan-speaking Native Americans originally from northwestern Canada and Alaska. Some of these tribes migrated over the millennia into the southern great plains of the present-day Oklahoma and the Texas panhandles. They were driven west into New Mexico, Arizona, far west Texas, and northern Mexico by their plains rivals, primarily the Comanche, Kiowa, and Arapahoe. These prairie peoples were related by language, but hostile to the culturally different Navajo tribes. The Mescalero Apache settled primarily in the mountainous southeast part of the territory between the Rio Grande and Pecos Rivers. Calling themselves Mashiende, "people of the mountains," the Mescalero joined, for mutual protection, neighboring Mexican tribes of Lipan Apache from Chihuahua, Chiricahua Apache from lands west of the Rio Grande, and Jicarilla Apache from the north. The Mescalero were semi-nomadic hunters and ranged far and wide when searching for game. This is certainly one of the reasons they were resistant to the Spanish and Mexican settlers, and later to settlers coming from the

United States. The Mescalero and their southern cousins in west Texas operated out of the Guadalupe Mountains to the north, and the Davis Mountains to the south. This tribe was known for raids along the roads from central Texas to El Paso. Their raids took them as far west as the Rio Grande and north into the Jicarilla Apache areas of the New Mexico Escarpment. After the Jicarilla wars in northern and northeastern New Mexico, the U.S. government realized that a long period of relative peace with the Indians in New Mexico had ended,

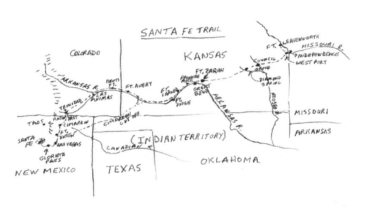

and that even the Santa Fe Trail supply line was threatened.

Construction of a number of forts was authorized in New Mexico. Fort Stanton in southeast New Mexico was built to provide protection from Apache attacks on the southern trails and settlements along the Rio Bonito, a tributary of the Pecos River. By 1856, the situation in New Mexico led the Army to reassign the Regiment of Mounted Riflemen to reinforce the dragoons who had been in the Department of New Mexico since the end of the Mexican War. This was in order to bolster the mounted patrol and escort duties which were becoming increasingly necessary. Five companies of the regiment, including Jacob's, were assigned to Fort Stanton due to the intensity of Apache raids. The supply line traffic was steady from Fort Union and Fort Bliss to Fort Stanton, the center of the Army effort against the Mescalero raids. Hostile activities ranged across southeastern New Mexico and along the stagecoach and commercial routes from central Texas. The Mescalero could strike anywhere without warning. Travel in the sector required mounted escorts. Jacob's first assignment was with an escort troop protecting delivery of food and ammunition from Fort Union to Fort Stanton. Fort Union was built as a depot in northeastern New Mexico in 1851 as a receiving site on the Santa Fe Trail for goods and supplies shipped to the Department of New Mexico from the Missouri River bases of Independence and Fort Leavenworth. After nearly 250 years of Spanish and Mexican dominance, the territory was now controlled by an American territorial government supported by the U. S. Army. In addition, the presence of multiple hostile Indian tribes required a strong, but limited military presence to protect commerce and settlers. A series of forts was established in western Kansas and New Mexico to provide law and order until the final closing of the American frontier.

FT. UNION 1856

Chapter VIII. Fort Union and the Trail

After overthrowing Spanish rule in 1821, the new government of Mexico tore down barriers with the United States. American traders were allowed to enter New Mexico without fear of imprisonment. Starting in 1822 with William Becknell's second trip to Santa Fe, wagons pulled by mules and oxen were used to make the long journey from Missouri, making larger scale commerce possible. The U. S. government finally got into the act in 1825, having the Army survey the wilderness route which became known as the Santa Fe Trail. Two routes were actually used, the more direct route crossing the Cimarron River directly southwest toward the junction of the Mora River and Sepullo Creek in northeastern New Mexico. From there the wagon trains were only two or three days from Santa Fe itself. The problem with this Cimarron cutoff was that it traversed the arid desert plains of southwest Kansas, and the winter hunting grounds of the Comanche and Kiowa tribes. Even large trains with military escorts were in constant danger from hundreds or even thousands of Indians suddenly attacking on horseback. The alternative Mountain Branch of the trail, following west along the Arkansas River was safer in terms of more available water and fewer Indians, but it was nearly 100 miles longer. It also required traveling over the treacherous Raton Pass at the foot of the Sangre de Cristo Mountains. The two branches of the trail converged near the town of Watrous, then threaded south and then west along the mountains to Santa Fe, through Glorieta Pass.

Many attempts were made over the years to establish outfitting stations in the northeastern corridor of New Mexico. The area of convergence of the trail branches was a natural place to station replacement animals for the trains. In addition, there were settlements in the Rayado, Springer, and Cimarron areas anxious to receive goods carried on the wagon trains. After the War with Mexico, the Army established Fort Union as a suitable location for a depot to receive and distribute supplies to the far-flung posts, camps, and stations throughout the Department of New Mexico. Fort Union would become a major commercial trading post, as Santa Fe Trail trade grew from about $50,000 annually by 1850, to more than $5,000,000 only a decade later. The trail also carried thousands of California-bound immigrants, trying to find their fortunes in the gold fields. A number of them decided to go no further, staying in New Mexico. In 1851, acting on War Department orders, the newly designated commander of the department, Lieutenant Colonel Sumner, began reorganizing the Army posts in the territory to better defend the population along the main supply line, the Santa Fe Trail. Fort Union had been chosen due to strategic location, availability of fresh water and grassland for animal fodder, close access to timber, and distribution routes for the rest of the installations in the territory. Fort Union would become the key to the defense of the entire territory, control of hostile native tribes, and access to the trading routes and mineral wealth of the west. Two hundred and fifty years of Spanish and Mexican rule over the native Indians had been refined into a more or less mutually cooperative arrangement, important for both cultures. Although interrupted by episodic conflict and occasional raids, there had been no major dislocations since the Pueblo Uprisings at the end of the seventeenth century. The sudden overwhelming influx of the Americans in the middle of the nineteenth century, with their Anglo-European culture, had many disrupting influences on both the Indians and Hispanic residents. There was a natural deep-seated resentment of the intruders, with Americans disinclined to tolerate the practices of the indigent cultures. Hispanic settlers were long accustomed to their system of traditional Royal Land Grants, whereby the aristocracy controlled the peons and Indians who actually worked the arable land, herded the livestock, or worked to extract the mineral wealth of the territory. Anglo-American tradition of private property rights and contract labor would clash heavily with the Spanish tradition, especially following the American Civil War. The Indians, for their part, believed that no man could claim the land personally. The earth was there for the use of all creatures without ownership, taking from the land only what was required for sustenance. Despite the cultural differences, the Americans were in the Southwest to stay, and accommodations would be made, sometimes peacefully, often with strife.

Jacob's escort detachment made the trip from Fort Stanton without wagons, following the Pecos, and cross country from Anton Chico, arriving at Fort Union on the 21st of August. There had been no Indian encounters on the trip north, and the escort made the trip in four days. After two days' rest, they picked up the supply train at the depot, twenty wagons with teams and drivers, carrying all classes of supplies back to Fort Stanton. Reaching Las Vegas on the Santa Fe Trail, they followed a small tributary of the Pecos south, to Anton Chico, crossing the Pecos itself and climbing up the plateau south of the river. The terrain did not seem difficult to Jacob, compared to what he had been through earlier in the summer in Texas. The Pecos River Valley was shallow with easy fording in the northern part, but deep and tortuous further south. Roads and trails fifty or more miles west of the Pecos were much easier traveling with wagons, and a more direct route and approach in the southern part of the route. This route required crossing high mountain desert areas of the Mesa de la Vista and the large salt flats further south, and there were water points west of Piedra Pintada Canyon along the eastern slopes of the Sierra Jumanes Mountains. The Springs at Lagos de Los Partes was the last watering hole before reaching Fort Stanton, passing between Cariso Mountain and the Sierra Capitan Range just to the north. The post was located near the Rio Bonito, also called the Rio Hondo, a tributary flowing east into the Pecos River. The trip had been smooth and without hostile contact, but the supply train had been watched at various points along the trails by Indian hunting parties. The mounted escort set out listening posts in all directions from the wagon circle every evening, with relief posted every two to three hours. This allowed the men to get chow and adequate rest. The mess wagon stayed open all night with hot coffee and biscuits. Soldiers and teamsters with the wagons were responsible for the care of the animals, corralled within the camp circle. Jacob was told that the Indians watching them during the first few days were mostly Jicarilla

Apache and Kiowa hunting parties, who had little interest in getting into a fight with the soldiers. They would usually keep their distance, but had been known to attack settlers and small parties of civilian travelers. These tribes were usually not as aggressive as the Mescalero groups south of Fort Stanton. Mescalero were not as nomadic as the northern Jicarilla and other plains tribes. The Mescalero bands tended to stay in the higher country of the Sacramento and Guadalupe Mountains. Feeling threatened by the encroachment of the white man, they were more prone to raids and ambushes than the plains Indians. This was due to a more intense history of hostile interactions with the Spanish settlers, and the threat to their hunting areas. There was adequate game in the mountains, but nothing like the seemingly unlimited herds of buffalo enjoyed by their northern cousins. The Mescalero jealously protected their hunting grounds from European encroachment.

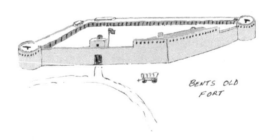

BENTS OLD
FORT

On the sixth night, the wagon train camped at Lagos del Los Partes, and arrived at Fort Stanton by early afternoon on September 2nd. Cheering and a few pistol shots rang out from the isolated Army post as the wagons approached the fort. This supply run was the first of many from Fort Union to Fort Stanton as the route would prove to be much less risky than the supply route from Texas through Fort Fillmore via Fort Bliss. It was a day longer from Fort Union, but the volume of freight from Missouri had begun to surpass that from San Antonio. Santa Fe Trail traffic resulted in Fort Union becoming the primary supply point for the entire Army operation in New Mexico. This included military essentials, but increasingly commercial and even luxury goods from St. Louis and the East. Jacob and the other soldiers were very happy to complete their first mission without a fight. They rode to the post corral area, unsaddled their mounts, making sure the animals were rubbed down, watered, and fed before they walked to the enlisted barracks. The troops washed up and put on clean shirts and headed for the parade field and the flagpole for the retreat ceremony. Afterward the soldiers entered one of the four commissaries, or mess facilities. After a supper of beans, bacon, fresh hot bread, butter, and coffee, the exhausted troopers signed in at the post returns register in the day room for their barracks and collected their mail. Charlotte had written a letter that was waiting for Jacob, which he quickly opened as the sun began to set behind the barracks.

"Lieber Jacob, I am missing you so much every day, Schatze. Even though we have many nice Army wives and laundry ladies here, even a couple of German women, we are very lonely without you. William cries for his papa almost every day. He is getting so big now, and walking better and even running a little. He does trip easily, but that will get better soon. He speaks English with two other little boys here, and I try not to talk much in German. We both hope you will come back to Fort Craig very soon, my dearest. I am doing well, but the living space in these quarters is very crowded. Sometimes I volunteer to help the other women with laundry and cooking. When our work is done and the children are put to bed, we sometimes sit together in the evening and sew or knit. One Irish lady is teaching us some card games. We have no chaplain here, but every Sunday one the priests or friars from a local mission comes to give a brief Mass, as most of the workers in our vegetable garden are Mexicans. We are supposed to have an evangelical pastor from Socorro here once a month, but I haven't seen him yet. The commanding officer's wife is very kind, calling on us weekly to see that we and our children are provided for. The quarters for families are very cramped with mud floors and straw mat ceilings covered with adobe, and still leaks when it rains. I don't see how women and children could survive a winter here. For now, the food is adequate with plenty of flour, sugar, bacon, eggs and chickens, and occasional beef or venison. Please come back as soon as you can, William and I are waiting for you. Love, Charlotte."

Jacob suddenly felt very empty and alone without his family. He was determined to get back to Fort Craig as soon as possible and find a way to move his family to more suitable quarters. He had seen some decent housing for families at Fort Union and thought his family would be better off there. It also looked as if he would now be doing escort duty trips to and from Fort Union rather than Fort Craig. The next morning he reported to the regimental day room to see the senior non-com, Sergeant Major Riley. Jacob told him about his situation, which was somewhat unusual, in that most private soldiers at this time were not married and had to obtain permission from the regimental commander in order to marry. This was already a reality for Jacob, and he had a child. The Sergeant Major knew that he was a good soldier and had recently reenlisted. He agreed to talk to the regimental adjutant on his behalf. This might be possible soon, he was told, as Jacob's detachment had already been tasked for escort duty in the Fort Union area, guarding supply trains from the depot to one of its sub-posts southeast on a branch of the Pecos River, known as Hatch's Ranch, about 65 miles from Fort Union. This station was strategically located in an area recently plagued by raiding Jicarilla Apache and their Comanche and Kiowa allies. Large herds of livestock were common in this part of northeastern New Mexico and were convenient targets for the plains Indians when there were no buffalo herds in the southern plains hunting grounds near the Cimarron and Canadian Rivers. Hatch's Ranch was at the southern end of the Gallinas Range northeast of the Pecos, and well situated for interception of invaders from the east. By November of 1856, Hatch's Ranch was established as a military sub-post supporting Company A of the Regiment of Mounted Riflemen, tasked with protecting the settlers and stock breeders as far as the Texas border, ready to intercept Comanche and Kiowa raiders.

About the same time as plans were being made to garrison Hatch's Ranch, a peaceful era along the Santa Fe trail was coming to an end. William Bent, a fur trader, with a trading fort near Big Timbers, on the Arkansas River, had begun to have new trouble with the Kiowa Indians in that sector of the trail. Bent wrote to Ceran St. Vrain, his friend and former partner, who had some influence with the military due to his rank as a Colonel in the fledgling New Mexico Volunteers. St. Vrain went to Fort Union from his home at Mora to receive the letter sent there from Bent. The letter warned that there were not only a large number of U. S. Army supplies at Bent's New Fort, but that travel on the Santa Fe Trail could be greatly endangered unless troops were sent there soon. St. Vrain forwarded the letter to Colonel Bonneville, the department commander in Santa Fe.

Bonneville then ordered Lieutenant Colonel Loring, the Fort Union commander, to send a detail to Bent's New Fort to investigate and safeguard the military stores if necessary. Since Fort Union's garrison was greatly depleted at the time, Loring called for Mounted Riflemen from other posts to form the detail. This included seven enlisted troopers of Co. C, Jacob's unit. They were ordered from Hatch's Ranch to Fort Union, where they were joined by Lt. McCrae and fifteen troopers from Cantonment Burgwin, a small post in the Sangre de Cristo Mountains near Taos. After outfitting at Fort Union for two days, and taking two wagons of provisions for two months, they set out for Raton Pass on November 19th. Jacob was supposed to be on his way back to Fort Stanton soon, but that would have to wait. He sent a letter to Charlotte at Fort Craig to let her know he would be delayed and probably wouldn't get to see her and William until after Christmas. Jacob was deeply disappointed at the prospect, having been away from his family for more than two months already. He was a little excited, on the other hand, to finally be on the famed Santa Fe Trail, and the Great Plains, the prairie lands he had heard so much about. He would also get his first taste of winter on the high plains of the Rocky Mountain West.

After crossing Ocate Creek, fifteen miles north of Fort Union, the detail traveled another fifteen miles north to Rayado, the first stop, and the Maxwell Ranch. Lucien Maxwell, a former Santa Fe trader, had inherited a huge area of land in northeastern New Mexico, originally a Spanish land grant of more than a million acres. Maxwell founded Rayado in 1848 as the first plains settlement east of the Sangre de Cristo Mountains. It was also an Army sub-post and staging area on the Santa Fe Trail until Fort Union was established. Travelers on the trail could obtain mules, horses, and provisions at Rayado. Maxwell in his youth had been a mountain man and hunter, a close friend of Kit Carson, and had accompanied Carson and John C. Fremont on western expeditions in the early 1840s. Maxwell and his Hispanic wife, Luz, built a large home at the Rayado Ranch, which they rented to the Army. After Fort Union was built, thirty miles to the south, the Maxwells moved to nearby Cimarron where they built a huge home and compound including a hotel, saloon, and dance hall, which were elaborately furnished and covered a city block. Rayado continued as a stagecoach and wagon stop on the mountain route on the Santa Fe Trail.

Jacob's unit departed Rayado Ranch the following morning, November 20th, following the trail to Raton Pass. The group camped the next day at Clifton House on the Trail. Crossing the pass required two days and was without incident except tor the shooting of a large black bear, which had spooked the horse of the Ute Indian guide near the summit. Jacob was amazed at the view from the top of the pass looking to the west. The impressive Spanish Peaks were backed up by the Sangre de Cristo range running to the north and south. To the east, the Great Plains stretched out into the Kansas Territory as far as the eye could see. The column arrived at Trinidad on the 24th of the month. The road over the pass was still hazardous for large wagons at the time, but posed no special problems for men on horseback and the two small Army field wagons. Four sure-footed mules were able to carry the wagons over fairly rough ground, even though the crossing was hard on some of the horses, slipping on loose rock. Fortunately, the Trinidad station on Purgatoire River was near, able to supply fresh mounts and water. The next morning the soldiers departed northeast on the trail toward the stagecoach station at Timpas Creek. No hostile Indians were seen on the way, only a small Cheyenne hunting party just south of the Arkansas River. The Cheyenne told the Army scouts that a migration of Kiowa and Comanche was already more than a hundred miles southeast of Bent's Fort on their way to winter encampments along the river. Lt. McCrae was greatly relieved that his small unit was now unlikely to encounter hundreds of warriors around the Big Timbers rendezvous area on the Arkansas. He decided not to pass this information on to the troopers at this point, in order that they should remain vigilant for the duration of the mission. The column moved quickly across the plains, reaching Iron Spring on the trail on the 26th. Camping here overnight, it would be only two more days to Big Timbers and Bent's Fort. They crossed the Arkansas at the ford west of Bent's Old Fort, the original trading post. The Bent brothers had abandoned and burned the old post in 1849 after sixteen years as a fur trading post and supply stop on the trail. After the Mexican War and General Kearny's march to New Mexico, the location began less useful for trade with the Indians, and they had failed to sell the property to the Army. William Bent moved his fur trading operation to Fort St. Vrain on the South Platte River further north, just east of the front range of the Rocky Mountains. When he returned to the Arkansas River in 1852, Bent would open a log trading post, about 30 miles east of the old fort, at Big Timbers, a traditional gathering and trading area of the plains Indians. He later built a stone fort nearby known as Bent's New Fort. From this location he could enjoy closer proximity to his Indian clients and still remain an important provisioning stop on the Santa Fe Trail. A large storehouse in the stone fort was used for stockpiling government supplies. Bent had returned from a trip back east in October of 1856, to find that one of his employees at the fort had been illegally selling whiskey to the local Kiowa tribes. When the employee was fired by Bent and whiskey was no longer available, the Kiowa were angry and attacked the fort, threatening to kill Bent. Fortunately for him, he was supported by friendly Cheyenne living around the trading post. Bent had been married to two Cheyenne wives and had developed a great deal of trust with that tribe over the past twenty years. This fact probably saved his life at the time. When the reconnaissance detachment arrived at Big Timbers, things were quiet. There were no Kiowa warriors in the area, and Lt. McCrae confirmed that they had moved to the Cimarron basin with the rest of their nation, joining them in winter quarters. Without a present threat to the military stores in the stone fort, the detachment decided to return to Fort Union, arriving there on January 8th, 1857, with Lt. McCrae briefing Lieutenant Colonel Loring. This information was passed on to Santa Fe. Loring informed Colonel Bonneville that the stores were safe. He also informed the department commander that any plans to move against the Kiowa encampments would require 400 to 500 mounted soldiers with Ute and Cheyenne guides, and wagons with three months of supplies to support the campaign. The ideal time would be late winter or early spring when adequate grass forage was available. Although preparations for a plains campaign were begun at many installations in the department, things remained quiet through the winter. The only scare was the failure of the January mail coach from Missouri to arrive in New Mexico. Because of this, the February mail from Fort Union to Independence was escorted as far as the Arkansas River well into Kansas, following the Cimarron route, by a large military escort of Mounted Riflemen, including Jacob and others from his unit.

While at Fort Union in January, Jacob had followed up with his friend, Sergeant Major Riley, regarding the possibility of moving his family from Fort Craig to Fort Union. Riley had good news for Jacob. The regimental adjutant had obtained the commander's permission for Charlotte and William, and some other family members of Mounted Riflemen, to travel north with a supply train returning from Fort Craig to the depot at Albuquerque, and then on to the headquarters in Santa Fe. Jacob would have to complete the escort mission safeguarding the mail to the Arkansas crossing, and after returning from this mission, he would be given two weeks furlough for travel to Santa Fe to meet his family and escort them back to Fort Union. Jacob was ecstatic, nearly jumping for joy. "Oh, thank you so much, Sergeant Major Riley! Das ist wunderbar, oh excuse me, it is wonderful news."

"Now don't get too excited, Private, Sergeant Major Riley said. "You know there is no official support for families of the lower ranks. The adjutant only authorized this because the commander was sympathetic due to your good record, and the fact that you were already married with a child when you came from Texas. Your wife and child are not eligible for regular quarters, and they will have to live in the quarters for the laundresses. You will have to stay in the barracks, and there will be no special privileges for your family. But, at least, your wife can make a little money as a laundress, and food and medical care will be available."

Jacob didn't care. "I know the rules, Sergeant Major. I will do whatever I have to do to be closer to them. You don't know how much this means to me. I'll be forever grateful."

Jacob ran back to his barracks to write a letter to Charlotte. He scrambled to find pen and paper. He was so excited that he spilled half of the ink from the bottle as he opened it. The quill was shaking in his hand as he began.

"Charlotte, Liebchen, my Sergeant Major just gave me the very best news. Since it looks like I am going to be doing escort duty for some time out of Fort Union, the regiment is going to allow you and William and a couple of other wives and families to move to this area. It looks like you can get work here and live on the post. I am sorry I couldn't be there for Christmas, but I just got back from a trip to Kansas, up the trail, and it looks like I will be gone again soon on escort duty. We will meet in Santa Fe by the middle of March. The Army will help you get our wagon and possessions there with a supply train. I am due a furlough then, and afterwards I will bring you back here to Fort Union. I am sending a spinning top to William with this letter. I miss you both terribly, but we will be together again soon. Love, Jacob."

Jacob sealed the letter and took it to the sutler's store, bought a little spinning top, put it in a box for William, and gave both to the mail service at the store. He was told that it would reach Fort Craig in about a week. He hoped that he would hear from Charlotte by the time he got back from his upcoming mission.

The fact that the regular mail from Missouri to Santa Fe had not reached Fort Union by the end of January, renewed fears that the Kiowa and Comanche were going to cause problems on the Trail again. If the mail couriers had been intercepted by the Indians on the westward run, the eastbound mail could not be sent without adequate protection. An escort of two officers and forty troopers, including Jacob, were ordered to travel with the mail, not as a mounted escort, but in wagons. Jacob and his comrades thought this was odd and were crowded into the wagons very uncomfortably. They were informed that several factors were in play, including a shortage of Army mounts at the time, and orders to avoid provoking Indians, unless attacked. If the plains Indians were found to be peaceful along the route from the Cimarron River, the escort could return to Fort Union after reaching Walnut Creek on the Arkansas River. As it turned out, there was not even a threat of hostilities by the time they reached the Cimarron.

Completing their mission, the group returned to Fort Union by February 25th. The escort troopers were tired and bored after traveling 500 miles without encountering hostiles, with little excitement beyond the occasional shooting of a deer or antelope to supplement the tedious diet of beans, bacon, and pan bread. Jacob didn't really care about that during this time, only about starting his furlough as soon as possible. He was dying to see his wife and child. The additional prospect of being with them in a real town was also pretty exciting after three months of life on the road. Soon they would be living close to him. He would do everything he could to increase his time with his family, and to secure better living conditions for them. Approval was forwarded by his platoon sergeant and signed the next day by the Adjutant. The dispatch rider from Santa Fe had arrived at Fort Union that morning with news that Charlotte had left Fort Craig with other families of the Mounted Riflemen and their dragoon escort and had safely reached Albuquerque on the 28th. They were expected to arrive in Santa Fe by March 1st and would be put up in an old inn across the street from the plaza, near the Army headquarters at the old Palace of the Governors. Jacob and two other soldiers going to meet their families would be leaving for Santa Fe in the morning on the mail coach with escort, the trip normally taking two to three days, depending on the weather. Bed and meals would be provided at Las Vegas, and Kozlowski's Ranch the second night. They were expected to reach Santa Fe on the third day to meet their families for a ten-day stay. They would be expected back at Fort Union by March 15th, traveling the same route with the east bound mail. Jacob was nearly beside himself by this time. He thought that this was all very generous of the Army, especially for such low-ranking enlisted men. He recalled, however, that his regiment had been having problems with recruitment and retention. A large number of enlistments were due to expire in the next few months, and the rest of the year might be worse. The Mounted Rifles had been stretched thin with all the extended escort duty during the past year, along with deployments into Navajo and Apache lands, trying to keep a fragile peace on multiple fronts. Colonel Loving, the regimental commander, and now also the commander of Fort Union, had concerns that there could be a real shortage of deployable troops if increase hostile Indian activity should arise. He needed to keep as many soldiers in the department as possible and do everything possible to encourage men to stay in the service. Although the eastern plains were quiet now, he knew that the Kiowa and Comanche tribes were unpredictable. Growing expansion of the northeastern New Mexico settlements would soon drive the plains tribes to strike out against encroachment onto their hunting grounds. In addition, Gila Apache groups southwest of the Rio Grande were raiding the stagecoach routes through southern Arizona. A campaign was being planned at headquarters to quell the disturbances. In the northwest part of the department, the Army had been at odds with the Navajo for years over traditional grazing rights claimed by the tribe. Even the establishment of Fort Defiance and Fort Fauntleroy, and several treaties, had not stopped the violence. The long hated established Spanish settlers, and other Indian tribes continued to encroach onto Navajo lands. More violence was almost certain in the coming months. Despite the ongoing fighting, Jacob had earned his two-week furlough, and was preparing for a long-awaited reunion with his family. He had also been lucky to run into a trader from St. Louis and had purchased a small bottle of French perfume for five dollars, nearly half a month's pay. Charlotte had not had such a luxurious gift since they had left San Antonio. Jacob looked forward to delivering it in person when he got to Santa Fe. Arrangements for travel to Santa Fe with two other soldiers on the mail wagon were made. They would all drive their families back to Fort Union in their own wagons.

PALACE OF GOVERNORS

Chapter IX. Santa Fe

Charlotte leaned her head out from under the wind flap of the wagon to ask the driver how much further to Santa Fe. "It's about one more day from here ma'am. We'll camp tonight at the Santa Domingo Pueblo, about an hour ahead from here."

"Thank you, Corporal," she answered. Charlotte had seen another pueblo, from a distance, at Isleta, half a day south of Albuquerque. They were fascinating structures, with their thick adobe walls, stacked one upon another like a hotel or resembling a desert fortress. Hundreds of people lived in these buildings, surrounded by small adobe-covered cooking ovens. The people of these villages seemed very friendly. It must not have been that way long ago, as she had heard stories of ancient wars with other tribes and with Spanish and Mexican colonists. There had been very few conflicts with the Americans so far, nothing major since the Taos uprising a decade before. That horrible event began with the murder of Governor Benton and others. The American Army had quickly crushed the revolt, ending tragically with over a hundred renegades being killed by cannon fire into a church where the rebels had barricaded themselves. This massacre had been a painful punctuation to the American conquest of New Mexico. The uprising seemed to have been a limited revolt by Mexican and mixed-race dissidents against the annexation of New Mexico by the United States. It was not

68

something the Americans had expected, since General Kearney had taken the territory with hardly a shot. Most of the bloody fighting during the two-year long War with Mexico took place in the heart of Mexico itself, with the northern borderlands being spared for the most part. In the New Mexico territory, most the fighting seemed to be a continuation of the centuries-old struggle of the Indian tribes against the Europeans, no longer just the Spanish, but now including English, German, Irish, Italian, Polish, and other recent immigrants to the United States.

"I suppose it has always been this way," said Charlotte muttered to herself. "You just can't expect a proud people to accept conquest without putting up a fight." Her experiences in this new cultural transition had actually felt fairly peaceful. She remembered enough Latin and French from school that picking up Spanish wasn't too difficult. She talked to the Mexican women as often as she could and found them to be friendly and generally accepting of the new reality of American rule. From what she could gather, the people had already begun to feel dependent on the States for supplying New Mexico with goods they would rarely receive from Mexico. Machine-made goods from the States were usually superior to handmade items from Chihuahua or Mexico City, and less expensive. New Mexico, and California were finding geographic advantages in being aligned with the United States. Since the beginning of sanctioned trade between the Missouri bases and Santa Fe, the annual tonnage carried over the Santa Fe Trail had grown from a few hundred tons in the 1820s to nearly ten thousand tons by the mid 1850s.

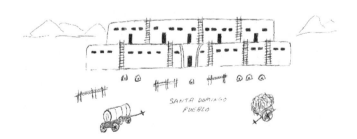

SANTA DOMINGO
PUEBLO

Santa Domingo Pueblo was an ancient and important site for the Pueblo people and culture. When the Anasazi ancestors moved out of the canyons and cliff dwellings in medieval times due to drought, important settlements were founded near more reliable sources of water. The upper Rio Grande Valley became heavily settled over the next few centuries in order to produce predictable harvests of maize, developed in Mexico thousands of years earlier, and other crops such as beans, squash, and melons. It was still winter in the valleys, but the residents of the pueblos were already looking forward to spring planting. The grain stores were running low, and game was especially scarce at this time of year. As the military wagons pulled into the central gathering area of the pueblo, the Lieutenant in charge of the small train dismounted, and went to greet the elders of the village, and offered them a few small gifts of blankets, woven cloth, and a small barrel of flour. The elders were happy to have these items, in exchange for overnight camping privileges for the white soldiers and civilians. The officer ordered the wagons circled about a hundred yards away from the pueblo. Charlotte watched about a dozen small children with fascination, as they ran along beside the wagons. It was late winter, and the children wore buckskin leggings and moccasins, but their shirts and skirts were calico and gingham cloth. Charlotte also noticed some of the women baking flat bread in the small, domed adobe ovens in the yard of the buildings. Dried strips of meat hung from small racks and trellises nearby. The permanent settlement lifestyle was strikingly different than from that of the plains Indians, with their tipis and wicker dwellings she had seen when she first came west from Texas. Southwestern deserts had slowly changed the living habits of the once nomadic people who had moved into this region over the past few thousand years. The lack of plentiful game in many areas had slowly forced a shift to an agricultural society living in fixed settlements. Maize was the staple crop, supplemented with squash, peppers, and a few gourds, melons, and herbs. Charlotte saw several women on their knees working dried corn kernels into a powdery flour. They mixed it with water to make a paste from which a flat bread patty or tortilla was formed. The finished tortillas could be folded or rolled up with meat or vegetables inside, eaten with the fingers, dipping in various vegetable sauces. Spanish settlers had added to the diet tomatoes and other seasonal vegetables of European and Central American origin.

Some varieties of potatoes from South America had found their way north over the centuries. The Anglo settlers and soldiers had also brought seeds and the art of canning fruits and vegetables in glass jars for preservation for winter use. The Spanish and Anglos also brought cattle, pigs, goats, and sheep, adding a sustainable source of meat, hides, wool and milk to the territory. Charlotte and the other Army wives settled into the center of the wagon circle, made cooking fires, and started making the evening meal for themselves, their children, and some of the soldiers guarding the campsite. William and a couple of the other young children were clinging to their mothers' skirts. It was after sunset by now, and the chill of the early evening was setting in. Reaching freezing temperatures after midnight was common in these mountain deserts. The women bedded their children down in the wagons on mattresses of straw, covering them with woolen blankets and homemade quilted comforters. These were topped with buffalo hides. After a last cup of coffee, the women crawled in with their children. Half a dozen soldiers were posted as a night guard, walking the wagon perimeter, relieved in two-hour shifts. Charlotte awakened periodically during the night, hearing only the soldiers talking around the campfire.

At first light, the teams were harnessed and hitched to the wagons. There had been a few scattered flurries during the night, and a light dusting of snow reminded the travelers that springtime in the Rocky Mountains was not assured until May. After a hasty breakfast of bacon, beans, pan bread, and coffee, the Lieutenant gave the order to move out. He wanted to reach Santa Fe before sundown that evening. The road was relatively easy heading on into Santa Fe, heading slightly to the southeast down a long shallow dry wash. After passing through a few minor arroyos, the route turned northeast following the Rio de Santa Fe toward the Sangre de Cristo Mountains. The territorial capital lay in the foothills below them. It was a chilly morning, slightly cloudy, as the wagons moved east from Santa Domingo, crossing the large arroyos south of the Santa Fe River. They then followed the military road south of the river, turning to the northeast. At noon the train stopped for the midday meal and watering of the animals. Santa Fe was only another dozen miles, and after an hour, the wagons were back on the trail, following the river road into the capital. The afternoon sun was warm now and the winds were calmer. Stands of cottonwood trees began to appear, surrounding the occasional ranch house and corrals. Charlotte recalled reading about

the early Spanish period and the establishment of Santa Fe de San
Francisco, the city of the Holy Faith of Saint Francis, which had been
the Spanish provincial capital for more than 300 years The site was
very near to the center of the ancient Pueblo Indian Kingdom, where
the culture developed around quaint looking adobe buildings, some of
the ruins still to be found, along with pieces of painted pottery. As the
wagons neared the center part of the city, the Plaza, a large public
square, came into view. It was the center of business for the town,
surrounded by most of the stores and shops of the merchants and
traders, as well as some public buildings. The largest building on the
north side of the street across from the Plaza was the old Palace of the
Governors, a whole block long, a low adobe building of rough
workmanship, fronted with a colonnade of covered posts and beams,
creating a sheltered promenade in the rainy season. It was occupied
now by the American Territorial Government offices. The U.S..
courthouse was there, and military headquarters for the department
and the 3rd Infantry at the rear of the building. Further north on
Washington Street were the ruins of old Fort Marcy, unoccupied since
the end of the Mexican War, but now used for storage of military
supplies. Across from the Plaza to the east and south was a hotel, a
large three-story rambling building formerly known as the La Fonda,
which had been built in the 1820s, but had been renamed the U.S.
Hotel after the Mexican War. Charlotte and the other Army wives
bound for Fort Union would meet their husbands there shortly. She
was getting very excited to see Jacob. It had been nearly six months
since they had been together. She was also anxious for Jacob to see
William, now nearly two years old. Before the women were taken to
the hotel, the Lieutenant pointed out the churches in the area, the old
Spanish military chapel, Our Lady of Guadalupe, and the more
recently built Baptist church for the American Protestants. In addition,
they were driven around the Plaza, where one could find more than
twenty stores, two tailors, two shoemakers, a bakery, an apothecary,
and two blacksmith shops. It seemed to Charlotte to be the most
civilized place she had been since leaving San Antonio. The military
train finally stopped at the U.S. Hotel, which had been expanded and
remodeled over many years of continuous use as the main hotel for
the Americans, going back to the establishment of the Santa Fe Trail
by William Becknell, who had stayed in this hotel many times. Its
name and shape had changed over the years, but Charlotte found it to
be a grand lodging, a great stucco palace, more luxurious than any

place she had stayed since leaving Europe. She checked in at the registration desk and found that Jacob had reserved a room for the family on the third floor overlooking the Plaza and the Palace of the Governors to the north. She was informed that the soldiers from Fort Union were expected on March 3rd, two days later.

At first, Charlotte was disappointed about the delay, but then realized that they would have more than a week together in this place. Looking out the window at the sunset on the distant mountain ridges to the west, she began to weep with joy, picking William up, hugging him and explaining that his Papa would be joining them soon.

"Papa coming?" William asked.

"Yes, William," Charlotte answered. "Papa loves you very much, and I know he can't wait to see you." Her heart was now jumping with joy and anticipation at the prospect of their husband and father being with them after nearly six months of separation. She was very weary after the trip from Fort Craig. She looked forward to a quiet meal that evening in the hotel dining room, and a warm bath for her child and herself. They would both sleep well that night in the warm double bed in this comfortable room. No bed of straw and buffalo hide covers this night or for the next week or two. Charlotte sat down for a few minutes in a rocking chair near the adobe fireplace in the corner of the room and rocked William in her lap. He had immediately fallen asleep. She dozed and dreamed of Jacob. About half an hour later, a knock on the door awakened her. The bellman from the lobby was there to announce that dinner would be served at 7 p.m., about an hour from then. Charlotte decided to have their baths before going down to supper. William would be too tired later, and she could feel her energy level fading rapidly. It would revive them, to wash away the trail dust, put on fresh clothes, and make it a lot easier to get William ready for bed. The bathrooms were located down the hall toward the rear of the hotel and built one over the other on the two upper floors, so that used bathwater could be flushed down a drainpipe connected to a basin inside the bathing area. This was unusual luxury, especially in New Mexico. After Charlotte found the bathroom, she pulled the bell cord just outside the bathroom, and a couple of minutes later a young Mexican woman appeared. Charlotte asked her to fetch some hot water for the metal tub and some towels. In about ten minutes, two Indian girls appeared with buckets of hot water and filled the tub. There was a dressing area screened off by sheets for changing into bathrobes. A couple of commodes were also located nearby.

Charlotte had returned to the hotel room and retrieved clean clothes for herself and William, then placed him into the tub and washed him. He cried a little at first, but then began to enjoy the water. Charlotte rinsed him and handed him to the attendant who dried him with a towel and dressed him while Charlotte had her own bath. The attendant handed her a large towel after she had washed and rinsed her hair. The girl handed her another towel to wrap up and stay warm and helped her dress. Charlotte had not experienced this level of luxury since leaving San Antonio the previous summer. She almost wept, thinking of the personal denial Jacob must have endured in order to save the money to pay for this comfort for his family. Thank God they would be back together in another day or two.

Dinner was wonderful that night. The soup was a beef stew with onions and a light touch of chili powder. This was a little spicy for William and the other children, two four-year-old girls, and a six-year-old boy. The cook made them some chicken soup with biscuits. The second course was mutton, not Charlotte's favorite, but well-seasoned with dried herbs. Fresh-baked bread, pickled vegetables, and jams were on the table. These hungry travelers were not complaining after more than a week of trail food. Dessert included a variety of Spanish cookies, flan, and coffee or tea. The families sat in the dining room for nearly an hour, relaxing and talking about their relatives, families they had left behind in their past lives, and about the husbands and fathers they had not seen for many months. About nine o'clock, the children becoming tired and fussy, and the women agreed to retire for an evening of well-needed rest in real beds.

Morning came too early. Charlotte had been up twice during the night, helping William use the chamber pot. She had slept well though. What a relief from the nights on the trail, sometimes waking up with frost on the covers. After awakening at first light and dozing for half an hour, she went over to stir the dying coals in the fireplace, adding some kindling and two pieces of a split log. William was now awake, and she reminded him where they were, and that his papa would probably be coming tonight or tomorrow. They dressed quietly and she brushed his hair and then her own. They went downstairs to a breakfast of fresh hot oatmeal and bacon, with biscuits and preserves. The other wives and children joined them shortly, and they all chattered excitedly about the expected arrival of their soldiers. The duty sergeant from the nearby headquarters stopped by the hotel for a cup of coffee and shared the news that the men were expected to arrive with the mail wagon, most likely by sundown that day, instead of tomorrow. A courier had passed the mail from Fort Union earlier and reported that they were ahead of schedule. They cheered the news and made plans for the day. After breakfast, the women decided to use the day to visit the shops around the Plaza. They didn't have much money to buy goods, but at least they could look in the shops. A yard or two of calico cloth could be an exciting prospect for a new skirt when one was so far from the States. These women had chosen a relatively hard life compared to many who had decided to stay in the East. It had been no small sacrifice from many of them to follow their men into the western wilderness and live sparsely in an unfamiliar culture. Small luxuries were few and far between and had to be enjoyed where they could be found. Charlotte, although not from a wealthy background, had received a basic grammar school and upper school education. She had completed nursing training, was reasonably well read, and could appreciate many of the lifestyle improvements becoming available to the rising European middle classes in the late eighteenth and early nineteenth centuries. The liberating influences of the Erklaerung (the Enlightenment) period in Germany and western Europe raised hope for millions, leading to aspirations for a better life for the common people. They had been trapped in the rigid class structure which had persisted since the Middle Ages. America was a beacon for those seeking even more freedom and opportunity, to a degree never before possible. Charlotte was practical enough to know that this transition could not be easy, that only hard work and perseverance could see a person through to a better life. She realized that, living here on the frontier of an expanding America, the challenge extended to life itself, surviving one day at a time. She was suddenly very grateful to be loved by a strong and faithful man and was desperately anxious to be with him again.

After a morning of walking around the Plaza and nearby streets, window shopping and tending to small children, the nippy March winds were becoming a little uncomfortable. The ladies and children returned to the hotel for a midday meal of beef stew and peppers, bread, and tea. The younger children became a little fussy and were settled into their rooms for afternoon naps. A warm fireplace was nice as Charlotte rocked William to sleep, and then settled him into the bed. Charlotte wrapped her shawl around her shoulders and rocked herself slowly in front of the fireplace. She closed her eyes and thought about sleep, but she was too excited at the prospect of seeing her husband, Jacob. It had been half a year since she was in his arms. She was musing about the reunion with Jacob when she was startled by William crying. She thought she had merely dosed off for a few minutes. But it must have been two hours or longer, she discovered as she looked out the window into the street below, noticing that the sun was much lower in the sky. Just then, an Army wagon with a team of four mules moved past the hotel, and her heart leaped when she saw the words, "U.S. Mail" on the canvas top. The wagon was headed up the street toward headquarters and the barracks beyond the Palace of the Governors. She went to the pitcher and basin on a small stand next to the bed and washed her face. William was fully awake now, as she picked him up and walked him around the room until he stopped crying. She changed his underwear and washed his face and hands, and put his little coat on, along with her own cloak and hat. They started down the stairs and made their way to the lobby two floors below. By this time the other wives and children were gathering there. Within twenty minutes, the three soldiers from Fort Union arrived to shouts of joy from their families. They rushed to and hugged their wives and children whom they hadn't seen in months. It was a joyous occasion. The men had been given a week in Santa Fe with their families before the three-day trip back to Fort Union. Jacob couldn't believe it! He was finally holding his wife and child in his arms. Those six months seemed to him an eternity. Charlotte wept happily while William squirmed to get free from the embrace.

"We had better let you breathe, little man!" Jacob finally managed, hardly able to get a word out of his mouth between kissing his loved ones and fighting back tears.

Charlotte laughed and cried at the same time, overjoyed with the reunion. "There is so much to catch up on, so much to talk about, Lieber Jacob," she blurted.

"You both look wonderful, Schatze," Jacob finally said, his eyes red and tearing. He was suddenly aware that the highs and lows of separation and reunion were the lot of military families. He had seen this reaction many times over the years in Bavaria, and Texas, and now here in New Mexico. He secretly vowed to himself that he would find a way to avoid long periods of separation in the future.

Thank God that his superiors had decided to let him bring his family to Fort Union.

The hotel guests dined on a fine supper of tortilla soup with chicken, rice, onions, and peppers, roast beef, pickled vegetables, corn cakes, coffee and tea. The meal was enjoyed by all and finished with sopas and honey. The soldiers and families stayed in the dining room for two hours, catching up on news from Fort Craig, Fort Union, and various items in the latest newspapers from St. Louis and the East. Finally, some of the children, including William, started to be whiny and tired. Everyone said good night and retired to their rooms. William was practically asleep on Jacob's shoulder as he carried him up the staircase. Jacob made a palette from a blanket for the boy, next to the bed, and gently covered him with his service coat. Charlotte let her hair down and brushed it over her shoulders. She slipped into a cotton night gown while Jacob took his boots and trousers off on the other side of the bed. He removed a small box from his travel bag, handing it to Charlotte and inviting her to open the small gift. She removed the wrapper and was delighted to find the small bottle of perfume from the sutler's store. She removed the stopper and dabbed some of the delightful fragrance on her neck and breasts. Jacob pulled her to him and passionately kissed his bride for nearly a minute. They fell into the bed together, quickly removing each other's nightclothes as fast as they could. A few minutes later, they rolled apart briefly, gasping after intense lovemaking, hugged each other tightly for a while, then exhausted, fell asleep. They would make love three more times during the night, between bouts of blissful sleep. Once, after midnight, Charlotte got up to find William crying. She changed his underwear and gave him some milk brought up from supper. He slept the rest of the night peacefully. About first light, Jacob startled and sat up in the bed. He must have been in the middle of a disturbing dream. He looked for his carbine but found only his unloaded pistol under his uniform hat. Suddenly realizing that he was in a safe place, he pulled on his long underwear, quietly walked over to the small adobe fireplace in the corner, stirred the dying embers, placed three small split logs, and stoked up the fire. It was still cold in Santa Fe in mid-March, and the fire was quite welcome. He placed William next to his mother in bed and returned to the small rocking chair in front of the fire, warming his feet, gathering his thoughts, and expecting the 0600 bugle-call to reveille. But wait, it's Sunday, he remembered. Peering out the window looking down on the Plaza, he detected no movement in the square. Up the street near the corner of the Governor's Palace, a lone figure appeared to be lighting a clay pipe. He wore a long coat, and his musket was leaning against the building. He was most likely one of the night sentries from the military headquarters, just finishing his shift. Jacob watched the soldier enjoying his smoke for a few minutes, when suddenly he banged the pipe on the bottom of his boot, stomped out the ashes, grabbed his musket, shouldered the weapon and began marching slowly. Less than half a minute later, a soldier with three stripes on his arm appeared, leaned into the face of the sentry, apparently reprimanding him for smoking on guard duty. The two figures began marching up the street to the north toward the military headquarters. Just then Jacob heard the notes of a bugle call coming from the garrison behind the Governor's Palace. It was 0600, and a bugler was bleating out late reveille, the call to waken the troops to a new day. Since it was Sunday, there would be no mandatory morning assembly, but if the soldiers in the barracks wanted to eat the morning meal, they would have to be up for chow by 0700 and eat within the next hour. It seemed out of place somehow to Jacob, since he was here in a comfortable hotel room, and would have a couple of hours to have a leisurely breakfast with his family. There was no need to hurry to get shaved and dressed and try to be near the front of the chow line, at least not for a few more days of blessed furlough with his loved ones. Crawling back into bed, he nestled in the pillows with Charlotte and William, who were still slumbering. About an hour later, Charlotte was awakened by William crying. She lifted him up into bed between them, and he went back to sleep for a few minutes. Finally, the boy started up again, hungry now, and awakened by the morning light in the windows. Jacob was still asleep as Charlotte quietly dressed herself and William, washing his face with cool water from the pitcher and basin on the nightstand. Deciding to let Jacob sleep for the time being, she quietly left the room with William on her arm and headed down to the dining room. One of the other Army wives was already at breakfast with her two children, sipping coffee as the youngsters finished their oatmeal porridge and milk. Charlotte ordered the same for William and coffee for herself. The two women chatted happily for the next half hour, both relieved to be reunited with their husbands. The men deserved another hour of sleep after the long wagon trip from Fort Union.

Charlotte and her companion, Betty Johnson, had met briefly at Fort Craig, just before the trip to Santa Fe. It turned out that she was from St. Louis, originally. Ben, her husband, had been in New Mexico for a couple of years with the 8th Infantry Regiment. Ben had been reassigned to Fort Union a year ago, but was unable to bring his family, as he had been out campaigning against Indian raiders in northern New Mexico. Initially, the settlers and the Army had blamed the Navajo tribes in the north and west regions of the territory, but they had been quiet for a couple of years following the signing of the treaty with Brigadier General Garland, the department commander. Eventually, it was decided that the culprits were actually Kiowa and Comanche raiding parties from the plains to the north and east. The authorities finally decided that there was no major threat to Fort Union or the Santa Fe Trail supply lines. Jacob's recent patrol had not found any looming threats, much to the relief of the small garrison at Fort Union. The raids had made clear that Fort Union was undermanned, and certainly at risk when a large number of assigned troops were out on operations. Brig. Gen. Garland was due to leave the department soon, and he and new commander of the post, Colonel Loring of the Mounted Riflemen, had been urgently requesting reinforcements from the United States. For now, the situation appeared to be stable, and safe for the families of soldiers to reside at Fort Union. Betty told Charlotte that her husband, Cpl. Ben Johnson, had been recruited to be the new armorer at the Ordnance Depot at Fort Union, and would soon be promoted to sergeant. This would make his family eligible for quarters. Charlotte suddenly felt a sinking feeling, knowing that Jacob, still a private soldier would have to remain in the barracks, and she and William would have to live with the washer women at the post laundry. Trying hard to not show her disappointment, she reminded herself that she was fortunate to at least be closer to Jacob. Everything would work out for the best, she kept telling herself. Just then Jacob and Ben Johnson walked into the dining room. They greeted and hugged their families, and Jacob exclaimed, "I am starved, how about you, Ben?"

"I could eat a whole stack of buckwheat cakes, and a couple of fried eggs and some bacon," said Ben.

"Me too!" roared Jacob. They ordered their breakfast from the waiter, and he poured out their coffee. Charlotte was relieved that Jacob and Ben were already friends. She decided she could handle her disappointment about the living arrangements, for now. The families ate a leisurely meal and talked about their experiences in the Army. Betty Johnson was intrigued to hear about Charlotte's life in

Germany, and she was amazed to hear the story of the trip from San Antonio to El Paso. Jacob congratulated Ben on his upcoming promotion and new opportunity at the depot. Ben talked about his boyhood apprenticeship as a gunsmith. Jacob recounted his more recent experience working with Paul Schmidt as a blacksmith and wagon master. He told the story of his trip up the Santa Fe Trail to Bent's Fort. He had met teamsters and wagon trains on the trail and heard stories about fortunes being made hauling freight from the United States to New Mexico. Maybe someday after his enlistment was over, he might try that business. Promotion for enlisted men in the Army, especially those who were foreign born, was agonizingly slow, and he might never make more than a lowly private's pay. For the next few years, he would just have to be content with his present lot and learn as much as he could about this barren land. He had to admit, however, that New Mexico was beautiful, in its own rugged and desolate way. Ben agreed with that sentiment and was very happy that his wife, Betty, also loved the land and the mix of cultures. Having been born and raised in St. Louis, he had long observed the westward movement of people from the East and Midwest.

St. Louis was the gateway to the West. As the population increased back in the United States, the lure of opportunity and free land out west was bound to grow in the popular imagination. Jacob mused to himself that he might have a chance someday to help guide others to this land. He could definitely see the need for freight haulers from Missouri to New Mexico and return.

The next several days were a heavenly respite for Jacob and his wife and child. The days were filled with cool crisp mornings, sun-filled afternoons, and very pleasant warm weather overall for early spring in New Mexico. There was some snow on the mountains to the northeast, but no snow or rain in the valley. They enjoyed long daily walks around the Plaza and the central part of the town, stopping to look in shop windows. Jacob and Charlotte admired the old Spanish mission churches and were amazed to learn that this town had been founded more than two hundred years earlier. Jacob thoroughly enjoyed the time with his family, chasing after his two-year-old son, who loved to run from his Papa, and squealed when Jacob caught up with him and lifted him overhead. Charlotte would yell out for William to be careful, but Jacob could see the delight in her eyes at the sight of her husband acting like a galloping horse with William holding on for dear life.

One day, the Stengers and the Johnsons rented a large carriage and drove along the river south of the Plaza, admiring the small adobe houses, stopping for a picnic lunch in a shady grove of evergreens on the north bank, just west of town. It was a lovely warm afternoon outing, sitting on blankets, watching the children toss pebbles into the stream, the Johnson children watching out for William, to keep him out of the water. Ben and Jacob had brought along a couple of bottles of Mexican beer, which they sipped after lunch while watching the children play. It didn't quite live up to the German beer they had both grown up with, but they enjoyed the day and the time together. That night, after William was fast asleep, Jacob and Charlotte cuddled after lovemaking. Charlotte confided to him, "Jacob, I have to tell you that I am a little envious of Betty. She told me that Ben will be promoted to sergeant soon, and they will be able to live in NCO quarters. I think it is wrong that we cannot have a place to live together at Fort Union. You have a family that needs you, too!"

Jacob knew that it was not possible to live together. He resented it himself but had reconciled the fact that they must be separated. "Charlotte, I know you are disappointed, but at least we will be in the same place when I am not on as mission. We will not be in the Army forever, you know. We have just over four more years on my enlistment. I will be gone on patrols and other missions from time to time, but I will always be coming back to you after a few days or weeks. I will not be reenlisting again, and we will be together permanently after that. I am going to be a wagon master one day, and guide trains back and forth from the States to New Mexico. You will be able to come with me whenever you like."

"Oh, Jacob, I love you so much," she replied. "You are a good man, and I will try to be at your side, always. We must find a place to live though, a place to raise our children. I know you will find the place. Until then, I can endure this Army life." They kissed and turned to sleep, but Jacob could not close his eyes for a while, thinking only of the year 1861, when his enlistment would be over.

The week of rest and relaxation was over. The soldiers and their families were met at the hotel with three wagons at nine a.m. on March 13th. The mail wagon took the third couple, a dragoon corporal, with his wife and six-year-old boy. The Johnsons had their own wagon and team, as did Jacob and Charlotte. A small detail of dragoon escorts, only a half-dozen mounted soldiers, fell in behind. Jacob checked the wagon and his mules, along with a small collection of furniture and household items brought from Fort Craig, packed in their bags, helped Charlotte and William on board the wagon, and climbed on to the driver's bench. He took up the reins and guided the team in behind the mail wagon. The hotel clerk waved from the doorway, and the small train slowly moved down the street. They passed many small adobe homes along the river, crossing a small bridge and heading south. They continued southeast into the narrow Apache Canyon, which led across the south end of the ridges extending south from the Sangre de Cristo Mountains. The wagons passed by the recently built Pigeon's Ranch and wound through the pass by the ruins of the Pecos Pueblo once occupied by Coronado when he visited the area in the 16th century. The early Spaniards had built a mission church here amongst the pueblo structures, but these buildings had been abandoned nearly twenty years before. After a brief stop for the midday meal, the wagons continued on, reaching the Kozlowski Ranch just before sundown. Martin Kozlowski was a U.S. Dragoon soldier who had decided to leave the service, and while serving at Fort Union, had purchased a parcel of land at the eastern end of Glorieta Pass. There was a natural spring on the property, and Koz had turned the place into a stagecoach stop on the Santa Fe Trail, with meals and overnight lodging for weary travelers. This beautiful area and its confining terrain would become a critical defile and battleground in a future struggle for control of the New Mexico Territory. Of course, those presently living in the area or just passing through, had no idea what an important place this canyon would prove to be in just a few short years. The stagecoach stop at Kozlowski's was a popular place for rest, and a trading post between Fort Union and Santa Fe. The food was always good and, being a former military family, Martin and his wife were always ready to welcome soldiers and the families. There was abundant water from the nearby spring, fed by Glorieta Creek, and a campsite provided forage for the horses and mules. Two bunk houses for the men stood near the main residence. Women and children were often able to sleep in the owner's adobe house when room allowed. There were no other travelers at the house when the families arrived, and the women and children were shown to rooms in a wing off of the main dining area. There was a nice fireplace in the front room of the house, where the families stood in front of the fire to warm up after the chilly ride up the pass. Mrs. Kozlowski offered the women hot tea, while the men took the horses and wagons to the spring and corral area. Kozlowski pulled several bales of hay from his small barn at the corral and drove his wagon over to the area where the horses and mules were tethered on a rope line. Once the animals were taken care of, the soldiers and their escort took their personal gear to the bunk house, where they warmed up around a small stove where a coffee pot was already steaming. They laid out their bedrolls on the bunk mattresses and washed up before heading to the main house for the evening meal.

Mrs. Kozlowski had been cooking a large pot of stew all afternoon. Her husband had shot two mule deer the day before and skinned them out. She harvested the back straps from one and cubed the meat, adding it to the slow-cooking kettle. She swung the pot on its swivel mount out of the fireplace periodically to add onions, potatoes, canned carrots, and a small amount of chili powder. It was too early for fresh garden vegetables, but she had canned the carrots and some pickles at the end of last season and had a good stock of corn in her larder, which she added to the stew.

There was a small wood stove with one oven in the kitchen. She made fresh bread every day for her guests and had made two mince pies and some sugar cookies to serve with canned fruit from her cellar. She fried several small blue grouse on the stove top in a cast iron skillet. Sergeant Kozlowski still had some connections at Fort Union and was able to trade specie, the U.S. paper money used to pay the Army, for coffee, tea, flour, lard, and sugar, and molasses from the post sutler, the manager of the exchange, the trading post at Fort Union. He in turn had bought these items from the commissary officer. Kozlowski also kept two cows in the barn for milk and butter. After a long day on the rough road from Santa Fe, the warmth of the fire and the smell of the cooking were almost overwhelming to the guests. The families huddled around the hearth as Mrs. Kozlowski made up small plates of food for the youngsters. Charlotte ate with William, and after the meal, as he started getting a little fussy, took him down the hallway to one of the guest rooms. Simple but comfortable, the room had its own adobe fireplace and a single bed with a feather mattress. William was already asleep before she could even get him out of his clothes and into a nightshirt. She pulled the sheet and woolen blanket over him and partially covered him with a buffalo robe, watching over him for a few minutes before walking back to the front room. The Johnson girls had just finished cookies and milk and were playing with their little stuffed rag dolls. Charlotte poured herself some coffee and sat down to chat with the other two women. After a few minutes, the men started coming in from the bunk house. The escort soldiers and mail crew sat down at the large table and were served by Mrs. Kozlowski. Jacob and the other two husbands joined their wives with cups of coffee and were served last. The pot of stew was soon emptied by the soldiers, leaving just enough for the Kozlowski's. After dinner the mince pies were devoured and washed down with more coffee. The hosts were happy to receive news and some mail from Santa Fe, and pleasant conversation lasted well into the evening. At nine o'clock the mail crew announced that the party should get to bed early, as the longest part of the trip was coming up on the second day of the journey. They needed to be up at first light and be ready to roll before sunrise.

Jacob awoke first in the morning and walked to the small window, noting the first hint of daylight in the sky to the east. He quickly dressed and walked to the room where Charlotte and William were sleeping. Entering quietly, he kissed her lightly and let her know he was going to help hitch the mules to the wagons. He walked out to the front room and found most of the soldiers eating a breakfast of biscuits, gravy, and coffee. They finished as the families were making their way to tables, the children still half asleep. They had their breakfast while the soldiers hitched up the mules and brought the wagons up to the front entrance of the main building. The sergeant in charge of the detail thanked the Kozlowski's and paid the bill.

With all aboard, the wagon party and their mounted escort left the station headed southeast along the south bank of the Pecos River toward the small town of San Miguel del Vado. About eleven o'clock, they reached this small town and farming community, used by the Spanish for cattle grazing for more than two hundred years. This headwater area was originally used as a route of passage by the Pueblo Indians for access to the eastern plains for buffalo hunting. It had been cultivated over the years by Spanish settlers and had become a land grant enclave of the Spanish governor in 1803. The wagon party watered the horses and mules here an bought some tamales and tortillas for lunch. They continued on to the village of Tecolote, passing by the trail landmark of Starvation Peak south of the trail after leaving San Miguel. Legend had it that the local Indians had forced some early Spanish settlers into a defensive position where they were surrounded and eventually succumbed to starvation. Continuing onto Tecolote, the wagons stopped to rest and eat the midday meal, while watering the animals. The trek to Las Vegas, the end of the second day of the journey to Fort Union, continued northward for four more hours over the foothills of the Sangre de Cristo Mountains. They followed the trail over the Kearny Gap, an improvement of the road finished by General Kearny's Army of the West during the invasion of New Mexico in 1846. Road improvements completed for the movement of the American Army and their supply trains made the movements of large wagons much easier. Along with improvements also carried out on the road over Raton Pass, further north, this eased travel and commerce on the New Mexico end of the Santa Fe Trail. After crossing the Galinas River, the group finally entered the town of Las Vegas. The town, established in 1835 as a Mexican land grant, was laid out in the traditional Spanish Colonial style. The central plaza was enclosed by buildings which could be barricaded together in case of Indian attack. A decade earlier, Gen. Kearny had announced from this plaza that New Mexico was being claimed by the United States as a result of the War with Mexico. Kearney made his announcement from the roof of a one-story adobe building which now served as a hotel or hostelry for travelers. The Army had used Las Vegas as a supply base from 1846 until Fort Union was built in 1851. The wagon party wound its way around the service roads of the acequias, the irrigation ditches which provided water for growing crops in the fields surrounding the town. This was a common method of watering cultivated land around many early New Mexico towns. The party reached the center of town and their lodging just after sundown, dropping off the women and children before taking the wagons and animals to nearby corrals for overnight boarding. After a meal of tortillas, chili con carne, and caramel flan, the travelers went to bed except for a guard detail posted to watch the corrals, relieved by a second watch after midnight. Las Vegas was frequented by rustlers and other unsavory characters. Previous incidents involving soldiers and freighters with these characters had resulted in losses of animals, wagons, and supplies.

After an early breakfast, the wagon party departed on the last leg of the trip to Fort Union. Charlotte was getting a little nervous about where she would be living. Jacob reassured her that the laundresses had better quarters there, and she would be closer to the commissary. In any event, they would be there soon Fort Union was only 20 miles away. The wagons would follow the trail through La Junta del los Rios, later known as Watrous, at the confluence of the Sapello and Mora Rivers. This important milestone was located at the junction of the Cimarron and Mountain branches of the Santa Fe Trail. This place had long been a meeting place where the plains Indians came to trade buffalo hides for goods from Mexico, corn, vegetables, and other wares. With the opening of the Santa Fe Trail, manufactured goods and non-native plants and crops from the United States were traded for hides, pelts, wool, and silver from the mountain mining areas. Samuel Watrous, a Vermont native, had come to New Mexico in 1835, as a trader in Taos. By 1846, he had set up a trading post in La Junta, eventually becoming one of the wealthiest traders in the area, taking advantage of the lush grasslands of the Mora Valley to raise a large herd of cattle. Watrous supplied the Army in northeastern New Mexico with most of its meat and many other items, especially fresh produce. Since the junction of the two rivers was also a major staging area for wagon trains headed for Missouri, over the next four decades, he became one of the most successful merchants in New Mexico. The group had a light lunch here and started up the road to Fort Union. Since Watrous was such an important supply point, most of the men had ridden this final stretch to Fort Union more times than they cared to remember. The mules of the mail wagon could practically follow the road with their eyes closed.

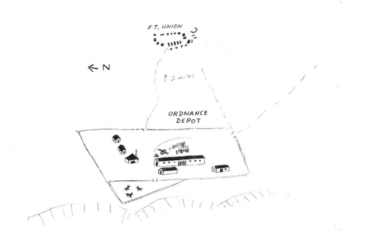

Chapter X. Fort Union and the Depot

After signing in at post headquarters, Jacob was given instructions and a letter of authorization for his wife and child to live in the post laundry quarters. Each laundress was allocated a separate room in the residence section adjacent to the laundry facility. Jacob moved their meager furniture into the building, located just behind the bachelor officer quarters at the north end of the parade ground. The commissary and the post sutler's store (trading post), since the establishment of the installation, were of a low single-story construction of logs covered with stucco. The ordnance depot and storage facilities were located about two miles west of the main quadrangle of the parade ground and surrounding housing and barracks. Most of the buildings were already considered to be inadequate and would be replaced by more permanent structures in the years ahead. The post was open with no outer perimeter walls, unlike Fort Craig. Charlotte immediately noted that the facilities, although not luxurious, were much less crowded than those at Fort Craig. She felt that she would have adequate space in her room and was happy to be close to the commissary and sutler's store, as well as being next to the post hospital. She would soon find out that she was pregnant again and was happy to be close to the medical facility. Charlotte also had a feeling that she would fit in and be congenial with the other laundresses. Fortunately, most of the women were easy to get along with, and there were very few conflicts. Many of the laundry workers were married to soldiers and had small children. Many were willing to share child-care responsibilities.

Jacob found out that he would be primarily assigned to garrison duty rather than escort duties. Most of the Regiment of Mounted Riflemen would be stationed at Fort Union during 1857, as the plains Indians were fairly quiet that year. In April, however, a large contingent of the regiment was deployed to southwest New Mexico with the commander, Colonel Loring, on a campaign against the Gila Apaches and other tribes. Loring returned in late September that year. Captain Jones, the interim post commander, felt that he had inadequate troops for the security of the fort, complaining that he had to draft soldiers from the band and the prisoner stockade in order to raise a guard detail.

Jacob was sent out with a small force in July to Hatch's Ranch in response to a request for military support from the local ranchers, who feared pending encounters with the Indians. He would be detailed to a couple of mail escort missions in the fall. Most of Jacob's days were dedicated to guard mount activities and ceremonial duties. Later he was assigned to stable duty, military horse and mule care, wagon and livery maintenance, and weapons maintenance and upgrades working with the ordnance depot and quartermaster sections. Jacob had some experience with quartermaster operations from his time in San Antonio. He appreciated the extent of the responsibilities of the quartermaster section, along with the commissary, ordnance, and medical departments, including everything from food and feed, livestock herding, housing and facilities construction, and maintenance, clothing maintenance, water supply, medical supplies, arms and ammunition, transportation of goods, civilian employees, and the complex process of contracting for all these goods and services. It took a huge logistical effort to equip and maintain an army. Between the quartermaster and the post sutler, a vast complex of activities evolved to support the U.S. Army, Department of New Mexico. Although his days were full, consumed with soldierly duties, he was now able to see his family almost every evening. It would turn out to be a busy, but uneventful year with one notable exception, the birth of the Stengers' second child, James.

Charlotte became obviously great with child by the late summer of 1857. She still worked hard every day in the laundry and raising young William, now nearly two and a half years old. Because of the miscarriage she had experienced the previous year, Charlotte wanted to be especially careful during this pregnancy. She already knew and trusted the post surgeon, Dr. Jonathan Letterman. He had taken care of her earlier in the summer, suturing a laceration of the palm of her left hand which she cut on a broken bottle. He had a kind and caring attitude and had done a careful repair from which she had no complications. He now examined her, nearly six months pregnant. She told him about how she had lost a fetus during the trip from Texas and was concerned that she might have similar problems. He told her that everything seemed normal and on course with her current pregnancy, and that she should not fear the loss of this child, although these matters are, as always, in God's hands. Jacob was also very happy that everything seemed to be going well. Their life had certainly been less stressful this year than the year before. They both looked forward to the birth, likely to be in late November. Jacob did eventually have two deployments before the year was out. The first one was an escort mission in mid-October, to the Canadian river crossing on the Santa Fe trail with Lt. Edson and twenty-five mounted troopers to meet the mail wagons. The mail had been joined on the trip down from the Arkansas River by Captain Chandler, 3rd Infantry, and a large company of recruits for the department. They were also accompanied by the new territorial governor, Abraham Rencher. The Kiowa and Comanche were quiet, and the combined groups reached Fort Union peacefully on the last day of October.

Jacob was elated that he was back at his post, as Charlotte was due to deliver soon, and she was thrilled that he was home safely. She had not been able to work of much of the past week or so and she was starting to have ankle swelling at the end of the day. Jacob had to find a way to stay on post until the baby came. Troop strength would be a little better for a few weeks, as the newly arrived replacements were in-processed at Fort Union before being sent out to their various assignments. Until these soldiers were sent to other locations, they would be available for casual duty details, relieving some pressure on the regular garrison troops. There were more than 200 new arrivals, both infantry and mounted soldiers.

Although the Department of New Mexico main supply depot had been moved to Albuquerque a few years before, the supply trains came primarily from Missouri and
Fort Leavenworth down the Santa Fe Trail. The ordnance depot at Fort Union, as well as the commissary and subsistence services were the initial recipients of the thousands of tons of Army supplies coming

down the trail each month. Only a fraction of the supplies came to the southern part of the command across the southwest deserts from San Antonio. Fort Union, although technically a sub-depot, had logically become the de facto distribution point for nearly all of the other posts in New Mexico.

The Ordnance Depot at Fort Union had been there from 1851 when the post was founded and was the armory for the department. Under the steady management of the ordnance section under Captain William Shoemaker, the department was nearly always well supplied with arms and ammunition. Shoemaker was a career arms and ammunition storekeeper. He understood the needs of the soldier in the field and constantly worked to provide the best weapons and ammunition based on the needs of the particular branches and units. Shoemaker did his best to keep up with technical advancements and upgrades, within the constraints of his superiors and the remote location of the Department of New Mexico.

In the late 1850s, Shoemaker managed a consulting trip back to Washington to update himself with the latest technology from the Army Ordnance Department. He was very interested in repeating arms, especially the newer repeating rifles and carbines. A few of the Mounted Riflemen who had been transferred to New Mexico from Texas had been issued Colt revolving cylinder carbines. Shoemaker was intrigued with this weapon, and had even performed maintenance on Jacob's carbine, repairing a faulty firing mechanism. The more reliable breech loading Sharps rifles were powerful and accurate and were adopted by the department, but the Sharps slower rate of fire, a few shots per minute, continued to limit the effectiveness of mounted troops in the assault. A number of additional Colt carbines were introduced to troops in New Mexico prior to the Civil War, but were not generally adopted due to bureaucratic infighting concerning cost and a reluctance to change. Jacob kept his weapon as he was able to overcome its potential hazards, and the ammunition was the same for his pistol and carbine. He would not change weapons until metal cartridges became widely available after the war.

Jacob spent as much time as possible with Charlotte after duty hours. Since she was married, caring for a small child, and about to give birth, she had managed to obtain her own room in the laundress quarters. During the final two weeks of her pregnancy, Jacob and a couple of the other women who worked with Charlotte, began to provide more care for William, and bring meals and do other chores.

She was very large by now and increasingly uncomfortable. Charlotte had seen Dr. Letterman on the fifteenth of November, and he told her that she was starting to dilate. It wouldn't be long now. Finally, she went into labor on the morning of the eighteenth and broke her water around two in the afternoon. The two women who had been looking after her alerted Jacob and called for the doctor. They began getting hot water and towels and linens together.

When Dr. Letterman arrived, he washed his hands and examined Charlotte. She was fully dilated and beginning to crown. He listened to her abdomen with his obstetric stethoscope and reported a rapid and strong heartbeat. As she was encouraged to bear down and push several times, she cried out in pain, doing her best to follow the doctor's commands. Finally, after 45 minutes, Charlotte seemed nearly exhausted and about to pass out. Letterman exhorted her to try very hard to push down hard one more time. He felt the top of the head slide into the birth canal and began to gently guide the baby forward. In another minute or two he lifted the head through the opening and turned the shoulders, guiding the child out and onto Charlotte's abdomen. The surgeon cleared the baby's mouth with his finger, removing a small amount of mucous, and the child let out a wail, and started crying loudly.

"Charlotte, it's a boy, and a right healthy one, I would say!" he announced happily. Handing the child to one of the women holding a clean dry towel, he quickly clamped the cord, tied it tightly with a gauze ribbon, and cut it free. Examining Charlotte again, he found the placenta falling into the canal, removed it, and packed her with a large gauze ribbon. The bleeding subsided very quickly, and he turned her care over to the other women, who proceeded to clean Charlotte up, bathe and re-gown her, and change her sheets. The two ladies then cleaned the boy, wrapped him in a small clean sheet and handed him to his mother. Dr. Letterman, meanwhile, had stepped outside onto the small porch of the building where Jacob was nervously pacing, carrying William.

"It's a boy, a large and healthy full-term boy, Jacob. And your wife is doing fine," proudly announced the doctor.

"Thank God!" Jacob sighed. His sense of relief was overwhelming. He almost dropped his son William, but caught himself on the doctor's arm. "Sorry, Doc, but I have been so worried since we lost the last baby over a year ago."

"Well, Jacob, it is not surprising, especially after hearing your wife's story of what you both had gone through on the way from Texas," said Dr. Letterman. "It appears that this time there will be no immediate problems. You know that life is challenging out here on the frontier. Civilization seems so far away, sometimes. But, I suppose civilization is where you plant it. You are strong parents, as I can see in this fine youngster on your arm."

Jacob was impressed with the kindness and manner of this man. They were lucky to have such a good doctor to take care of them in this strange land. "Thanks again, Doc, I can't begin to tell you how much we are indebted to you."

"No need, Jacob. It is reward enough, just to see that smile on your face. Well, I will look in on Charlotte, quickly, then I must be getting back to the hospital. I will come see her tomorrow, to make sure she and the baby are having no problems."

After the doctor had departed, Jacob entered the room to see Charlotte holding the boy in the fold of her arm and smiling sleepily. "What will we call him, Jacob?"

"I have been thinking about it for a while," he responded, "and I am starting to like the English names. How about James?"

Charlotte looked a little surprised at this suggestion, but it had seemed to work for William. "Then James it shall be, my husband."

Jacob kissed his tired wife on the forehead, and then showed the new baby to William. "William, this is your new baby brother, James."

The two-year-old was not sure what to think of this new person, this tiny baby. Charlotte leaned over and hugged William with her free arm, and reassured him that he was still loved, just as much as the new baby. With winter coming, Jacob tried to spend every spare minute not required for duty with Charlotte, and especially to help take care of William as much as possible. One of the other laundresses donated a cradle with rocker base for James. Jacob kept the little room supplied with firewood for the little pot-bellied stove in the corner. Charlotte was able to take care of the newborn for the first couple of weeks without much trouble, with assistance from the other ladies, and Jacob's evening visits. There was one tin bathtub kept in the quarters area of the laundry. Jacob heated water for it twice a week for Charlotte and the children to bathe. He brought whatever extra food he could scrounge at the mess facility and made sure the family cow was milked early every morning for William. Jacob was very thankful that his duty schedule allowed for this, at least for a few weeks. It was beginning to get cold at night on the eastern plains of New Mexico, and he was glad that Charlotte was able to avoid being outside for extended periods while she was recovering from childbirth. Dr. Letterman checked on her every week or so to make sure she and baby were well. Life was peaceful for a few precious weeks as Jacob was able to continue his garrison duties and was not sent out on patrol. Considering himself blessed, he enjoyed this period of relative calm with the family. It was to last until after Christmas, which was celebrated with a few other German families.

The Stengers were invited for Christmas dinner at the quarters of Sergeant Mueller and his wife, Beatrice, who had become friends with Charlotte and some of the other wives at the laundry. There was a traditional tree, decorated with small toys, hard candy, and candles. Beatrice made spaetzle and sauerbraten, while another family brought sauerkraut and sausages, and another wife who worked at the post bakery made a wonderful cake with marzipan filling. She had brought some almonds with her from Texas, and made marzipan, the crushed almond pastry filling with sugar and cinnamon. A few bottles of wine and some beer were purchased at the sutler's store, and a wonderful time was had by all. For a few moments, Jacob felt transported back to his earlier life in Germany. He had not been so happy in years.

Chapter XI. Fort Union 1858

From all appearances, this depot post near the terminus of the Santa Fe Trail was becoming more and more important to the Army in New Mexico. Even though the headquarters was at Santa Fe, Fort Union was the port of entry for the vast majority of supplies and replacements necessary to maintain the far-flung forts and stations in the department. New Mexico was becoming a vital outpost of national expansion and support for President Polk's doctrine of "Manifest Destiny," to consolidate American incorporation of the western territories all the way to the Pacific. The southern borders had to be protected, and the hostile natives subdued. While the mission of the Army in the Department of New Mexico was primarily containment of the Indian tribes, there was growing sectional tension surrounding the Missouri Compromise. As the country expanded westward, the southern states were increasingly concerned that the northern states might try to block any extension of slavery to the west. The Kansas-Nebraska Act of 1854, and the 1857 Dread Scott Case, had essentially done nothing to assuage the fears of the northern abolitionists and free staters. Eventually, these contentions would explode into armed conflict, including the invasion of New Mexico by Texas in the short-lived western theater of the American Civil War. Jacob and Charlotte, as well as most people in New Mexico, had no idea of the impending national crisis. They were concerned with their immediate lives and circumstances. Life on the western frontier had been for them so far a daily challenge for bare necessities and personal safety. This time together at Fort Union had been very welcome relief and comfort for their young family. They knew it would not last much longer. A soldier and his family had to be ready for deployment at any time, on very short notice. The time would come again in February, 1858. Jacob would be detailed as one of the twenty-three troopers under the command of Lt. John Van Deusen Du Bois, a flamboyant young officer of the Mounted Riflemen. Dubois had been involved in the1857 expedition from Fort Bliss against the Apache and Navajo in Arizona, the western area of the New Mexico Territory. He was a daring officer and prolific writer, well known for the wit expressed in the journal he kept, and often related strange or humorous events experienced on the trail.

The patrol was detailed to escort the eastbound mail party to the Arkansas River crossing. The trip was unusual in many respects, not the least of which was the scarcity of horses at Fort Union at the time. This made it necessary for the troopers had to ride in wagons drawn by four-mule teams. These wagons were uncomfortable for the soldiers and could not travel fast enough to keep up with the mail coaches. The coaches carried, in addition to the mail and dispatches, military and civilian passengers bound for the United States. There were many episodes of separation of the mail party from the escort troops, creating much confusion and concern about attacks by Indians reportedly in the area.

The winter route followed the Cimarron crossing on the original branch of the trail. Less water was available on this route up through the present-day Texas and Oklahoma panhandles, known as the dry route. In fact, the Cimarron crossings were frequently dry, and water sumps were often dug into the riverbeds and lined with barrels or wagon beds to collect water. Winter travel could also be hazardous due to severe cold snaps or winter storms. Between the Cimarron and Arkansas crossings in southwestern Kansas, parts of the trail were littered with the bleached bones of hundreds of mules, which had perished due to severe winter weather.

Because two escort teams were unable to keep up the forty miles per day pace of the mail party, Lt. Du Bois left them in camp at the Lower Cimarron crossing, and took the other two escort wagons and soldiers north with the mail to the Arkansas crossings near Fort Larned. He returned to collect the remainder of the escort at the Cimarron and wait there for the west bound mail. Du Bois had not seen nor expected hostile Indians and did not wait in Kansas for the mail coach. Along the way, however, he was warned of hostile Kiowa attacks on some Mexican traders, and he decided to rejoin his detached wagons.

The mail party arrived the next morning, running hard from what they estimated to be about a hundred Kiowa on horseback. The Kiowa warriors held off and did not attack due to the escort troops. The party moved on to Rock Creek crossing where they met the eastbound mail and escort led by Lt. Gibbs, another patrol leader for the Mounted Riflemen. After a one-night encampment, the groups continued on their separate ways, with the westbound mail and escort covering forty miles to the Canadian River. The next day the mail party and one wagonload of escort troops set out in a blizzard, which forced three of the escort wagon teams to stay behind at Burgwin Springs due to a number of exhausted or lame mules. Led by the determined Lt. Du Bois, the mail and one escort wagon fought through the storm, reaching Fort Union late that night after making the last forty-seven miles in nearly a foot of snow. The remaining wagons and troopers reached Fort Union a few days later. Jacob, who was with the last group, was very tired but glad to be back after this frigid expedition. As soon as he had finished helping with the mules at the post corrals, Jacob made his way to Charlotte's room at the laundry. He knocked on her door and was greeted by Charlotte, who was nursing baby James. She cried out loud, "Thank God, Jacob, I thought you might have frozen to death! It has been nearly a month."

"It was very cold, Schatze!" managed a tired and frigid Jacob. "A couple of soldiers may lose a toe or two, but we are all doing alright. We did lose three mules in the snow, but we were able to replace them at the corrals at Burgwin Station. We almost had a fight with some Kiowa near the Cimarron crossings, but they didn't attack, thank God!"

"Oh, Jacob, I am just glad that you are back," Charlotte said. Jacob hugged his wife and children for a few minutes, remarking how much the boys were growing, especially James. He raised three-year-old William over his head and told him how much he had missed him.

"Jacob, would you like some coffee?"

"I would love some coffee, Charlotte, I'm still shivering from the past three days in the snow," Jacob said. Charlotte handed James to his father and walked over to the pot-bellied stove in the corner of the room, pouring a cup of strong black coffee for her tired husband. They talked for about half an hour, and Jacob decided that he was so dirty from his long trip that he had to go back to his barracks and take a bath. It was late in the afternoon with the sun already heading for the horizon. He would clean up, change into a fresh uniform, go to supper at the mess hall, and bring some biscuits and cake back early in the evening. Charlotte made him promise to bring his dirty clothes back so she could clean them.

Jacob returned a couple of hours later, smelling a lot better this time. The boys were asleep already with William in a small child's bed, and James in a cradle. He would get a little fussy from time to time, but Charlotte would gently rock the cradle for a few minutes, and he would go back to sleep. Jacob was amazed how much he had changed in a month. He loved his boys and spent as much time with them as possible, whenever he was not on deployment. Charlotte poured a cup of coffee for her husband and herself, and they shared the cake he had brought back from the mess hall. They talked for the better part of an hour, huddling near the stove for warmth. After a while they fell into bed and made love briefly, before the exhausted Jacob fell asleep. Charlotte couldn't sleep as she was concerned that Jacob would miss his barracks call at taps at 10 p.m. She woke him up after a couple of hours, and he quickly dressed and kissed her goodnight, making it back to the barracks just as the bugle was finishing taps. Jacob dreamed of the time when he would finally be able to live with his family on a full-time basis, but he appreciated being with them none the less.

The next few weeks were a very happy time as Jacob was able to see his wife and children nearly every night and most Sundays. The weather was very mild for March, and they would often take walks to visit the other German families on post, and the Johnson family they had traveled with from Santa Fe the year before. Life seemed to be stabilizing, and an occasional short patrol or guard duty seemed manageable. This would not last long, however, and the next big separation would come in early April. Jacob was one of 25 mounted troops from Fort Union chosen for escort duty along with more than three hundred other soldiers from the department, to accompany a large drive of horses, mules, and cattle to the Utah Territory.

A 2,500-man expeditionary force from Fort Leavenworth, Kansas, under the command of Colonel Albert Sidney Johnson, had been sent the year before to present day southwestern Wyoming, in anticipation of trouble with the Mormons in the Salt Lake Valley. The Mormon settlers in Utah considered themselves to be an autonomous region, not subject to the sovereign control of the United States government. President Buchanan and the Congress disagreed. The armed Mormon Brigades under Brigham Young were prepared to resist, and U.S. troops were sent to enforce U.S. law and order, particularly regarding the illegal practice of polygamy by the Mormons.

Colonel Johnson created a base of operations at Camp Scott near present-day Green River, Wyoming, to enforce federal law in Utah, should negotiations fail. During this period, even though there were no battles fought, the Mormons raided U. S. Army supply trains and stole many animals. Colonel Johnson sent a small force under Captain Randolph Marcy to New Mexico to obtain 1,500 horses and mules to support the expedition. New Mexico did not have enough animals immediately available, and the roundup effort would take several months. The animals were finally assembled in southern Colorado by early April, and about 400 troopers under the command of Colonel Loring started the drive through the mountain valleys and passes under very cold and snowy conditions in the late spring. With the help of expert mountain guides, they arrived at Camp Scott with the herds, two months and 800 miles later. The horses and mules arrived in good condition, and after re-outfitting, the New Mexico troops returned home, arriving in early September, 1858.

Just as the animals had arrived at Camp Scott, the Mormon leadership began to negotiate with U.S. representatives, leading to an agreement by the LDS Church leaders to submit to U.S. authority. This peace settlement avoided what would have likely required major military action by the United States. The so-called Mormon War was thus avoided.

Jacob was looking forward to getting back to Fort Union and his family, after the long trip to Utah. Unfortunately, just before departure from Camp Scott, Jacob suffered a fall from his horse, injuring his right knee and bruising his right lung and liver. He was taken to the camp infirmary where he was treated for one week, including reduction of his dislocated knee. His internal injuries were not life threatening, and he was deemed fit to travel, but not on horseback. He traveled in a field ambulance with some other sick and injured soldiers for the first month of the return trip. The wagon ride was very uncomfortable throughout the mountains of Colorado, but at least it was the middle of the summer then, and the days were warm, even if the nights were chilly. Around the campfires at night, he dreamed of being with his wife and children for some extended convalescence. Jacob could ride by the middle of August, but the knee bothered him a lot after a long day in to saddle. He would recover from this injury in the short run, but arthritic complications with the knee would limit his mobility in later years. The anticipated rest and time with his family would be cut short to only a couple of days. After checking in on his return he was told that he would be leaving in a few days as part of a protective escort for a mail coach coming from the headquarters in Santa Fe. Brig. Gen. Garland, the Department Commander, was in ill health and was returning to the United States. He was turning over the command to Colonel Bonneville, who had been leading an expedition against the Navajo for raiding the Rio Grande settlements again. Two companies of Mounted Riflemen had already been deployed to Navajo country in northwest New Mexico, and Fort Union was shorthanded and awaiting reinforcement by the returning troops from the Utah expedition and new recruits coming from Fort Leavenworth.

Jacob was very disappointed that he had to go on deployment again so soon, but when he found out that he would be going as far as Fort Leavenworth, he sensed an opportunity to scout out the eastern end of the Santa Fe Trail. This might turn into an opportunity to find a place where his family could settle down after his hitch was up. Charlotte, though unhappy with his short turnover time right after another mission, agreed that Jacob should go and see what Kansas might hold for their future.

"TO THE STATES"

Brig. Gen. Garland left Santa Fe in mid-September, arriving at Fort Union a few days later. He traveled by mail coach with a few staff officers and a Sergeant, as well as the mail crew. Garland was very sick by this time, and Dr. Letterman, the assistant surgeon, was being reassigned to the East Coast. Letterman agreed to accompany the General as far as St. Louis. Jacob, with 18 other troopers, two Sergeants, and one Lieutenant, left Fort Union with the mail coach. The party traveled as far as possible each day, taking the Cimarron route, as the plains tribes had recently been relatively quiet during the summer along the trail. The only Indian problems recently reported were around the Pecos River ranches and settlements and along the recently constructed road from Fort Smith to Albuquerque. Additional troops were stationed at Hatch's Ranch, and scouting parties sent to patrol the areas to the east and south for possible Comanche incursions. Meanwhile, the mail coach traveled unimpeded along the Cimarron branch of the trail, stopping only one night for rest and water. After they crossed the Cimarron, the party encountered unusually warm weather, and found that most of the grass had been burned by recent prairie fires. The coach and escort had to slow the speed of travel to little more than a walking pace and stopped from noon to four p.m. to keep the horses from collapsing altogether. After two days, the party decided to stop and send a rider back to New Mexico for fresh horses, water, and supplies. Several days later the coach and escort were able to continue, crossing the Arkansas River near old Fort Atkinson, which had been abandoned three years earlier. After the Arkansas crossing, they camped the following evening near Pawnee Rock, a well-known landmark on the trail, to rest, water, and graze the animals. Brig. Gen. Garland was having a hard time making the trip and was continuously ill. Dr. Letterman diagnosed him as having lung congestion and chronic bronchitis, more than likely related to long-term complications of a severe chest wound suffered while leading his troops into Mexico City, a decade before. Letterman did his best to make the General comfortable, but knew that he would need to see a pulmonary specialist in the East. Garland would eventually succumb to his condition in 1861. Jacob would learn years later that Garland's son-in-law, Major James Longstreet, a popular infantry officer stationed in New Mexico, had become one of the most distinguished leaders of the Confederate Army, one of Robert E. Lee's Corps Commanders in the Army of Northern Virginia. Two days later, slowed by several stream crossings, the party would reach Council Grove, Kansas. Brig. Gen. Garland would rest there for three

100

days, before continuing on to Fort Leavenworth, St. Louis, and the East Coast.

Chapter XII. The Promised Land

Jacob was impressed. He had a couple of days to explore
Council Grove and the surrounding area before moving on to Fort
Leavenworth. His knee needed to rest also. This little town on the
edge of the open prairie was very inviting. There were shops, a
blacksmith, a couple of churches, a schoolhouse, a post office, and
two outfitters. Council Grove had been a steady settlement since the
1825 treaty with the Osage Indians under the great Council Oak Tree
on the banks of the Neosho River. It was the last town on the east end
of the Santa Fe Trail, where west bound travelers could obtain
supplies, mules and oxen, and wagon repairs. Large wagon trains
often assembled here before setting out for New Mexico and the
southwest. There was an outfitter on the west side of town named the
Last Chance Store. The town had just recently incorporated, and a
year ago Seth Hays, a descendent of Daniel Boone, had opened a
restaurant and store. Across the street was Gilkey's Hotel, where the
General and his entourage were staying. Jacob talked to a lot of the
folks in town and found them to be very friendly and helpful. He had
to be careful about his politics though, as there were a few
sympathizers for the southern cause living here, who had recently
moved to Kansas from Missouri and other southern states. There were
a lot of fears expressed about the fate of Kansas, whether to be a slave

state or free. Of the few black people he encountered, most were emancipated or freed slaves. Jacob believed ever since his Texas days, that all men should be free to enjoy life as the founders of this nation had intended, even though those founding fathers didn't always adhere to this principle in their own lives, especially the landholding southern planters. Many northerners felt that slavery would be ended at some point, although few could have imagined at what price that freedom would come. In any event, Jacob felt that this town was "free state" at its core and would be a good place to raise his young family. He would find a way to make it happen, eventually. His wife and sons deserved no less. His military enlistment would be up in less than three years, and he would move them here, God willing. Jacob knew he could make a living as a teamster, and Council Grove would be his base.

As he mused over these future plans, Jacob had time to write a short letter to Charlotte relating his joy over finding this place, and how the and the boys would finally be able to have a real home. He gave the letter to the westbound mail wagon, which was just heading for New Mexico. The next morning Brig. Gen. Garland was apparently much improved, and after a hearty breakfast at the hotel, Seth Hays saw them off, telling the General about his extended family in Booneville, Missouri. The coach rumbled across the ford the Neosho and headed east. The party passed the old camping grounds used by the Osage tribe during their migrations along the Neosho river. With a fast coach and mounted escort, the party expected to reach Westport Landing near Independence in three days, weather permitting, following the last 120 miles of the trail. They found dry roads and warm days, and crossed a few shallow streams along the way, the coach and escort maintaining a good pace. The group made forty miles and camped the first night near Dragoon Creek, rather than risk encountering southern sympathizers in the nearby town of Burlingame. There were tensions in the area between the "Free Staters" and some southern-leaning residents following the Kansas-Nebraska Act of 1854. Less than twenty miles away, Lawrence, Kansas, had been sacked by southern sympathizers only two years before, in retribution for other atrocities by anti-slavery zealots including John Brown and his followers.

As the coach party moved eastward the following day, they would pass through Baldwin City in Palmyra Township, where the Battle of Black Jack had been fought by Brown and Henry Pate, a pro-slavery organizer. Brown's forces had prevailed, but a legacy of violent conflict in the area, known as "Bleeding Kansas," was to follow. Some historians would later consider this incident to be the first true battle of the American Civil War, rather than the attack on Fort Sumter some three years later. In any event, Brig. Gen. Garland had no interest in stirring up passions because of his presence in the area and instructed his driver and escort to push on to the newly established town of Olathe, Kansas. Arriving after dark that night, the party quietly checked into a nearby livery stable, avoiding contact with the populace as much as possible. Westport was now only twenty-five miles away, and the General was anxious to book passage on the first river boat headed for St. Louis. Accompanied by his Aide-de-camp and Dr. Letterman, he bid his escort farewell, and instructed them to return along the Kansas River to the ferry crossing at Bonner Springs, then to proceed up the military road to Fort Leavenworth. He handed a dispatch to the sergeant in charge of the escort with instructions for his men to be given rations, quarters, new mounts, and to be placed on casual duty until they could be reassigned to an escort detail headed for New Mexico. The troops gave their beloved commander a salute and a hip, hip, hooray, as his boat pulled away from the dock. They believed that he was headed east to assume and important command and a promotion. Little did they know that only three years later he would pass away due to respiratory complications from his old battle wounds.

After the escort had crossed the river and were riding slowly north toward Fort Leavenworth, Jacob noticed how beautiful the ride was. It was the middle of October, and the leaves were beginning to turn to the wonderful autumn combinations of gold, orange, red, and brown. It was a very mild and calm day, and the sun was getting lower in the sky, but still warming the backs of the soldier's blue coats. Eastern Kansas was so different from the arid southwest he had lived in for the past seven years. He hadn't seen an autumn so beautiful since leaving Germany. He wished that Charlotte could be here to see this glorious day. For the time being, he was looking forward to some rest and good food, a bath, and a clean uniform. Hopefully he and his group would soon be able to join a west bound escort headed for New Mexico. Winter was coming!

Charlotte was surprised and delighted to receive the letter from Jacob. She was a little tired after a long day at the laundry and had been a little depressed that she hadn't heard from Jacob for a couple of weeks. Maybe the mail was just slow, but the weather was good after several days of thunder storms the week before in northeastern New Mexico. No one at Fort Union knew of any raiding activity on the trail. She was worried about Jacob's safety and wondered what he had found in eastern Kansas. In any event, the letter was here, and she could relax a little, knowing he would be home in a month, most likely. Neither she nor Jacob couldn't imagine what it was really like there, as he had never been that far east on the trail. She had heard of vast expanses of prairie land with waist-deep grass in places. Some of the women at the laundry told stories of great herds of bison, which they call buffalo in America. Trees were scarce in the western part of the territory, but plentiful in the eastern part. She quickly read through the letter and cheered to the boys that their daddy would be coming home in a few weeks. She was excited that Jacob had found a place that he thought would make a perfect home for the family. It was called Council Grove, but Jacob referred to it as the promised land. She had heard of this little town, the last chance place to get supplies on the way to New Mexico. He would tell her all about the place when he got home from his mission of seeing Brig. Gen. Garland off at Westport landing, and picking up supplies and horses at Fort Leavenworth along with replacement soldiers headed for New Mexico. Charlotte was buoyant. What good news this was! She could hardly wait to hear all the details. It was still several weeks until her soldier would be home, but this gave her a lot of hope for the future, and a lot to dream about, a more normal life in the future.

XIII. Replacement Troops and Mounts

Jacob and his detachment didn't have to wait long to start the journey back to Fort Union. They were assigned to participate in a large movement of men and horses from Fort Leavenworth to Fort Union. A new contingent of nearly 150 recruits and more than 500 cavalry mounts were dispatched to Fort Union only two weeks later. Along with a train of twenty small Army field wagons, loaded with arms and ammunition, the soldiers and about ten civilian wagons carrying dry goods and canned food from the States, departed Leavenworth on November 20th. With a goal of reaching Fort Union by Christmas day, the wagons were limited to 1,500 pounds of cargo, pulled by teams of four mules. This was a tight schedule to keep, and it would depend on the weather and some luck avoiding large parties of Comanche in southwestern Kansas. After the ferry crossing of the Kansas River, locally referred to as "The Kaw," the caravan moved quickly through the troubled areas of eastern Kansas, stopping only at night, or for brief watering stops, until they were well past Baldwin City. A few small groups of armed mounted men shadowed the movements of the military train, so the train commander ordered a picket line, stringing in trail all horses not under saddle. This entailed the attachment of a heavy rope picket line attached to each wagon, with the trailing rope used to attach the horses at six-foot intervals with short halters attached to the main ropes. A pair of steady lead horses were attached closest to the wagon, with the rest in pairs in double file with the halter ropes tied to the knotted main rope in between. This maintained good control of the horses, while still allowing them to graze and water at stops and streams. Up to twenty horses could be placed in trail behind each wagon, with the remainder placed in trail behind mounted troopers. This eliminated the need for herding of large groups of horses and discouraged Indian or other raiders from trying to stampede the herd. Resupplying New Mexico with mounts and troop reinforcements would be repeated many times over during the next few years to replace losses from attrition. The Comanche threat was becoming a growing concern, and operations against the Navajo and Apache raiders were ongoing. It would not be long before an even greater threat to U. S. interests in the southwest would arise from the deterioration of the political situation in the East. Texan sympathizers with the southern cause were already beginning to covet the southwestern territories they felt entitled to following the Mexican War.

The military train reached Council Grove in five days without incident. The transport herd was corralled and pastured, and the train took two days to make sure that their personal mounts and all the mules and wagons were fit for the following month on the trail. Council Grove was the last chance for outfitting and wagon repairs until they reached Fort Union. Jacob was happy to stop here again and took several hours to look around and talk to the locals. He became more and more comfortable with the place and was by now convinced that this would be a good place to live and raise his family. He met with Seth Hays, the hotel proprietor, and was assured by some of the local merchants and outfitters that this little town had a promising future, and that he could make a decent living as a freighter or wagon train guide if he moved here. That evening Jacob wrote a short letter to Charlotte telling her more about Council Grove. He gave the letter to the mail wagon the next morning which was headed west and would probably reach Fort Union at least a week before the wagon train.

After breakfast, the train reassembled and headed for the pasture site on the west side of town, to pick up the herd of horses. They were tied to their picket lines behind the wagons, as before, as this had worked well so far. The train pulled out around midday, heading for Diamond Springs, the next watering hole, half a day to the west. The weather was holding, the road remaining dry except for the occasional stream crossing. The days were still warm, although the nights were chilly now. They had the trail all to themselves except for an occasional small Indian hunting party. The train reached the Little Arkansas River after three days and Pawnee Rock on the fourth.

The troops and horses camped for two days at Pawnee Creek, at a site where Fort Larned would be built after 1859. A few horses and supplies were delivered to the small Army camp that had recently been established there to help protect the mail route. They had no reports of hostile actions to date, with Pawnee scouts informing the train commander, Lt. Flynn, that the main Comanche camps were already south of the Cimarron River, moving into winter quarters. They were following the buffalo herds, and there had not been any raids or attacks on travelers for several weeks. Lt. Flynn decided that it would be safer to avoid the Cimarron route, as the large number of horses might be too much of a temptation. Taking the mountain route would take a few days longer, but there would be more water sources along the Arkansas River. Without oversized wagons, crossing Raton Pass would be relatively easy with the smaller wagons sent on this mission. Wagon trains and horses were moving westward at a rate of 30 or more miles per day, encountering only small Indian groups along the trail. Most were Arapahoe and Cheyenne hunting parties, trailing the last of the buffalo herd stragglers into the winter grazing basins further to the south between the Cimarron River and the various branches of the Canadian River. The hunters showed no hostile intent and made no efforts to steal horses from the Army, presumably because they were outnumbered and the horses were tethered, not loosely driven. The scouts who talked to the hunting parties reported that the Comanche and Kiowa had not been around the Arkansas River for the past two to three weeks. This was confirmed by various small trains of Mexican traders who passed as they moved east bound to Missouri. The Army train reached Bent's fort on the mountain route on the 15th of December and laid over for a day of rest and care and feeding of the animals. A dozen horses were left at this station with two wagon loads of supplies. There were reports of four to six inches of snow on Raton Pass in the past week, and the train commander was anxious to get over the pass before another winter storm could make the road impassable. His concerns were realized four days later as the train was forced into camp just as it reached the summit of Raton Pass. Fortunately, the storm dumped only four more inches overnight, and two days later the weather cleared. The train moved slowly down the south slope road and set up camp at the base the mountains.

It looked like they might make it to Fort Union by Christmas after all. Jacob was getting excited to see his family, and he had brought a few small toys for William and James from Westport Landing, along with some calico cloth and sewing supplies for Charlotte. He could hardly wait to hold them all in his arms again and tell Charlotte all about Council Grove.

The train reached Fort Union about noon on Christmas Eve, 1858. There was a light covering of snow on the parade ground, and smoke was pouring out of every chimney in site. The first order of business was to deliver the new mounts to the post corrals and the wagon cargo to the quartermaster storehouses. One hundred and forty-eight new recruits were signed into the adjutant office and shown to temporary quarters pending assignments throughout the department. The troops were greeted by the post commander, Colonel William Loring, who had been in and out of Fort Union for a good part of the past year, as he and a large contingent of troopers from the Regiment of Mounted Riflemen had been periodically deployed to deal with renewed Navajo raids against New Mexico settlements. A coordinated campaign against the Navajo had resulted in a temporary truce, which had allowed most of the regiment to return to Fort Union by the end of the year. The garrison was now up to a strength of nearly 300 soldiers. The regiment would enjoy the holidays for now, but the eastern plains of New Mexico were about to erupt into a major confrontation with more powerful tribes, the Comanche and Kiowa nations.

Chapter XIV. Trooper of the Plains

Jacob was very happy to be back with his family. They had a wonderful Christmas together. The boys were growing so fast, he couldn't believe it. He was back in the arms of his wonderful Charlotte, and they were together every minute he could spare from his duties. These included several short forays into the eastern plains of New Mexico, as far as the Texas frontier. Many of the new recruits were distributed to the Mounted Rifles at Fort Union and the eastern stations including Hatch's Ranch, and as far south as Fort Stanton. Improvements to the military road from Fort Smith, Arkansas, had recently been completed by an Army engineering detachment over the past several months. The remainder of 1859 and early 1860 would see Jacob and his unit deployed frequently on the eastern plains. In February, he and other members of his troop were sent to Galisteo to escort an engineer unit surveying for water sources from artesian wells. They had been attacked by Comanche raiding parties which were fought off by a detachment of recruits sent west with the road construction party. After suffering many casualties, a group of Comanche had moved into the Cimarron River area to the north of Fort Union, and there were fears that they would attack Fort Union. Colonel Loring was concerned about having insufficient troops at Fort Union to ward off an attack. He kept many scouting parties in the eastern plains to keep track of any large concentrations of Comanche warriors. Patrols also ensured that the mail coaches bound for Fort Smith were safely escorted to the Texas border. The increased use of the Fort Smith Road would make encounters with the Comanche and Kiowa more likely in the future and ensure more clashes with troops from Fort Union. Jacob's unit was to be kept busy in the area for the next year and a half.

In addition to the growing Comanche threat, other tribes visited the area north of Fort Union and to the east. A group of Utes and Jicarilla Apaches with nearly 200 warriors gathered near Wagon Mound, stealing sheep and cattle in the area of the Sapello River. Jacob was part of a detachment led by Colonel Loring himself on a hasty expedition to the area to remove the Utes. Greatly outnumbered, the soldiers gathered every available man at Fort Union and moved toward the Indians at Mora. Loring had summoned the help of the Indian agent at Taos, where most of the Utes had come from, out of the Sangre de Cristo Mountains. The agent, Kit Carson, arrived just in time to help mediate a peaceful departure, and escorted the Utes back to Taos. Jacob admired the negotiating skill of Carson, who helped prevent unnecessary bloodshed that day, securing the transfer of much needed wheat and grain to the Indians in return for their peaceful return home. At least one threat to Fort Union and the eastern plains had been averted.

Jacob admired Kit Carson, himself once a soldier in the Regiment of Mounted Riflemen during the Mexican War. Carson had become the agent at Taos and married a local woman. He would become a valuable asset for the Army in New Mexico, both as a civilian mediator and later as a commander of New Mexico Volunteer Cavalry during and after the Confederate Texan invasion in 1862, and later during the Indian campaigns including Adobe Walls. He was part of a small force sent to Hatch's Ranch to set up a supply base for a battalion which would patrol the Fort Smith Road and the Canadian and Pecos Valleys during the summer. Along with mounted units from Fort Stanton and a company of 8th Infantry soldiers, they were tasked with scouting for hostile Comanche groups, supporting survey and road building crews along the Canadian and Pecos Rivers' basins. Later in the summer of 1859, Jacob was sent as one of 100 troops from Fort Union to escort a road survey crew from north-central New Mexico to the San Juan River in the far northwest part of the territory. He would not return until fall. Other than a couple of mail escort trips to Fort Larned, Jacob was mainly deployed with his company to provide local security at Fort Union. Comanche and Kiowa raids were increasing on the eastern plains, and the raiders had threatened to attack Fort Union if the Army attacked their camps. Manpower issues became so severe that the new department commander had to pull in troops from as far north as Fort Garland in Colorado Territory to protect Fort Union. Infantry units from Santa Fe and other stations were moved to provide additional security.

In June 1860, with reinforcements arriving from Kansas, Jacob's company was transferred back to their original posting at Fort Stanton in the southeast section. There had been reports of plains Indian raiding parties as far south as the Bosque Redondo, and two companies of Mounted Riflemen were tasked to clear the Pecos Valley on their way to Fort Stanton. They had initially been included in the planning for a large three-column attack against the Comanche and Kiowa base camps in the Cimarron and Canadian Valleys. This campaign had to be postponed due to a devastating epidemic of equine black tongue disease, which had rendered many of the Army mounts incapable of a sustained campaign on the prairie. This major effort against those tribes would have to wait for several months for the horses to recover or be replaced. Now there was an urgent need to reinforce Fort Stanton due to a resurgence of raids in southeastern New Mexico by Mescalero Apaches. Jacob had only a few days at the end of May to get his family ready to move back to Fort Craig. He was told that this was a permanent move, and his family would be safer in the more secure location on the Rio Grande. Three other families were likewise affected, and they were quickly packed, loaded in their wagons, and escorted with the next mail coach. Charlotte was three months pregnant and having no problems. There would not be another good opportunity to relocate. Jacob and the three other soldiers were granted ten days leave to accompany their families to Fort Craig. Jacob was more likely to be able to visit the family at Fort Craig than at Fort Union. Charlotte cried in his arms when he told her what she must do. "Jacob, this is crazy. We are just fine here!"

Jacob insisted, "We just don't have a choice. Please do this one more time. You will be safer at Fort Craig, and I only have one more year on my enlistment." He reassured her that she had only one more year to endure this insanity, then his enlistment would be up. Then they would make their way to Council Grove, where they could finally have a chance for a more normal life. Charlotte was very disappointed, "Only for you Jacob, only for our family, but there must be an end to this madness. This is no way to live, and this is no way to treat a good man like you."

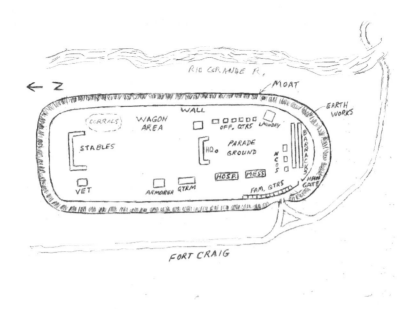

FORT CRAIG

XV. The Desert Fortress

Charlotte and the other wives relocating to Fort Craig were not exactly happy about returning to the crowded walled fortress on the Rio Grande. It was a confining place, and the laundry building and other quarters had not been substantially improved. These women knew that during rainy weather, they and their belongings were more than likely going to get wet. Also, the average temperature in the valley was at least five to ten degrees higher in the summer months than Fort Union. Winters were at least as cold in the desert as the northeastern plains. The only compensation was that they were more likely to see their husbands, at least on a monthly basis. Even though the men were officially quartered at Fort Stanton, it was only a couple of day's travel to Fort Craig. The soldiers usually made at least one supply escort trip a month. Assuming their husbands were not on a campaign against the Mescalero, the visits could be fairly frequent.

The small train of wagons followed the mail wagon to Santa Fe during the first week of June. There was no time for delay as the soldiers had to report to Fort Stanton by the middle of the month. Sergeant Baker from Jacob's Company C was the ranking soldier in the small group of families. He took the lead position after the mail wagon and two mounted escort troops. The party arrived in Santa Fe in three days, spending two nights camped on the trail, one night at

Kozlowski's Ranch, and a night in Santa Fe at the U.S. Hotel, a blessing to Charlotte, as she recalled the wonderful time she had there two years earlier. The next morning they left early, attached to a supply train bound for Albuquerque, reaching the depot there in two days. They reached Socorro two days later, and Fort Craig the following day. This was a fast pace and not pleasant for the families, but it allowed the group two days to register and move the families into quarters newly built inside the northwest wall of the compound, near the post laundry. This was new family housing, finished only a few months before, and a big improvement over Charlotte's previous quarters sharing arrangement in the past. She and Jacob were relieved and thought that made things wouldn't be so bad after all. Charlotte was given a room of her own due to her larger family, with a baby coming in the fall. The next day she visited the post surgeon, Dr. Williams, to inform him of her expected date of delivery. He examined her and confirmed to her that she appeared to be having a normal pregnancy and that he would like to see her once a month or immediately if she had any problems. She and Jacob were pleased with the doctor and excited about the arrival in the late fall of their third child. Jacob spent the evening with his family until taps, and then returned to the enlisted barracks. He was scheduled the next day to join a detachment escorting a small supply train to Fort Stanton.

A large supply train from Fort Bliss and Fort Fillmore had arrived at Fort Craig three days earlier with the monthly allocation or rations and military supplies. Merchant wagons had joined the convoy hoping to sell various wares from Texas. They brought hard-to-get items and dry goods to the occupants of Fort Craig and the Socorro area. Fort Craig was in a difficult supply area, at the end of the supply lines from both Fort Union and Fort Bliss. Non-military items were scarce and the families at Fort Craig were happy to receive what they considered to be luxury goods and food items unavailable in the vicinity. Southern supply lines from San Antonio and south Texas had been fairly secure for the past couple of years, and occasional goods from Chihuahua or even central Mexico would make their way to this isolated desert area. After unloading most of the military rations and staples, and hay and oats for the horses at Fort Craig, about twenty wagons were sent on to the even more isolated Fort Stanton, near the Pecos Valley. Most of the ammunition would be sent on to Fort Stanton, as the number of raids by Mescaleros in that area had been steadily increasing. Most of Jacob's company and one other company had already arrived at Fort Stanton by way of the eastern route through the Pecos Valley from Fort Union.

The supply train and escort arrived at Fort Stanton after two days, traveling a little slower due to the rocky roads through the San Andres Mountains, and eastward into the Three Rivers Area, north of Sierra Blanca, and through the gap to the Rio Bonito River and Fort Stanton. Jacob and his Army companions signed in at post headquarters and were billeted in the Company C barracks of the regiment. There had been a few improvements since his first posting here in 1856, with a new headquarters building, mess, and small infirmary. Three companies of Mounted Riflemen were now stationed at Fort Stanton, along with two companies of the 8th Infantry. After their mounts were taken care of at the post stables, the men settled in for a hot supper, a bath, and a good night's sleep. The following morning, after a breakfast of bacon, biscuits, and coffee, the new arrivals were given a briefing by the post adjutant. The department commander, Colonel Fauntleroy, had decided to strengthen the garrison at Fort Stanton in response to increasing Apache raids in the area. The threat affected both southeast and southwest New Mexico, but there were already adequate deployments of troops in the southwest sector, stationed at Fort Craig and Fort Fillmore. Mescalero raids threatened the lower Pecos Valley and the mail and travel routes in the southeast. In addition, there was an ongoing campaign to protect the eastern part of the territory from the plains tribes raiding from the Texas panhandle area. The Mexican Comancheros, renegade bandits, had long been known to be trading the Kiowa and Comanche in the area east and south of Anton Chico, exchanging powder, shot, and weapons for buffalo hides. The Colonel felt that a stronger presence was needed in the Pecos Valley in case of raids conducted to the south. For these reasons, patrols in the Pecos Valley and the mountain valleys just to the west would be increased. Details of 25 troopers would be dispatched for a period of seven to ten days, alternating with escort duty to and from Fort Craig. Jacob was not happy about the prospect of at least two weeks on patrol each month, but he was encouraged that he would likely be able to see his family at Fort Craig twice a month. After all, the number of American settlers and ranchers did need protection, and that was why the Army was here. He could certainly do this mission for another year. He thought it improbable that Fort Stanton would have to deal with the Kiowa and Comanche any time soon. They were too busy worrying about losing their buffalo hunting grounds to the stream of settlers coming from the East. The Mescalero were mostly concerned about the while settlers and ranchers in this part of the country encroaching on their mountain hunting grounds. He and many others would later appreciate the tenacity of the Apache nations, resistant to the growing presence of American settlers, and their ability to create big problems for another half century.

A few days after arriving at Fort Stanton, a detachment of 25 soldiers from Company C outfitted for a patrol of the Rio Bonito and Rio Hondo Rivers, from the post to the junction of the Pecos River. There had been several reports in the past month of Apache raids in this area. A few ranches and homesteads in this area reporting cattle rustling by Indian raiders coming into the valley from the west. Livestock theft had plagued Spanish settlers in the valley who had come east from the Rio Grande Valley in the fairly recent past. Now, white settlers were starting to move into the area due to drought in Kansas and other plains states. The abundant grasslands made it suitable for ranching but not large-scale farming. Decades later, the discovery of large aquifers would lead to the development of artesian wells and spawn a large farming and fruit orchard community. Early ranchers did not displace native inhabitants, as the area was previously uninhabited except for the transient groups of Indians who came to the river to fish and hunt. The Mescalero Apache tribe, which lived mainly in the mountains west of the Pecos, were hunters of deer and elk and smaller mountain game. They had been pushed into the area of the Sacramento Mountains long ago by the plains Indians, especially the Comanche, who had driven them out of northern and central Texas. This made them very apprehensive about the prospect of displacement or encroachment by the new and unwelcome invaders from the east. Apache tribes in western Texas, New Mexico, and northeast Mexico had resisted and fought the Spanish and Mexican settlers for over two centuries. The incorporation of New Mexico into the United States, and the American homestead acts of the 1860s, would ensure continued settlement pressure in the territory, and continued resistance and hostility on the part of the Apache nations. Although the American Civil War would place this problem on the back burner for a few years, the mounted troopers of the U. S. Army would not quell the resistance until the end of the century. On this patrol, however, the detachment from Company C would encounter no hostile parties of Mescalero Apache.

A dozen ranches and grazing camps were visited where they discovered no casualties among the Hispanic or American ranchers. A few dozen cattle and five horses had been taken from three of the herds, but no buildings or corrals had been invaded. The rustling had occurred at night and only one encounter had resulted in shots being exchanged, all at long range and in near darkness. The ranchers expressed gratitude for the presence of the soldiers in the area, providing food and fodder for the patrol when they camped overnight at some of the ranches. In the absence of sustained attacks on the settlements, and with no casualties involved, it seemed that an encounter with hostiles would be only by chance. Perhaps the presence of the patrols would be enough to prevent a major attack against settlers and keep livestock losses at a minimum. This pattern would prove to be the case for the remainder of the summer and fall of 1860. Not until winter weather came, would any serious incidents be encountered in the Pecos Valley or the Llano Escondido, the escarpment lands of eastern New Mexico. Jacob had finished his first patrol from Fort Stanton. He would soon be escorting wagons back to Fort Craig.

Late July and early August in southeastern New Mexico were just plain hot. Even the first day of the ride from Fort Stanton to Fort Craig, through the mountains and the Three Rivers area, were uncomfortable. The detail of 25 troopers and half a dozen, mostly empty, Army field wagons were moving along at a quick trot in the morning, but by mid-afternoon had slowed to a crawl. The men had taken their blue tunics off during a brief water stop an hour earlier. They were looking forward to a quiet night on a small tributary creek near the Three Rivers confluence in the valley west of Sierra Blanca. Camp was set up in an area of the petroglyphs, a strange area of large volcanic rocks with images of birds, animals, plants, geometric symbols, and human likenesses, believed to have been etched into the rocks by ancient occupants of the area. Jacob was fascinated by these images and was always glad to have some time to explore the area when camped in the area. The Apache were quiet so far, keeping their distance from the soldiers, with only one small hunting party seen in the mountains earlier in the day. The detail had sufficient food for the two-day trip, and the soldiers were ordered not to shoot any game animals, to avoid antagonizing the Indians. Beans and bacon, bread, and coffee were the staples of troopers on the trail. There would be plenty of beef and corn and other garden vegetables to look forward to when they reached Fort Craig. Jacob finished his coffee and reported to his sentry detail corporal, who posted him to guard the roped and corralled horses during the first watch of the evening. It was a clear night, and the stars were brilliant. His thoughts drifted back to his boyhood star-gazing days in Bavaria. At 2200 that evening Jacob was relieved from guard, and he relaxed with his pipe, then pulled his blanket over him, and let his thoughts turn to his family waiting for his arrival the next evening at Fort Craig.

Four o'clock in the morning came early, when the third watch sentries woke up the camp. The troopers and wagon drivers got up, made coffee and the usual breakfast of bacon and biscuits. They were hitched and saddled before sunrise, and the column moved out to the west, through the volcanic rock fields and up the ravines of the central gap in the San Andreas mountains. They were determined to make it to the desert floor and across the ancient trace of the Camino Real, which ran from the Jornada del Muerto on the south end up to the Socorro area to the north. The afternoon heat would be intense in the dry basin where the trail led westward to the Rio Grande and Fort Craig. They carried extra canteens and barrels of water from their overnight stop. They would stop every hour to water the horses and mules, as there would be no more water until the river crossing at Val Verde, a few miles north of Fort Craig. The desert floor was indeed hot that day, slowing their progress to a slow walk with a couple of water breaks. By early evening, they reached the Rio Grande, encountering a small Army patrol, which was checking the crossing for any signs of Apache raiding parties reported south of Socorro. Only a few old tracks were seen, none fresher than a week old were noted. The scouting patrol joined the wagons for the final five miles back to Fort Craig on the west bank of the river, arriving just after sundown.

Charlotte was thrilled to see the soldiers ride in through the main gate at Fort Craig. She was coming into late term of her pregnancy and had her hands full with her five-year-old, William, and his nearly three-year-old brother, James. She had just recently stopped working in the laundry, except for her own family's needs. The heat was nearly overwhelming at this time of year in the Rio Grande Valley. In the mornings she tended a small garden near the western adobe wall of the compound, but the afternoons were just too hot for anything other than seeking shade from a small porch overhang outside her quarters. Sally Mills, her neighbor, brought her two large buckets of water each morning, and helped with some of the cooking, which was almost always done in the morning when it was cooler. Charlotte saw Jacob's patrol ride into the compound and watched and waved with the boys as the detail rode to the corrals. They spotted their father near the end of the column and waved wildly. Jacob tipped his hat and yelled that he would see them in an hour or so. Charlotte took the boys inside to wash up. She fed them a small supper of shredded chicken, beans, and flatbread with some cantaloupe the post sutler had bought in Mesilla. She knew the boys would not eat once their daddy got there. She would have a bite to eat with Jacob after the children were tucked in for the night. About an hour later, Jacob walked over from the corral area where he had taken care of his horse and signed in at the adjutant's office. The boys ran to Jacob and he lifted them in turn over his head and hugged them as they squealed wildly. The family hugged for several minutes before retiring into Charlotte's quarters.

"My goodness, Frau Stenger," exclaimed Jacob, as he beheld her protruding abdomen, "you look like you might have the baby any day now!"

"I would gladly deliver your child tonight, Jacob," Charlotte retorted, "but I saw the doctor yesterday, and he thinks it will be at least another month. Everything seems fine, and the baby's heartbeat is strong. It is just that the baby is large, and with this late summer heat, the waiting is nearly unbearable."

"Well, it will come soon enough," Jacob observed. "I only hope that I will be able to be here when it comes. I have requested assignment to escort duty between Fort Craig and El Paso for the next two months. Things have been quiet recently in the Pecos Valley and the eastern mountains. Who knows what will come this winter when the Mescalero start moving down out of the mountains looking for food. The news from Fort Union is that the Comanche are raiding the northeastern plains again, even moving down into the upper Pecos valley. There may be a winter campaign against them if enough troops are available. There are also problems in the northwest with the Navajo, and in the southwest with the western Apache in Arizona. I could be sent anywhere later this year, but for now my sergeant is trying to help me stay as close to Fort Craig as possible, at least until the baby is born."

"Thank God, Jacob!" Charlotte sighed. "It would be a blessing for you to be here for a while after the baby comes, at least for a week

120

or two until I get back on my feet." Jacob told her that he would try to get casual duty for a couple of weeks working at the corrals here, but he would first have to go to Fort Bliss in El Paso for a few weeks to escort supplies to Fort Fillmore. There were frequent supply trains moving military and commercial goods from San Antonio to El Paso and Mesilla. Once most of the supplies were distributed to the southern area, the remainder would be coming to Fort Craig and Fort Stanton. Jacob would likely be back to Fort Craig by the end of September.

CATTLE DRIVE

XVI. Cattle Drive

Jacob relished his time with his family for another three days before riding out with a detail of 25 Mounted Riflemen. The detachment headed south toward Fort Fillmore, following the Rio Grande, arriving three days later, and quartered there overnight before moving on to El Paso and Fort Bliss. The area around Mesilla and Fort Fillmore appeared little changed to Jacob since he first passed through in 1856, except for the constructions of several new corrals and a new wagon repair facility. Mesilla was now a major stop for wagon trains moving westward to California along the southern route. Fresh draft animals, strong wagons and wheels, and food and water were essential for completing the final desert crossing through the southwest. Fort Fillmore also provided military escorts for trains moving through Arizona, where hostile Apache raiders could strike travelers in the desert mountain passes. Jacob and his detail rested well that night after three days in the saddle, making good time in spite of the late summer heat. At least they were following the river and had plenty of water for themselves and their mounts. The following morning, Sergeant Johnson, the detail commander, rustled the tired troops out at dawn for the trail breakfast of bacon, biscuits, and coffee. They saddled their mounts and headed south just as the sun broke over the eastern horizon. Stopping only to water the horses every three hours, the detail made good time, reaching El Paso before sundown, arriving at Fort Bliss half an hour later. Their horses were unsaddled and turned in at the post stables, as they would be issued fresh mounts for the return trip. The escort troopers were assigned to bunk rooms in the barracks. Attending a short meeting at the adjutant's office after supper, they were briefed on the escort mission scheduled two days later. The assignment was to accompany two supply trains recently arrived from San Antonio, with twenty wagons scheduled to move north to Fort Fillmore, Fort Craig, and finally to Fort Stanton. This had been the pattern of distribution of supplies in the southern zone of the department for nearly six years. Jacob had come to New Mexico on this route, and it supplied the needs of the Army in the southern sector well, supplementing the main supply route from Fort Leavenworth and the Missouri bases to Fort Union. The troops were informed that the convoy would be delayed for an additional two days as a large purchase of Longhorn cattle had been made by the quartermaster. Mounted riflemen, aided by about fifty cowboys and Mexican vaqueros, would be moving over 500 steers up the river, most of them destined for Fort Craig. Jacob and his comrades were not very happy to hear about this new development. Although needed for feed the growing population at Fort Craig, this large herd would really slow down the supply train and could add at least a week to the trip north.

Security would be difficult, as the convoy and the herd were tempting targets for any opportunistic bands of Apache raiders encountered along the river. A stampede of this many animals, either intentional or not, could be disastrous for the mission, and all the experienced soldiers knew it. Jacob was concerned that he might not make it back to Fort Craig in time for the birth of his third child. He knew that Charlotte was due about the first week of October. God willing, he would be there with her for the great event. He thought about his wife constantly, knowing that she was suffering through the late summer heat. At least she had a good doctor and many experienced Army wives to help her with the care of the baby and two young boys. In any event, she would be well cared for, but Jacob wanted desperately to be there if possible. It was already mid-September. For now, he was simply exhausted and needed to wash away the trail dust and get a good night's sleep after many days in the saddle. He would worry about things tomorrow, but for now his mattress promised the rest he needed. The sun was down now, and the bath and the cooling evening air of the desert evening allowed the hot and tired men to relax and recover. Tomorrow, as always, would provide enough trouble of its own.

Sleep came quickly. Reveille came too early. Sergeant Johnson was already rousting out the wranglers, some of whom had managed to find a couple of bottles of tequila the night before. The tough veteran of the Mexican War had some choice words for a couple of men who had trouble getting up, holding their heads, which were splitting from an excess of the sweet biting liquid. Sarge detailed them for a couple of hours of mucking out the post stables that morning, to work off the hangover. The remainder of the detail shaved, dressed, and finished breakfast by 0630, and marched to the corrals. They picked out new mounts, saddled them, adjusted the cinches and livery, and trotted the horses around the exercise pens. Most of the animals had been broken and initially trained for military use, but a few were still skittish, and bucked their new riders off. The remainder of the day went well, however, with all but two horses achieving successful trail and skirmish line maneuvers. The following day they were replaced with better mounts and the unit was declared ready for duty. On the third day at Fort Bliss, the escort troops spent the day at the shooting range, learning how to use their newly issued Sharp's carbines. These .52 caliber, brass cartridge, breech loading, falling block rifles were a vast improvement over the muzzle loaders and revolving cylinder carbines previously issued to mounted soldiers. The newer Sharps could sustain a rate of fire of 8-10 shots per minute and had a muzzle velocity of 1,200 feet per second, giving them a maximum effective range of almost 500 yards, with open ladder sights. The men were amazed at the accuracy they could achieve and the ease of use, especially on horseback. These new carbines promised their users a whole new level of confidence, being able to quickly reload and maintain a range advantage, to keep swarming bands of hostiles outside the effective range of their own, usually older firearms. After instruction on care and maintenance by the Fort Bliss armorer, the weapons were cleaned and inspected, then stored for the night. The troops were held over for an hour after supper for a briefing on the escort mission scheduled for the next day. The cattle had arrived from the southeast that day and were being fed and inspected by the quartermaster and post veterinarian to cull out any animal unfit for the drive north. The escort detail would split into three squads of eight or nine men, with a squad outriding on either flank, and one following the herd. Drivers and vaqueros were instructed to follow closely behind the line of twenty wagons carrying supplies and ammunition. The convoy commander and his sergeant would lead the train and control the overnight campsites and water stops. Due to the heat, the wagons and herd would stop for rest from noon to four p.m. each day. Reveille would be at 0400 and move out time at 0530 each day. Two extra water wagons would be assigned for use of the soldiers and herd drivers.

Escort detail, wagon crews, and herders were up at four in the morning, quickly ate, drew weapons, and saddled up and harnessed teams. After marshaling the wagons, the herds were moved out of the pens and started moving by 0530. Jacob's squad was the trail element behind the cattle. Since it was impossible to keep from stirring up dust with all these cattle, the detail squads would rotate every two hours to get relief from the dust. The soldiers had to wet their bandanas to keep the dust out of their mouths and noses. Movement was very slow at first, and the train and cattle had to skirt the village of El Paso to reach the Rio Grande before heading north. Captain Ross, the train commander, planned on making only two to three miles per hour with a herd this large. Hopefully the pace would pick up a little after the first 100 cattle were left at Fort Fillmore, in two to three days. He thought it unlikely they would encounter Apache raiders in this first phase. Most attacks on wagon trains in the past few months had occurred along the east-west road much further to the east of the Rio Grande. The areas south of Mesilla and Fort Fillmore had been quiet during the past year. True to expectation, the train and herd arrived at Fort Fillmore at the end of the third day. The wagons, mules, and mounted troops were reported to have had no injuries or losses. The first leg of the drive with the cattle was also calm except for the loss of five or six Longhorns out of the nearly 500 starting the trek. This was felt to be a successful start, as most herd drives of this size and distance were expected to have around ten percent attrition of the herd. A couple of the steers were lost with broken legs or lameness after the crossing of a small arroyo and had to be shot. Two died of heat exhaustion and another one or two were unaccounted for when heads were counted on the second morning. There were no reports of rustlers, and they may have wandered off during the night. Animals with broken limbs or lame were usually shot and field dressed and quartered, then carried in a cook's wagon or mule pack until the evening stop. They were then butchered for the evening meal. Fresh meat was always welcome on the trail, when the normal rations were bacon and beans. Left over beef was used for stew meat for as long as possible, and the waste left for the scavengers.

The garrison at Fort Fillmore were delighted when the train commander had the drovers cut out 100 head of cattle for the use of the post. After two days of feeding and watering, the remainder of the herd and the wagons moved north following the Rio Grande. They were 120 miles from Fort Craig, but with cattle, travel would be slow. With only the wagons, the distance could probably be covered in a week or less. Ten miles per day was about the best they could hope for with this herd. Jacob figured that they could make it in less than two weeks, but it was already the 12th of September. Anything that would spook the herd, like an Indian attack, would complicate the situation by scattering the herd and losing control of the drive. Captain Ross had been involved in a situation like this once before. He had no intention of allowing a chaotic event to jeopardize the mission. The night before leaving Fort Fillmore, he briefed the drovers and the mounted escort regarding the need for great vigilance at night, and to look out for diversionary tactics by an attacker which might draw them away from the main herd. The most important task was to prevent a stampede. Losing a few cows could be tolerated, but a stampede could lead to massive losses. Herd control was the highest priority. The Captain also established an enhanced perimeter patrol scheme for the escort, with a shift change every three hours between the three squads.

The drovers were encouraged to keep ropes and hobbles on the most agitated animals at night. The first three days and nights were pretty quiet. Occasionally a loose steer was run down and roped back into the herd by a drover or escort. These cattle were mainly descended from the original animals brought over by the Spanish hundreds of years ago. Most were purchased from ranchers in northern Mexico and the lower Rio Grande Valley. Some of the herd had even been feral animals for decades or longer, rounded up from the chaparral and deserts of west Texas and Chihuahua. Although some sprouted long, even menacing horns, the Spanish breeds were inherently gentle, intelligent animals. Some remained undomesticated and needed extra watching. They were likely to take advantage of any opportunity to escape their keepers.

On the fifth day of the march, the group stopped for the night near the junction of the Rio Grande Road, and the El Camino Real de Tierra Adentro, which ran more directly north to Socorro. Very few travelers chose this route running through a very dry high desert valley between the San Andreas Mountains to the east, and the Caballo Range to the west. The infamous route was known as the Jornada del Muerto, the journey of the dead man. Even a small group with extra water would have been in danger of perishing in this very hot and dry environment, especially in the summer or fall months. With the number of draft animals and large beef herd, there was really no choice but to follow the river route. The drive also needed to cross the Rio Grande to the west bank for the rest of the trip, as the fords were shallower here than further to the north. Additionally, the river became marshy in places making passage on the east bank more difficult. The slow flow of the river in these areas also provided small areas of vegetation in oasis like areas known as bosques, which could be used for animal fodder.

All went smoothly during the evening, as the large herd was moved down to the river for water and feeding on the abundant shrubs and grassy areas. Jacob and his squad of mounted escorts were posted on the east side of the river, taking turns in twos or threes patrolling the flank of the herd. Another squad was posted on the west bank, trailing the herd and the circled wagons of the train. About 0200, Jacob and his patrol partner noticed some movement of horsemen about 300 yards to the northeast. The riders appeared to have come out of the Jornada in the direction of an escarpment known as Point of Rocks, a low plateau forming the eastern boundary of the entrance into the desert valley. Suddenly there were flashes of light over the area of encircled wagons, with fire-arrows striking the canvas of the wagons, flaring quickly into flames, engulfing three or four of the canvas wagon tops. As this was unfolding, some of the riders galloped into the edge of the herd of cattle, shooting and yelling, stampeding some of the herd away to the east. Jacob turned his mount back toward the camp where his squad was kicking dirt on a small fire, then scrambling to saddle up. He yelled to his corporal that about twenty Indians, most likely Apache, were trying to stampede cattle out of the marshland toward the east. The squad leader sent three soldiers with Jacob toward the escaping rustlers. He told them to set up a hasty ambush and shoot as many Indians as possible, but then to try to recover as many cattle as they could. Meanwhile, the squad leader rode to the drover camp, rousting out all the men he could find to help get control of cattle trying to run to the east. By this time, the sergeant in charge of the escort had come on the scene with the reserve squad. The corporal told him what had happened, and that the fire arrows were not followed by an attack on the wagons. This had been a diversion to help the rustlers get away, and this was nearly successful as more than 200 cattle had been spooked out of the herd. Apparently, there were not more than two dozen Apache involved. The half-moon high in the sky allowed for some visibility on the desert floor. Jacob's squad had ridden hard to the east and outflanked the rustlers driving the cattle. Half of the soldiers dismounted about 500 yards ahead with their new carbines and were staring to pick out their targets on horseback, riding in the middle of the stampeding cattle. Several Apache were shot from their ponies. Jacob felt certain that he had hit at least two riders. The remaining soldiers had ridden ahead and were trying to turn the stampede back by shooting over the cattle attempting to turn the cattle to the south. They were also able to pick off some of the leading Indians, dropping about half a dozen. Unfortunately, two troopers were shot out of their saddles in a running battle. After another five minutes or so, about half of the cattle began to turn to the south and west back to the river.

By this time Lt. Stevens, the second in command of the convoy, arrived on the scene with another ten troopers. They pursued the remaining cattle and Indians, managing to turn another fifty or more cattle back to the river. The commander, Captain Ross, had stayed with the wagons, directing firefighting efforts, which extinguished the fires, but only after the total loss of two wagons, and part of the cargo in two others. Apache infiltrators, who had shot the fire arrows, had briefly exchanged shots with the soldiers at the wagons, but quickly broke contact to join their comrades escaping to the east. Captain Ross, learning that most of the stampeding cattle had been recovered, ordered the pursuit halted, and sent as many herders and soldiers out to help round up stray cattle and care for any casualties. One squad of escorts was posted to ward off any further attacks. By dawn, all of the recoverable cattle had been brought back to the camp, and a head count conducted. It turned out that the rustlers had gotten away with over fifty cattle with another twenty steers lost to injuries or shot during the stampede. Seven attackers were found dead, and one Apache was captured after breaking his leg falling from his horse, which had been shot from under him. There were four military casualties with two troopers killed, one wounded in the arm, and one suffering moderate burns while fighting the wagon fires. One drover had been killed trying to stop stampeding cattle.

Captain Ross was certainly not happy with the losses, but all things considered, he had not suffered devastating losses of men, and he still had more than 300 cattle and most of the supplies. Fortunately, the raiding party had been small, but their leader had achieved near total surprise, and made off with a substantial number of cattle. Most of the raiders were probably halfway to their sanctuaries in the San Andreas Mountains by now. The commander would be more vigilant after this, doubling his patrols each night. After all this, wagons and herd would not move this day, but would recover, treat wounds, repair wagons, and inspect the herd for injuries, culling animals as necessary. There would also be a briefing on lessons learned and changes in security procedures.

The captured Apache was interrogated with the help of a Mexican drover who could speak enough of the Indian language to learn that the raiding party was about 30 braves, Mescaleros, from the mountains south of Fort Stanton. They had been hunting the area south of Sierra Blanca, and game was scarce. Their leader, a sub-chief of the tribe, had seen the large herd moving north and found it irresistible. Unexpectedly, the rapid-fire weapons of the soldiers proved to be more than they could deal with. Captain Ross thought the prisoner's story believable enough that these Apache hunters were working alone, and not part of a larger force. He warned the prisoner, through the interpreter, that he would be the first to die if the soldiers were attacked again. The Indian's leg was splinted for travel, and he was allowed to have water and biscuits.

Early the next day the train was ordered to move north with the herd being tightly controlled, which was a little easier after losing nearly 100 steers. The train managed to make twelve miles along the west bank of the Rio Grande by mid-afternoon, and it was very hot. Watering the herd was a priority, and there was a large bosque with shallow water, that would accommodate the whole herd. Except for large swarms of mosquitos, the area seemed safe. It would be more difficult to steal cattle out of the boggy river bottom. Two squads were posted on the east bank, each pulling two hour shifts with outriders 400 yards farther out. The night was uneventful, and the train and herd continued the march north at dawn. Three days later, Elephant Butte, a prominent mesa, was spotted at the end of a gorge, a traveler's landmark. Captain Ross knew he was within a week of Fort Craig at this point, and there had been no more threats to his unit. The remainder of the trek was peaceful, except for the loss of one of the fire damaged wagons, and another dozen cattle. The mission was successful, despite the losses.

Fort Craig was a welcome site, though it was in the middle of nowhere, even by New Mexico standards. As the wagon train entered the main gate, a great cheer rang out from the post occupants gathered to welcome it. The corrals and pens were huge within the large adobe walled compound. More than 300 cattle had survived the trip, and all but fifty would stay at Fort Craig. In three days, those fifty cattle and seven wagon loads of supplies would start out again for their final destination, Fort Stanton. Jacob was almost certain that he would have to make the trip to Stanton. It was his primary duty assignment, after all. At least he would have a couple of days to see his family.

Escort troopers helped the drovers finish moving the cattle into the holding pens, before heading for the horse corrals where they unsaddled, brushed their animals down, and made sure they had water and hay. The men signed in at post returns at the headquarters before heading for the barracks. The few married men, like Jacob, walked over to the family quarters area to meet wives and children. Jacob had no sooner reached the northeast family quarters of the compound, than his five-year old, William, came running toward his Papa. He dropped his saddle bags and carbine, and picked up the boy, tossing him overhead, William squealing and hugging his father's neck.

"Come inside Papa," urged William, "Mrs. Brown next door brought us chili for supper. She also baked some cornbread this morning."

Jacob was hungry since the detail had not stopped for a midday meal, trying to make Fort Craig before sundown. "That sounds fine, Will!" Jacob responded. He put the young man on his shoulders and moved toward the door of their quarters. It was hardly a set of quarters, more an adobe roof and walls built against the inside of the perimeter walls of the fort. The roof, with straw over a few log rafters and covered with adobe mud, was alright in dry weather, but could turn into a leaking overhead mess when it rained hard. Father and son entered through the low doorway, and there she was, great with child. Jacob couldn't believe the change in only the few weeks he had been gone. Charlotte turned to embrace and kiss her husband.

"Jacob, it is very close now," she gasped as the tears welled up in her eyes. "Only a week or two. Are you going to stay with me now?" she pleaded, searching his face for the answer.

130

"I wish it were so, Liebchen, but we have to deliver some of the cattle to Fort Stanton. I have to leave early, but I will be back in a week."

Charlotte face showed disappointment, but she fought back tears and hugged her husband. "Hurry back, Jacob, I need your strength," she implored.

"I will do everything I can to get back here in a week," he promised, "If you can wait a week, I will be at your side."

They were about to have a quiet dinner provided by the neighboring wives; the boys having already finished their evening meal. William was a very bright five-year-old by now, and he had a few questions about his father's recent trip and all those cows. Jacob explained why cattle were so important to provide meat for the soldiers and their families. The animals were also useful as occasional gifts to the Indians to help prevent them from raiding farmers and ranchers for food. William didn't quite understand all of that, but he somehow knew that Papa did important work to protect people and keep them safe. James, his three-year-old brother, was just getting out of the toddling stage and always exploring his surroundings. He was intrigued at the moment, playing with a spinning top that Jacob had bought for each of the boys in El Paso.

After helping tuck in the boys, Jacob and Charlotte cleaned up from supper, and returned the terra cotta dishes to the neighbors. A few pleasant moments were spent talking to their friends, before Jacob went to the barracks and returning after a quick bath and shave. For the next couple of hours, Jacob shared his stories of the trip with Charlotte, enjoyed her talk about anticipating the coming birth of their child, and relaxing with a last cup of coffee until the first note of taps reminded him it was time to return to the barracks for some precious sleep before starting his duty routine all over again.

Reveille came early. It was darker earlier in the morning as the late fall days were getting shorter. Jacob dressed quickly, ate, grabbed his saddle bags and weapons, and headed for the corrals. After saddling their horses, the escort troopers helped the drovers separate out just over fifty healthy looking animals for delivery to Fort Stanton. Ten drovers accompanied the herd and the small train with a dozen troopers on this last leg of the drive. There were five supply wagons, two water wagons, and half a dozen extra horses tethered to the wagons.

Departing Fort Craig at sunrise, they moved up the west bank and crossed the Rio Grande at Valverde, allowing the herd to drink their fill. Following the river up the east bank, they turned to the east after a few miles. By mid-afternoon the train and herd were in the Jornada del Muerto, having passed around the northern end of Oscura Mountain. Even at the end of September, it was still a slow, hot trek across the high desert wasteland, with the steers able to make three to five miles an hour. Sergeant Johnson decided to stop on the eastern edge of the desert floor as four steers had already collapsed during the crossing of the Jornada. He ordered the drovers to take buckets of water from the wagons to give the animals half a gallon each to drink. The cattle were tethered together in groups of ten, to prevent them from wandering off in search of water. One of the dead steers was butchered for dinner for the men, and a perimeter guard of four soldiers was posted with a shift change every three hours.

This route to Fort Stanton had the advantage of running north of Sierra Blanca Peak, away from Apache villages further to the south and east. There was no sign of raiding parties during the night, and the train and herd broke camp and moved out at first light. Another two cattle had died during the night, but over forty head appeared to be doing well. Abundant water for the herd would be available when they reached the springs in the valleys that night, after crossing the lava fields and moving east around the north end of Church Mountain, the second night's stop. Here the north branch of the Rio Bonito, which would be followed to Fort Stanton, merged with the main part of the river, itself a tributary of the Pecos River. The evening was calm, and no Apache were encountered except a small hunting party seen at a distance near Capitan Mountain. Deer and antelope were abundant in this area, and this small group did not shadow the herd. The train and herd arrived at Fort Stanton in the early afternoon of the next day, to the cheers of the garrison and a few nearby settlers. Two companies of Mounted Riflemen were stationed here numbering over one hundred, but many troopers were detached for numerous escort details, as was the case with Jacob.

Because his family was living at Fort Craig, and especially since his wife was due to deliver very soon, Jacob was allowed to return the following day to Fort Craig. He would be sent out with Sergeant Johnson, and another soldier who was going to Albuquerque to deliver important dispatches for the post-adjutant's office and to pick up some small rifle parts. Two other men were headed on to new assignments in Santa Fe. Jacob would accompany them to the Rio Grande and then ride south to Fort Craig. It would be a hard ride, traveling nearly 100 miles in one day, traveling light except for a couple of extra canteens of water. A ride of that distance wasn't unusual, especially for couriers who did it routinely. Sergeant Johnson wasn't taking any chances though, and requisitioned two extra mounts, in case a horse came up lame. The group left the gate at dawn, and quickly settled into a trot. They could make ten miles an hour that way without totally exhausting the horses. Two miles from Fort Stanton, they turned west into the open valley they had followed the day before. By nine in the morning, the group had reached the artesian springs north of Three Rivers, stopping briefly to water the horses. Continuing northwest across the lava fields, by evening they were over the crest of the San Andreas escarpment, and the horses were beginning to show signs of fatigue. They slowed the pace to a walk due to the heat. When the group had crossed the Jornada and were coming into the approaches to the Rio Grande, Jacob's horse stumbled after stepping into a hole and fell, throwing Jacob over the reins, tumbling a couple of times. He hurt his right knee, which had been dislocated a couple of years before during the Utah expedition. He could walk, but was limping, and fortunately the knee did not dislocate again. He thought he could still ride. His horse was not so lucky. It had fractured the left front leg below the knee and could not stand on it. The other soldiers unsaddled the mount, transferring the gear to one of the extra horses. Jacob knew what he had to do, but it filled him with dread. This chestnut gelding had been one of his favorites for several months now and had performed wonderfully. Making the poor animal kneel down and then roll onto his side. Jacob calmed him by stroking his neck gently and cooing to him. He then cocked his pistol and gently place the barrel behind the horse's ear, and slowly pulled the trigger. The noble beast twitched for a few seconds and then went limp. It was always difficult for Jacob to put down a mount, especially one he had spent so much time with on the trail. He knew it was the humane thing to do but hated it all the same. He stood over the animal for a moment, then turned to mount his new ride. She was a roan, two to three years old with strong conformation, probably of mustang stock, but with some Morgan lines. He began to mount, cringing and barely made it all the way to the saddle. Jacob bent forward in the saddle with his right knee on fire. Sergeant Johnson immediately recognized that Jacob was in severe pain.

"Stenger!" he barked, "You are only two or three hours from Fort Craig. Do you think you can make it alone?"

"Yes, Sergeant!" he answered.

"Then you better get going. Take the trail down to Valverde, and get to the post surgeon at Fort Craig, as soon as possible, and get that leg splinted. I am going to need you in two or three weeks, but for now you need to take care of yourself, so you can see if that baby has arrived yet." Jacob just smiled, turned his filly south and down the gentle slope to the river. Desperately wanting to be there when the baby came, He didn't know when it would come exactly, but the sooner the better. It was a very kind gesture by his sergeant, and he was grateful.

An hour later, Jacob reached Valverde, crossed to the west bank and followed the road to the fort. He knew he could be there in an hour, but he couldn't trot or gallop. The knee was not painful now, except when his horse lurched to avoid the deeper wheel ruts in the road. Before long it was possible to see the outline of the fort in the distance, the sun now lower in the sky and reflecting off of the northwest wall. As he neared the main gate, a sentry yelled at him, and Jacob yelled back the greeting. Young William must have recognized the voice of his father and came running to see his horse passing through the wooden gate. With considerable grimacing, Jacob pulled the boy up by the arm and hugged him. They rode across the compound to the housing area until they reached Charlotte sitting outside in a rocking chair, and when she stood up to greet her husband, she appeared bigger than ever. She looked uncomfortable, and with great effort, he dismounted and limped over to her, embracing and kissing her.

"Jacob! What is wrong?" she cried out. "It is nothing, dear, I just had a little tumble off of my horse, nothing to worry about," he lied. Charlotte knew better, this was the same leg that had once before kept him from walking normally for several months.

"We need to get you over to the hospital right away, so Dr. Williams can have a look at that."

The next-door neighbor, Sally Mills, had come out to see that was going on. "My husband can fetch a wagon and drive you over there," she offered.

Jacob thanked her for her concern, but he told her that he was more concerned about Charlotte's condition right now, not his own.

Turning to Charlotte, he asked, "Have you had any contractions yet, Schatze?"

"Last night I had some cramping, but it didn't last long, a few minutes. It is not my time yet, Jacob, another two or three days yet." Jacob wasn't convinced, but she was still on her feet. "Jacob, Sally has some training as a midwife. She will be here to take care of me until the doctor can come. Now, you need to go to the doctor right now. You are not going to be any good to me if you can't even walk. You may need a splint and some crutches for a while, now go! You need to get that leg elevated tonight, and I will see you in the morning. I have an appointment with Dr. Williams in the morning for a progress check. Maybe we will have a better idea when the baby will come." Jacob was not happy with the idea, but he knew that his wife was right. He just thought that the timing was all wrong, with Charlotte in such a condition. Corporal Joe Mills, who worked at the Quartermaster office, had brought the wagon around. He helped Jacob aboard, and tied his horse to the back of the wagon. As they rode to the hospital, some three hundred yards away, Mills told Jacob that he would help him inside with this gear, then take his horse to the stables, and get her watered, fed, and stabled. Jacob expressed his sincere appreciation for Joe's help.

At the hospital Jacob was helped into the reception area, waiting about half an hour before Dr. Williams came out to inspect his knee, which was quite swollen by now. The Dr. admitted him and had the leg placed in an elevated sling over the bed. He ordered supper for Jacob, and he prescribed some laudanum if his patient should have trouble sleeping. Jacob reluctantly accepted the facts of the situation, happy that he had at least made it back in time to be with Charlotte. He wolfed down his meal, sipped his coffee, and nearly forgot about the pain in his knee, thanking God for his family and good fortune. He fell asleep in about an hour. Except for the need of the urinal, and two doses of the pain medicine, Jacob was able to sleep until the sun came through the hospital windows in the morning.

XVII. Christian Stenger

Charlotte had little time to muse over names for their third child. She naturally hoped for a girl, having two boys already. She and Jacob had agreed, just in case he did not return from his trip to El Paso, that a girl would be named Christine, the name of Jacob's favorite sister. If a boy, he would be named Christian, after Jacob's father. That having been settled, they both just prayed for a healthy child. They had relocated during a pregnancy once before and had lost the child. That bitter memory lingered, but they were more confident this time because the travel had been less traumatic, and Charlotte had not shown any signs of problems. After her final progress check this morning, Dr. Williams had found nothing to worry about, with a strong heartbeat, no bleeding, a normal crowning posture, and only a slight amount of dilation. She had not been experiencing any severe contractions, only intermittent light cramping once or twice a day, and no signs of imminent delivery. Charlotte relayed this to Jacob as she gave him the doctor's report. Dr. Williams had seen Jacob earlier in the morning, and he recommended that he stay in the hospital with his leg elevated for at least another day or two, then they would see if he could ambulate with crutches. Jacob wanted to be with Charlotte, but she assured him that it could be another couple of days or maybe and long as a week. In any case, she had very kind neighbors who would bring her to the hospital, or summon the doctor, depending on her condition. Jacob would be better served by staying where he was and following the doctor's orders. He was not very pleased about being there, but he really didn't think the leg would bear weight yet, so he would do as he was told. Charlotte spent the next two hours with Jacob, before returning to her quarters, assuring his that everything would be just fine. Jacob was nearly exhausted from the last few weeks on the trail, needed rest, and would just take advantage of the opportunity. In the back of his mind, though, he thought it unlikely that Charlotte would be able to hold out more than another day or two.

Charlotte appeared at Jacob's bedside the next morning along with Sally Mills, and with a great smile, asked how he felt. He did feel a little better today, having only called for pain medication once during the night. "Any changes with you?" he asked.

"Doing just fine, good night, but a little tired." As she sat down in a chair next to his bed, Charlotte suddenly started, and gasped, "Oh, my goodness, I think my water just broke!"

Jacob shouted out, "Orderly! We need the doctor!"

Sally helped Charlotte to lie down in a bed adjacent to Jacob and pulled a couple of privacy screens around her bed. By the time the doctor arrived on the ward, coming from the exam and surgery room, Sally had already removed Charlotte's skirts and undergarments and covered her abdomen and upper legs with a sheet. Dr. Williams immediately ordered hot water and towels and some basic instruments. By this time Charlotte was beginning to have heavy contractions and starting labor. Dr. Williams, after examining her, said that the baby was going to be born within the next half hour. Charlotte was gasping and crying out, while Sally coached her to control her breathing, and wiped her brow with a cool wet cloth.

Jacob couldn't believe this was happening so fast. When William was born in San Antonio, Charlotte's labor had been slow and seemingly took all day, although it had really been only a little over two hours. It had been similar with James at Fort Union. Jacob felt totally helpless being flat on his back with his leg in a sling. Fortunately, they had the entire ward to themselves, with no other bed patients admitted at the time. Jacob wanted to get up and pace the floor, like an expectant father was supposed to do. He even tried to take his leg out of the sling, but a sharp shooting pain changed his mind right away. For the next fifteen to twenty minutes, Charlotte moaned and cried out while the doctor and Sally coached her to use and bear down.

"Here it comes," announced the doctor, as he maneuvered the baby's head into the open. He cleared the mouth and throat of the newborn, held it up by the feet and after a moment, slapped the baby's bottom, and the child began to wail. He placed the infant on a clean dry towel and passed it to Sally who began to clean the baby with warm water, while Dr. Williams clamped and tied the umbilical cord with a gauze strip.

"It's a boy," he cried out. Sally placed the baby, wrapped in a clean towel, in Charlotte's arms. Jacob couldn't believe it, another boy. Charlotte would really have her hands full, with three boys less than five years apart. But now, the excitement was over, and it was a moment to be grateful that mother and child were healthy, safe, and he was blessed to be there with them.

What a day this had been. Sally volunteered to take care of the other two boys for a few days, and she would help Charlotte with the baby until Jacob could get back on his feet. He thanked her profusely and assured her that he would be able to come home in a day or two when she was discharged with the baby. Later that evening, after Charlotte had nursed the baby and slept for a couple of hours, Jacob told her that he loved her very much and was so happy about the whole event. He knew she was a little disappointed that she didn't have a daughter, but they could try again for a girl in a year or two. Charlotte replied that she was perfectly fine with three boys, but she didn't know if she could handle any more children. Whatever happened would be what God wanted. Jacob felt honored that he was able to name the boy after his grandfather, Christian. In another year or two, Christian would be called "Kit," after a man that Jacob served under and had tremendous respect for. Jacob couldn't get over the fact that he was in the hospital with a seemingly minor injury, and even more bizarre, that he was in a bed next to his wife, who had just delivered their third boy. He was very thankful that everything had come out well, but was frustrated that he couldn't attend to her needs. He felt useless in this situation, sharing his thoughts with Charlotte, but she would have none of it.

"Jacob, you have always done everything for me, at least when we have been together. You haven't always been there when I needed help, but that is just the lot of an Army wife. The families help each other when their men are away. You and all the other soldiers are there to protect us and all of the people the Army is responsible for. What you do is important, and I don't want you to feel guilty about anything."

Jacob gathered his thought for a minute or two and replied, "You are so strong, Charlotte. You have been so understanding and patient. I promise you when my enlistment is up next summer, we will move to Kansas, where we can have a more peaceful life, and raise our three sons in our own home."

"I know we will, Jacob, and I am so looking forward to that time. But don't worry about me, we are a family, and we can endure almost anything as long as we love each other."

Two days later, Jacob was fitted for crutches and was able to get about on his own after a little practice. Charlotte and baby were doing fine, ready to be back at their quarters to take care of the other two boys. The doctor gave Jacob a two-week medical furlough, pending clearance to return to duty when he could ride again. Cpl. Mills brought a wagon over to the hospital and drove the Stengers back to their quarters. He set up a cot for Jacob, assuring him that he would be there to help him on short notice, if the family needed anything. Sally brought Will and James over from her place, along with enough food for the rest of the day.

"Don't worry about cooking for a few days, Charlotte," insisted Sally. "Several of the neighbors have volunteered to bring food for the rest of the week." Charlotte and Jacob thanked the Mills and expressed their sincere gratitude. Finally, they settled down for the day, with Jacob playing with the two boys, while Charlotte nursed Christian.

The next two weeks went slowly for Jacob. He didn't like being on the crutches, but he realized that he needed to rest and heal, and after the swelling went down later in the week, he was able put weight on his right leg and walk with one crutch. By the end of the second week he was able to walk, but still stiffly. He got permission to begin riding again. Fortunately, his left knee was strong, and he was able to mount his horse normally. He was placed on casual duty, temporarily working at the quartermaster office with Joe Mills. A couple of weeks later, Dr. Williams examined the knee, which was considerably better, and gave him clearance to return to escort duty. Luckily, Sergeant Johnson and the rest of his detachment were on a mission to Albuquerque picking up supplies and replacement horses for Fort Stanton. Jacob would have another week to recover before returning to trail duty. He made the most of it, enjoying his family. He had a great time taking care of the two older boys, sometimes walking with them down to the stables, or exploring other areas of Fort Craig like the sutler's store, exploring the post, or even standing out at Retreat, listening to the bugler signaling the end of the duty day, and saluting as the Stars and Stripes were pulled down from the tall flagpole flying above the parade field. He realized, more than ever, how lucky and blessed he really was.

XVIII. The Gathering War Clouds

The remainder of 1860 was routine and uneventful for Jacob
and his family. He had only one more deployment in November and
was back to Fort Craig by the third week of December, after another
supply escort assignment from El Paso and Fort Fillmore. There were
no attacks on the train coming up the Rio Grande this time, and the
small contingent that went on the Fort Stanton was not bothered. The
Mescalero had apparently found sufficient game in the mountains
during and after the fall rut. Elsewhere in the department, operations
against the Navajo in the northwest were concluded by the end of the
year. Raids by the Comanche and Kiowa tribes during the last part of
the year were only notable for an incident of theft of about a thousand
head of cattle in the Cimarron River area. In addition, there were
reports of raids against travelers along the Santa Fe Trail. These
activities prompted the new commander of the Regiment of Mounted
Riflemen, Lieutenant Colonel George Crittenden, to send out
reinforced patrols without much effect, until under his personal
command, a reinforced squadron of more than one hundred troopers
surprised a camp of Kiowa and Comanche near Cold Spring on the
Cimarron in early January 1861. With minimal casualties themselves,
they routed the camp, killing and capturing a large number of Indians
and horses. Crittenden had hoped to put together a larger campaign to
really punish the Comanche nation, but was hampered by lack of
sufficient troops and horses.

Another distraction was the resurgence of settlement raids in the Pecos Valley by the Mescalero Apache tribe. Crittenden and Colonel Fauntleroy, the department commander, decided to wage a serious campaign against the Apache, but as they were organizing for the campaign, Fauntleroy was recalled to Washington due to increasing tensions between the Union and the emerging Confederate States. The new commander, Colonel Loring, a previous commander of the Mounted Riflemen, was forced to cut back on transportation and other resources as Union Army priorities shifted to the East. With a reduced force, Lieutenant Colonel Crittenden still pursued the Apache in southeastern New Mexico, but no battles were engaged, and by March, the Mescalero agreed to negotiate for peace. The task force was recalled to Fort Union. The officers in the department who identified with the Confederate cause, including Loring, Crittenden, and dozens of others, began to resign their commissions and left for service to the Confederacy. Unlike the commissioned officers, most of the enlisted men were bound by their enlistments, and were not free to leave the Union Army, under threat of arrest and prosecution for desertion. Very few NCOs and enlisted men left for the South. Jacob, even though he had served many years in Texas, felt no obligation to support a government that championed slavery; however, it might have been justified under the guise of state's rights. He thought the Union should be preserved in any event, but it seemed very unlikely that he would be involved in any coming conflict, as his term of enlistment was about to end. He just wanted to take his family to Kansas and begin a new life in that "promised land" that he had discovered. He owed that to his beloved wife and children who had suffered his absence and dislocations, having to live in less-than-ideal conditions. Before that could happen, however, a national cataclysm would intervene, altering the family plans for at least a couple of years. Jacob believed that the Army in New Mexico might be drawn down to support Union forces back east, but that the western territories would still have to be defended against Indian attacks. There were rumors that the Texans, with a long-standing desire to annex New Mexico, might try to take over the territory for its mineral wealth. Now, the Confederacy might want to take the territory as a gateway to California and the Pacific Ocean. As far as Jacob was concerned, it wasn't his problem, as he was only a few months from the end of his enlistment. He had absolutely no intention of reenlisting. He had been a private for nearly ten years.

After Texas seceded from the Union in February 1861, it became clear to Colonel Edward Canby, the incoming department commander in New Mexico, that following the surrender of federal property and stores in San Antonio, the only lifeline remaining for the Army in New Mexico was the Santa Fe Trail. Colonel Loring resigned in June and left Fort Fillmore to wait for acceptance of this resignation by President Lincoln. Colonel Canby assumed command at Santa Fe. His first priority was to secure the territory against invasion from Texas, and to secure the Santa Fe Trail, his lifeline from the Missouri bases. Reinforcements were requested from the East, and more arms and logistical support. Horses were especially in short supply. Washington had its hands full trying to build the Army of the Potomac, and New Mexico was put on the back burner. It was determined that the department would have to become more or less self-sufficient, raising volunteer regiments, and arming them with weapons stored at or made by the ordnance depot at Fort Union. Captain Shoemaker, Jacob's old acquaintance, who had repaired his Colt carbine a few years ago, told Colonel Canby that he would be able to arm two regiments of volunteers within a few months by refurbishing some older muskets turned in by the infantry units. The arms were shipped out to the depot at Albuquerque, Fort Craig, and Fort Stanton, where many of the volunteers were being mustered in. A large number of the recruits were Mexican, which created some language barriers, but the command required that new volunteer unit commanders speak Spanish or at least have an interpreter present to help with translation. Some training was conducted at Fort Union for the volunteers, and they were assigned to companies, wherever possible with Spanish-speaking NCOs.

While troops were being recruited and trained, Colonel Canby kept patrols active on the Santa Fe Trail, as one of his main concerns was the possibility of Texans infiltrating the area of the Texas panhandle and raiding or interdicting the supply routes, especially around the Cimarron River crossings. He kept scouts out on the eastern approaches, and even though the Confederate threat never materialized in this area, no chances were taken. The only incidents in this part of the department were the usual run-ins with the Comancheros, the Mexican renegades who made a living running guns to the Comanche and Kiowa tribes. Surprisingly, the Indians were fairly quiet during this period, while the department prepared to block the expected Confederate invasion.

The main invasion was expected to come from the south and up the Rio Grande Valley. The Confederates had already occupied El Paso, operating out of Fort Bliss, which was abandoned to the Texans after the opening of hostilities in April 1861. Taking Fort Union, the arms depot for the department, located in the northeastern sector, was recognized by both Union and Confederate leadership as the key to control of New Mexico and indeed the entire southwestern desert area.

Colonel Canby set the defense of this post as his highest priority. In its original position, it was deemed to be indefensible if attacked from the high ground to the west of the fort. Plans were rapidly made during this time to move the main part of the installation out of artillery range of the bluffs to its west. A massive octagonal earthen fortress, the Star Fort, with outer ditches, was quickly built about a mile to the east of the original post, to provide protection against artillery fire and to be able to return cannon fire from its elevated ramparts.

As the reconstruction of Fort Union continued during the summer of 1861, Canby prepared to defend the southern approaches from invasion up the Rio Grande from El Paso, which was already controlled by the Texans under Colonel John Baylor, commanding the 2nd Texas Mounted Rifles. Baylor was occupied initially with battles against the Chiricahua Apache, who were attacking settlers in the Arizona region of the territory. By late July 1861, Baylor had control of the southern border areas and was ready to move against the Union forces at Fort Fillmore, under the command of Major Isaac Lynde. There was a minor battle, on July 25th, at the town of Mesilla, where Baylor routed the numerically superior Yankees. Casualties were light, but Lynde, fearing a follow-on attack, withdrew to Fort Fillmore, then abandoning the post the next day. He began a retreat northeast toward Fort Stanton, with a depleted and demoralized force. He was lacking adequate supplies, horses, and especially water. It was later discovered that many of the Federal soldiers had filled their canteens with whiskey, which later made them easy prey for the pursuing Texans, and many dehydrated stragglers were captured or killed. On July 27th, approximately 100 remaining Union troops were overtaken and forced to surrender at San Augustine Pass as they retreated toward Fort Stanton. The Confederates continued on, occupying Fort Stanton, which had been ordered abandoned by Colonel Canby. The garrison commander, Major Roberts, led his troops northwest to Albuquerque, sending some as reinforcements to Fort Craig.

This disgraceful chain of events eventually led to the court martial of Major Lynde and his dismissal from the service. Some aspects of his failure of proper leadership became controversial in later years, but at the time, his actions were held to be directly responsible for the humiliating defeat by the Texans. This disaster in the southern sector of his command caused Colonel Canby to rapidly reinforce Fort Craig with thousands of additional troops and to speed up the reconstruction of Fort Union. Nearly everyone on the Union side was certain that the Confederates would be invading central and northern New Mexico within a few weeks. The Texans, already in New Mexico, however, were too small a force to wage a major campaign moving north. The major engagements would have to wait for the arrival of a much larger invasion force, the twenty-five hundred Texans then being organized and brought westward by an old New Mexico hand, the former U.S. Army Major Henry Hopkins Sibley, now a Confederate Brigadier General. Canby had known Sibley for many years, as the two West Pointers graduated only a year apart in the late 1830s. They had both served in the Indian Wars in Florida and in the War with Mexico. Sibley had the personal backing of Jefferson Davis, the president of the Confederacy, who had agreed to Sibley's proposal to invade New Mexico, take the territory away from the Union and claim the mineral wealth for the South. Sibley had been busy raising a brigade of troops in Texas, during the late months of 1861, while Lieutenant Colonel John Baylor had been steadily taking control of the southern regions of New Mexico, which included much of present-day Arizona. Sibley had served at Fort Union and recognized that controlling that installation was the key to winning the campaign for New Mexico.

While all the preparations for war were unfolding, Pvt. Jacob Stenger had been preparing himself and his family to escape the coming conflict. Jacob had reached the end of his second five-year enlistment and had been mustered out at Fort Stanton, just ahead of the loss of the fort to the Texans. He and a few other members of Company C, Regiment of Mounted Riflemen, recently renamed the 3rd Regiment of U.S. Cavalry, had gone to Fort Craig. Those with families at Fort Craig had been allowed to move north with other families being evacuated to Santa Fe for final out processing and further movement on to Kansas, Missouri, or points east. Jacob and another married soldier were encouraged to quickly move their families north to safety and out of the war zone. They took their wagons and teams, escorted by a small detail of cavalry, to Santa Fe. From there they could join wagon trains transporting soldiers reassigned to the war in the East, moving the civilians out of harm's way.

XIX. Crisis of Conscience

The four-day journey to Santa Fe went by quickly for Charlotte and the boys. The weather was good, a little hot with the afternoon sun, but the clear nights were good for sleeping after the evening stop and supper on the trail. The second night found the group at Albuquerque. With numerous troop movements, supply trains in transit, and civilian evacuation in progress, there was no lodging available. The group circled their wagons near the depot, due to lack of adequate camp sites, which was not unusual for areas expecting imminent military hostilities. Jacob, reflecting on his haste in removing his family from the imminent war zone, began to feel torn between the need to move his family to safety, and his sense of duty to his adopted country. He had spent a lot of time during the move north pondering his options. It seemed to him there was no easy course. Certainly, he would make sure that his wife and children were in a safe place. He just couldn't help feeling an obligation to resist the southern cause. He had spent enough time in Texas to realize that the sentiments of many southern sympathizers didn't match up with the constitutional ideals of the American founders. After learning to speak and read English well enough while living in San Antonio, he had found a small library at the Army depot at the Alamo. Jacob had received a fairly good education, including seminary, and he had an appreciation of history. There were copies of the Declaration of Independence, the Constitution and Bill of Rights, and a couple of books explaining the history and causes of the American Revolution. He realized that the coming struggle was all about individual freedom and equality under the law. The government was important for protecting the security of the citizens, and looking out for their rights, freedom, and well-being in general. But here in America, unlike the kingdoms of Europe, the most important consideration was the individual, rather than the state or the ruler, or the hereditary wealth of the upper classes. Government was supposed to represent all the people fairly, not just the powerful. It seemed to Jacob that many southern sympathizers, who supported leaving the Union, were more loyal to the idea of an older feudal form of government controlled by the landed aristocracy. Even though government officials were elected democratically, the electorate was limited to white males, who were in turn controlled by the wealthy landowners and plantation economy. The lower classes were often discouraged from voting due to inadequate education and the social hierarchy. Slaves had no franchise at all. Jacob felt that this system denied freedom to untold thousands or even millions of Americans, keeping them from improving their own lives. It slammed the door in the face of the promise of America: Life, Liberty and Pursuit of Happiness. Jacob knew that he could never support the other type of system, vowing to always resist the spread of this evil culture.

By the time the soldiers and families reached Santa Fe, Jacob had shared his feelings with Charlotte, and as expected, she was quite upset with the prospect of being separated from her husband again, especially with the threat of war looming on the horizon. "Jacob, we have endured too much time apart all these years. You have done your duty, and now it is time to stay with your family. Christian is not even a year old, and I need your help raising these children. We need some stability."

Jacob wanted to be with his family, and start a new life in Kansas, but he was conflicted. "I will have to wait and see what the situation is when we get to Santa Fe. I want to keep moving north and east, but if I am needed, I must serve. It is rumored that the Texans might even try to take over the supply lines of the Santa Fe Trail. If that happened there would be no safe place for us to go. I would never be able to live with myself if I felt that I had shirked my duty."

Charlotte knew he was right, but she could feel her new life slipping away. She would remain quiet about it for now. Camping that night near the Santa Domingo Pueblo, she recalled that she had been in this place three years before. She felt as if she was destined to spend her years as a migrant Army wife, and she decided to put the dream of a stabile family life on hold. She knew her husband would not in good conscience run away from the coming fight. Charlotte was not as political as Jacob, but she knew and respected his views that this country was worth defending.

By the time they arrived in Santa Fe the next evening, on August 4th, Charlotte had reconciled herself to whatever might happen. Fortunately, there was room for their family at the U.S. Hotel. The men, even though recently discharged, had to complete final out processing at Fort Marcy, and stayed in barracks. Military headquarters at the Palace of the Governors was frantic with activity. There was great alarm following the news that Fort Fillmore and Fort Stanton had fallen. Troops were coming and going constantly through the city with long wagon trains coming through Fort Marcy heading

148

south. Colonel Canby was trying to pack Fort Craig with men and supplies to block the Confederate advance. Jacob heard the terrible news and was greatly distressed. Other recently discharged soldiers were deciding to re-enlist and stay in New Mexico volunteer units being formed at Santa Fe headquarters. Jacob, seeing all of this, began to have a change of heart about his duty to stay and defend New Mexico. He inquired about joining the volunteers. About an hour later, he walked down the street to the hotel, and found his family waiting for him in the lobby. Charlotte didn't even let Jacob get the words out of his mouth.

"Jacob, I read your mind. You don't have to say anything, you have to do your duty. But, where will the boys and I be?"

Jacob was completely surprised by her statement, hugging her as she started weeping. "Charlotte, I will take you all to a safe place. I just re-enlisted for three years in the New Mexico Volunteers, and they are going to give me a commission as an officer. We will continue to Fort Union, to train volunteers for my new company, mostly New Mexico natives. Our regiment will then relieve the regulars at Fort Lyon in Navajo country. You can stay at Fort Union, and if the worst happens you will be evacuated to Fort Leavenworth."

Charlotte thought for a moment. "You mean you will be an officer, after ten years as a private?" She couldn't believe it. "Maybe now you will get the respect you deserve, Jacob."

"All I need is your respect, Charlotte." They hugged and took the boys into the dining room for supper.

New Mexico map showing Confederate Invasion 1862, with locations: Colorado, New Mexico, Rio Grande, Santa Fe, Ft. Union, Battle of Glorieta Pass, Albuquerque, Battle of Valverde, Ft. Craig, Pecos R., San Augustine Pass, Mesilla, Ft. Fillmore, Ft. Bliss, El Paso, Texas, Confederate Invasion 1862

XX. The Texans are Coming

Colonel Canby had decided to make a stand at Fort Craig,
which stood as the last major obstacle blocking the Confederates from
sweeping north and taking the vital main depot at Fort Union. A direct
attack from the Pecos Valley seemed less likely now, as more troops
and materiel were coming into New Mexico from Kansas and
Missouri. Canby now believed that the main threat from invading
Texans would be up the Rio Grande Valley to seize Fort Craig, the
depot at Albuquerque, and the capital, Santa Fe. The department
commander knew the Texas commander, former U.S. Army Major
Sibley, now Brigadier General of the Confederate States of America.
Sibley had most recently been stationed in New Mexico before
resigning his commission and offering his services to the
Confederacy. Not only did he know the territory, but he had a plan to
take New Mexico, then eventually the entire southwest, California,
and parts of northern Mexico. Sibley, after leaving the Union, had
made a long journey to Virginia, presenting his idea to Jefferson
Davis, the Confederate President. Davis agreed to the plan, thinking
such a victory might give Great Britain an incentive to come into the
war as an ally of the Confederacy, enhancing the chances for the
South to become a two-ocean power, and split the continent. President
Davis gave Sibley his blessing, a commission as a Brigadier General,

and authority to return to Texas, raise a brigade, and to invade and capture the southwestern desert territories, and California. Unfortunately for the Texans, there was no promise of men and money to help build an invasion force. Undeterred, Brig. Gen. Sibley rode west to San Antonio to recruit his brigade.

Union forces were working non-stop to finish the earthworks of the new fortress at Fort Union, while at the same time, constantly guarding against an unexpected attack from the Texas panhandle or Pecos areas. The Santa Fe Trail approaches to New Mexico were improved to make wagon travel easier. Colonel Canby also had requested Governor Weld of the new Colorado Territory to be prepared to send volunteer reinforcements to help block a Confederate invasion. This would prove crucial in the spring of 1862, after the Texans had seized Santa Fe and were within striking range of Fort Union. All of these events would have to wait until the Confederates could muster enough force to push north. Lieutenant Colonel Baylor, having won the initial round of fighting in the southern part of New Mexico, did not have enough troops to launch the invasion by himself, and spent his time consolidating control and waiting for the Sibley Brigade to arrive. This happened just before Christmas 1861, when Union spies discovered an estimated 2,000 mounted Texans, with a good supply of artillery, encamped about twenty-five miles north of El Paso. Colonel Canby decided to move reinforcements from Fort Union and Santa Fe to Fort Craig, where he moved his command post to personally take charge of the blocking force. He left fewer than a thousand troops at Fort Union under Lieutenant Colonel Paul. Canby also sent a courier to Colorado requesting the Union volunteers march to Fort Union without delay.

During this time, platoon leader Second Lieutenant Jacob Stenger with his C Company, 2nd New Mexico Volunteers, having finished training at Fort Union, was posted in the northwest corner of New Mexico at Fort Fauntleroy, the newly renamed Fort Lyons, to help quell a new episode of Navajo attacks against the Mexican settlements and ranches. There wasn't much fighting, and Jacob spent much of his time chasing deserters and other soldiers who were often in trouble, not least because they had received little or no pay since they were inducted. There was very little loyalty to the United States from many Hispanics who felt considerable resentment about the imposition of American culture on their people, many of whom had been born under the older Spanish rule, prior to the Mexican War.

Despite the cultural disconnects, the majority of the volunteers were loyal to the Union cause. Many New Mexicans hated the Texans because of a history of invasion or mistreatment of New Mexicans after the Texas War of Independence in 1836. Some of the Mexican people were more afraid of the Texans than they were of death. When Colonel Canby confirmed that the Texans were moving north, he ordered the volunteer regiments to move rapidly to Fort Craig to back up the Union regulars. By late January and early February 1862, Union forces at Fort Craig numbered nearly 4,000. Jacob's unit was assigned with others to a reserve role. They were to back up units of the 5th, 7th, and 10th U. S. Infantry, two companies of the 1st U.S. Cavalry (formerly Dragoons), five companies of the 3rd U.S. Cavalry (formerly Mounted Riflemen), Captain McRae's Artillery Battery, Company B of 2nd Colorado Volunteers, and Colonel Kit Carson's 1st New Mexico Volunteers.

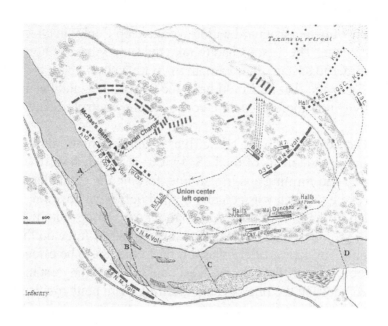

Union center
left open

Texans in retreat

Infantry

XXI. Valverde

Sibley's Brigade, of the Confederate Army in New Mexico, arrived and camped a few miles south of Fort Craig on February 13th. They deployed in a line for three days trying to lure the Union troops away from the fortification, to engage them in the open. Colonel Canby didn't take the bait. Sibley was outnumbered, having limited supplies and about 2,500 troops. Canby had placed fake replicas of large cannons on the ramparts of the fortress, and sensing that a direct assault on Fort Craig would fail, Sibley and his staff decided to attempt a flanking movement on the east side of the Rio Grande. Canby discovered the strategy and moved a blocking force about five miles north of the fort, to oppose a Confederate crossing of the Rio Grande at the Valverde ford. This was where the major fighting would take place. On the morning of February 21st, the 2nd Texas Mounted Rifles, under Confederate Major Charles Pyron, moved to the fords, followed by the 4th Texas Mounted Rifles, Lieutenant Colonel Scurry commanding. These two units were to secure the crossing and the west bank of the Rio Grande, with the rest of the brigade and trains to follow. Sibley had hoped to avoid a major battle here and wanted to move north to Albuquerque, cutting off Canby from his lines of communication and the headquarters at Santa Fe. From there the main objective, Fort Union, and its depot would be in easy reach while a rear-guard action would keep Canby in check, if he chose to pursue. The Texans had to take the supply base at Fort Union soon, in order to sustain their campaign. With a strong base at Fort Union, Sibley felt that he would have the upper hand, and be able to defeat any Union forces in detail, consolidating control of New Mexico.

The Texans, arriving at the river at mid-morning, found fierce resistance from elements of the U.S. 1st Cavalry, which were dismounted and forming a skirmish line, forcing the Confederates into a dry creek bed, which was actually a good defensive position. Pyron then called for help from Scurry, who moved his troops into the dry creek on Pyron's right. The Texans had the superior force on the field at this point, but their artillery was too far to the left to be effective against the Union artillery on the west bank of the river. A standoff developed between the lines by late morning, with neither side able to advance. About this time, Canby ordered most of the remaining troops at Fort Craig to march north on the west bank to the fords, leaving only the militias to guard the fort. Arriving at the battlefield at mid-day, Canby ordered most of the Union force and Captain McCrae's artillery battery across the river. Colonel Kit Carson's 1st New Mexico Regiment and Colonel Miguel Pino's 2nd New Mexico Regiment were held in reserve on the west bank. Pino crossed Companies A and B to the east bank with Jacob's Company C, held on the west bank, instructed to stay in reserve. Company C was

CHARGE OF TEXAS LANCERS

154

instructed to be ready to cross on short notice, but the order never came.

Colonel Green, the Confederate second in command, had taken over from Brig. Gen. Sibley who had reportedly become ill, but was more likely incapacitated from the excessive intake of whiskey, something he was well known for. Green ordered a charge into the left flank of the Yankees by a company of lancers. The charge was gallant, but a company of Colorado Volunteers stood fast, decimating the Confederates, with most of the lancers' horses killed or wounded. This action represented the first and the last lancer charge of the American Civil War.

The fighting continued with repeated charges by the Texans against the Union left. McRae's battery continued to wreak havoc, breaking up one assault after another until late in the afternoon when the Texans appeared to be gaining the upper hand. Colonel Canby ordered Kit Carson's mounted regiment with additional artillery support on the right, to attack the Confederate left flank. This was initially successful, and the left flank of the Texans was pushed back, with additional confusion created in the Confederate rear and trains area, which was harassed by Colonel Pino's and Stapleton's cavalry. For a while it looked like the Union cavalry might roll up the Confederate left flank. This was a short-lived hope, however, when Colonel Green marshaled an attack on the Union center and the artillery position. Three waves of Texas infantry, totaling more than 750 men, aided by cavalry, finally overran the Union artillery. McRae and his battery were wiped out in the savage close and hand-to-hand fighting with the enraged masses of Texans, many of them armed only with sawed off shotguns and Bowie knives. What followed was a panic-stricken retreat by Union regulars and New Mexico volunteers. Jacob's company was preparing to cross the river and join the melee, but the Union lines were already broken. Colonel Canby, fearing a rout, decided to send a rider with a white flag to request a truce to remove the dead and wounded. Brig. Gen. Sibley, who had finally regained his presence late in the day, agreed. The Texans held the battlefield, and Canby ordered a retreat to Fort Craig. He had lost more than 400 men, including deserters, to the reported Confederate loss of fewer than 200 casualties. Canby fortunately realized that it was more important to protect and hold Fort Craig and its stores, rather than chance losing the logistical advantage of the overall campaign. Even though the Texans claimed victory, they were bloodied and spent, momentarily. Half of their trains had been destroyed or captured by Union raiders hitting them from the rear, and they were in dire need of supplies. Sibley knew he couldn't take Fort Craig by siege and decided to move north to Socorro and Albuquerque. Jacob and his men, as they marched back to Fort Craig in the dark with the other surviving men, felt great sadness and disappointment, humiliation, but relief to be alive. They would soon learn of the success of Kit Carson's regiment, which included the destruction of a major portion of the Confederate trains, the wagons full of ammunition and supplies. This tactical defeat at Valverde would, in a few short months, be seen as a strategic victory.

Colonel Canby was more than a little humiliated by the loss at Valverde. In retrospect, he should be given credit for saving his bastion at Fort Craig, along with the bulk of his command and nearly all of their supplies. Brig. Gen. Sibley was not happy with the loss of half of his supply trains. He felt that he had to move on to the major objective of taking Fort Union, the key to controlling the territory. After recovering the bulk of his force, and tending to his casualties from the battlefield, Colonel Canby decided to pursue the Confederates with harassing tactics to hinder and complicate any quick thrusts Sibley might make toward his main objective, Fort Union.

XXII. The Rebels take Santa Fe

Sibley was now desperate for supplies. He felt that if he could get to Albuquerque and seize the small depot there, he would then be able to make a rapid thrust to take Santa Fe, the political capital, which would allow his troops to live off the land, help the morale of the brigade, and then be able to maintain the momentum and push on to Fort Union. The strategy worked for the next two weeks, and Santa Fe fell with little resistance. The Union officers there were able to discern Sibley's plan, however, and had evacuated the bulk of Union supplies and ammunition from Albuquerque and Santa Fe, sending them on to Fort Union, where they planned to make a last stand. This strategy was a major setback for the Texans, who found living off the land very difficult, especially in the late winter in northern New Mexico. The delay in resupplying the Confederate advance toward Fort Union proved to be an important factor in the outcome of the campaign. Not only did the Union forces have additional time to complete the new star fortress at Fort Union, gathering militia and volunteer units at the site, the Colorado governor had more time to march his 1,200 volunteers to New Mexico just in time to reinforce the defenders at Fort Union. The Colorado companies consolidated and rested for a couple of days at Fort Union. These tough men, recruited mostly from the front range mining camps of the Rocky Mountains, were eager to move forward and make contact with the Texans. These miners and teamsters were a rugged and rowdy bunch. Some had already proved themselves at Valverde, stopping the lancer charge of the Texas cavalry. They were tired of marching and anxious to fight the Confederates.

Colonel Slough, a Denver lawyer and legislator led the Colorado regiment out of Fort Union, against the orders of Colonel Canby, who had planned to move the bulk of his forces north from Fort Craig, to attack from the rear, trapping the Texans between two large Union forces, and crush Sibley from two directions. The impetuous move by the Colorado commander would eventually cost him his job, but this would prove to be the most serendipitous event of the campaign against the invading Confederates.

Battle of Glorieta Pass 1862

(map labels: GLORIETA, SANTA FE PASS, TO SANTA FE, CSA, RETREAT 28 MARCH, APACHE CANYON, JOHNSONS RANCH 28 MARCH, TO CANYON 26 MARCH, PIGEONS RANCH 28 MARCH, TRAIL, ROUTE TO CONFEDERATE TRAINS, KOZLOWSKI RANCH, TO APACH, USA, TO FT UNION)

XXIII. Glorieta Pass

After a two-day march from Fort Union and a bivouac near the town of Las Vegas, Slough sent his second in command, Major John Chivington, with more than 400 men to the eastern approaches to Glorieta Pass, near Kozlowski's Ranch and the abandoned Pecos Pueblo. Confederate Major Charles Pyron, commander of the Texans occupying Santa Fe, was informed of the march of Union troops from Fort Union toward Santa Fe, and advanced more than 250 men from the capital to the western approaches of the pass at Apache canyon. They were the smaller force, having only two pieces of artillery. The Union had captured the Confederate scouts, enabling them to surprise Pyron in the canyon. Even though he had no artillery, the Union commander was able to position riflemen high on the sides of the canyon with tree cover, enabling them to fire down on the Texans. He also sent a cavalry troop leaping over a ravine, disrupting Texas infantry positions. Both sides withdrew at dusk for a truce to take care of casualties. Chivington's troops went back to Kozlowski's Ranch for the night. The encounter was a technical victory for the Federals, but it was not a decisive blow. On March 27th, Colonel Slough brought the main force up to join Chivington and bivouacked that night. The rebels brought up several hundred reinforcements to Johnson's Ranch at the western approaches to Glorieta Pass, along with the brigade trains, and prepared to engage Slough's regiment the following morning. Lieutenant Colonel William Scurry, now assuming command of the combined Confederate forces in the pass, moved up the road with 700 men and three howitzers. Slough met them with 900 men and eight howitzers. Unknown to Scurry, Slough had dispatched 400 men with Chivington, over a secret mountain trail and southeast of the canyon onto the mesa behind the Texans, overlooking the canyon south and west of the pass behind the Confederate trains waiting at Johnson Ranch. More than seventy wagons were attacked and burned, and a large number of mules shot or bayoneted. This turned out to be the decisive action of the campaign. The Texans pushing up the pass had won a narrow tactical victory, driving the Union forces from the field, forcing them back to Pigeon's Ranch and then back to Kozlowski's Ranch. Without their trains, however, the rebels could not exploit the offensive advantage. They had also missed an opportunity to capture Slough's supply train, and the advance ground to a halt. Exhausted and nearly out of ammunition, food, forage, blankets, and medical supplies, the Confederates were forced to withdraw to Santa Fe that night.

The loss of their supplies dictated the end of the war in New Mexico, as the Texans began a slow retreat back down the Rio Grande Valley. They were under constant harassment by Union cavalry, including raids on their trains by Jacob's unit at Peralta. There were a few skirmishes along the way, but Sibley's forces were pursued all the way back to El Paso and Fort Bliss. Colonel Canby, the Union commander, in his after-action report, made reference to reports of Brig. Gen. Sibley's incapacitation at critical times in the campaign. This certainly was an important factor in the failure of the Texas offensive.

While the brigade was struggling to escape New Mexico, Colonel James Carleton, who had been stationed at Fort Union years before, arrived from California with 1,500 men, and drove Baylor's forces from their positions in Arizona. In a few weeks, even Fort Bliss itself was abandoned, and the Texans limped back to San Antonio and central Texas.   There was never again a serious effort to invade New Mexico, as the South could not afford another attempt to become a transcontinental, two-ocean power.

Although the campaign failed to attract much notice back east, historians would later give more credit to the Union efforts to hold onto the southwestern territories. Many have referred to the actions at Glorieta Pass as the Gettysburg of the West. If the Texans had taken New Mexico, the Confederacy might have been able to take over the southwest all the way to California. The course of the war could certainly have been altered. Great Britain, whose industrial revolution and textile industry were increasingly dependent on southern cotton supplies, might have even come into the fight on the side of the South, if the outcome of the war had become less certain. Jefferson Davis had certainly been open to the possibility. Fortunately for the Union, he had no extra resources to commit to the efforts in the southwest.

Chapter XXIV. Transition

Jacob's 2nd New Mexico Volunteer Regiment had been formed in crisis during the anticipation of the Confederate invasion of the territory. The War of the Rebellion had lasted only a short time in the southwestern territory. With the Texans no longer considered a major threat, his duties would now drift back to the original mission, fighting or at least controlling hostile Indian attacks against settlers and other civilians. He had begun to think again about leaving the service, moving his family to Kansas. Jacob was obligated though for two more years under his commission terms. Things were a little better now with an officer's pay, and at least a little more respect. Jacob had no way of knowing that his unit would be disbanded and mustered out in another month. As part of the reorganization of the New Mexico volunteers and militias, the 2nd New Mexico was eliminated, and some of the units were consolidated into the new 1st New Mexico Cavalry, using the nucleus of Kit Carson's regiment. Jacob's entire company was mustered out, and even though the officers were obligated to fulfill their service commitment, there were no positions available pending formation of a number of new companies within Colonel Carson's regiment.

In May of 1862, Jacob was informed that he would be offered a commission and promoted to First Lieutenant in October, when Company M, 1st New Mexico was to be formed. In the meantime, there was no duty position for him. He agreed to join Company M in October and decided to take advantage of the intervening few months to relocate his family to Council Grove. Jacob left Fort Craig in late May and rode with other soldiers to Fort Union, where Charlotte and the boys were still waiting for him. The details of his future commission in the 1st New Mexico Cavalry were taken care of during a two-day stop in Santa Fe. He then rode on to Fort Union, arriving in the last week of May.

Charlotte was ecstatic to see Jacob's smiling face. He had been gone for a long time. Thank God he had survived the fighting at Valverde, and here he was, finally. Jacob explained the situation, that he still had a two-year obligation, but with no job yet available, he was free for the next four months, He intended to move her and the children to a permanent home. Her head was spinning, trying to absorb all this information. At least they were together, with positive plans for the future. Jacob had four months to move the family to

Council Grove, before returning to Santa Fe for activation of the new regiment. Since he had mustered out of the Regiment of Mounted Riflemen, he was temporarily out of a job, on leave without pay. He needed to make a little money in the meantime to feed his family and rent a small house for them in Kansas. Jacob visited the sutler's store to see if he could deliver any goods to Council Grove and bring something back after resettling his family. The sutler, Mr. William Moore, was skeptical at first, but was more receptive of the idea once Jacob explained his situation, along with his plans to leave the Army after completing his obligation. He would make his living as a freight hauler and wagon guide between Council Grove and Santa Fe. As luck would have it, Mr. Moore had been providing some Indian trade goods to points along the Santa Fe Trail, including Council Grove. He told Jacob that he personally knew Seth Hays, and traded occasional items such as Navajo blankets, pottery, turquoise, animal pelts, and buffalo hides to Hays in exchange for hard-to-get luxury items such as perfumes, jewelry, and wine and liquors from the United States. Moore liked to save on freight costs and would usually try to send smaller lots with eastbound customers for a fraction of what the large commercial freight companies charged. Jacob explained that he would gladly bring back a wagon load of goods from Kansas by the end of the summer when he had to report for duty in his new regiment. Mr. Moore seemed happy with the prospect of having a private connection to Kansas in the future. Jacob seemed like an honest fellow, and he willing to take a chance on what might turn out to be a profitable future for both of them.

Jacob raced back to Charlotte's quarters to share the good news of his deal with the sutler. "Charlotte, we have a way to pay for our move to Kansas!" He was so excited that his bear hug nearly crushed her ribs. She pushed him away so she could breathe. "I made a deal with Mr. Moore, the sutler, to deliver a load of hides and Indian blankets to Mr. Hayes in Council Grove, and he will pay me fifty dollars."

"But, what about our possessions?" she asked. "We don't have much, but we do have a couple of small beds, some chairs, and a table and chest. What about the kitchen ware and the children's things?"

"Don't worry about all that, we have a fairly large wagon, and the trade items will only take up half the space. It will be a little crowded, but now I can afford to rent a small place for the family until I start getting my Army pay again in October. Then I can send money each month until I finish my obligation in two years. Who knows, maybe the war will be over by then and they will let me go earlier. This first freight hauling job, small as it is, may lead to a profitable future for us."

Charlotte was dumbfounded. She didn't see how this could all work out, with three boys to raise by herself for a couple of years. It would be a strain, but she could always take in laundry to help make ends meet. Charlotte swallowed hard and suddenly blurted out, "When do we go, Jacob?"

Jacob grinned and told her, "I already checked with the adjutant's office. There is a large party of wagons leaving next week, bound for Missouri, mostly families headed home, as soldiers are being reassigned to fight the war in the East. I feel very lucky that I wasn't picked to go fight back there. I won't be so awfully far away. There are some good people in Council Grove, and you will all be safer there. I will try to get escort duty on the Santa Fe Trail whenever I can, so I can visit you and the boys as much as possible."

"Two years is a long time, Jacob," said Charlotte, not happy with the prospect.

Jacob didn't have a retort ready, but reflected that it was a time of war, and at least he wasn't headed to the eastern battlegrounds. The newspapers, when they received them at all, were full of reports of thousands of casualties from Virginia to Mississippi. She would rather have him take his chances fighting Indians, at least he had survived nearly ten years of that. She couldn't believe that he had barely missed being a casualty at Valverde. If the fight had gone on much longer, he would have been right in the thick of it. Whatever people said about Colonel Canby, he had made the right call as far as she was concerned.

"Alright, Jacob! We will do what we have to do then. We will go to Kansas and make a home there, and we will wait for you."

Jacob was able to make all the arrangements and pick up their household goods that week, and the family joined a stagecoach and a small group of wagons escorted by twenty mounted soldiers being reassigned to the eastern battlefields. They camped overnight in Rayado, before heading north over Raton Pass and reaching the summit in two days. The following morning the group descended down the north side to the growing little town of Trinidad, where they exchanged some mules and stocked up on a few supplies. With only the stagecoach and five mule-drawn wagons, the group was able to travel fairly fast, reaching Bents Fort on the Arkansas in three days. There were no hostile encounters on this portion, as the Kiowa and Comanches were already north of the trail, following the spring calving of the buffalo herds. The soldiers with the group were able to shoot a lame, straggling older bull buffalo and a couple of antelope for camp meat, which they shared with the traders at Bents Fort. Following the river to the east, the small group reached Fort Larned by the end of the first week and rested the animals for a day. Two mules and three horses were replaced at Larned, and the garrison there reported that a few Comanche hunting parties had passed by over a week ago, without incident. Arapahoe Army scouts, who met with some of the Comanche hunters, passed on that the Comanche only wanted to reach the Nebraska grasslands to set up summer quarters and take advantage of a late and wet spring, which promised lush forage, attracting many large buffalo herds.

As the small group followed the Arkansas east and northeast toward the great bend in the river, they passed the westbound mail, and a day later, a twenty-wagon Army supply train escorted by cavalry recruits from Fort Leavenworth. They camped together at Pawnee Rock overnight, exchanging news from the war in the east, and answering the recruits' questions about life in the desert southwest. Jacob was interested in any news about Council Grove and was pleased to know that the Army had created a small sub-post in the town including a blacksmith shop to support troop movements on the Santa Fe Trail. There had been some rumors that Confederates from Missouri were planning to raid certain main stops on the trail to disrupt Federal operations. The commander at Fort Leavenworth was aware of the risks and helped organize home guard units at Council Grove and other towns further east. Jacob asked about Seth Hays and found that he was doing well and was a strong leader in the community and one of the leading merchants. Jacob reassured Charlotte that he would introduce her to Mr. Hays and that she would know who to turn to with any problems. He would also be a good source of information regarding available housing in town, and possible part time work for Charlotte. It would be nearly impossible for her to work full time and care for three young boys. Jacob had been saving some money, enough to pay the typical rent of ten dollars a month for a two-room boarding house rental. He expected to be paid at least a hundred dollars commission for his present load of hides, blankets, and a few Navajo silver and turquoise bracelets and necklaces. This would keep them solvent for nearly a year, and after the return trip to New Mexico with a full load of luxury items from Seth Hays to the sutler at Fort Union, he expected to make at least as much again on commission.

The next morning, the two groups camped at Pawnee Rock, bid each other goodbye and moved out in their opposite directions. Jacob's eastbound train followed the trail to the east, reaching the Walnut Creek crossing north of the Arkansas River above Big Bend. The water was about three to four feet deep at the fording site, consistent with the late spring runoff of the Arkansas backing up Walnut Creek. The creek bottom at this location was improved with a firm rock and gravel base and the wagons crossed quickly in the slow current. There were no huge cargo loads, and the mules were more sure-footed than the teams of oxen used to pull the larger Conestoga wagons. After half an hour the troops and mule teams were safely across with no tipped or floating cargos. There was plenty of light left after the train formed up again, and the commander decided to push on to the trading post at the Rath Ranch. This was a stagecoach stop on the trail and would later serve as the site for Fort Sarah, a popular rest stop on the trail until 1870, when the trail began to be marginalized by the advance of the railroads. Arriving before dusk, the soldiers and other travelers circled the wagons and made camp, with the first order of business to make fires and dry out any wet clothing or goods. They settled into the evening for dinner, posted sentries, and planned for an early departure the next morning. At this point Council Grove was just over one hundred miles away, and they would probably be there in three to five days. The only major obstacles were the crossing of the Little Arkansas and Cottonwood Creek. Charlotte was amazed at the number of waterways in this middle prairie land, compared to the few and far between rivers and streams in New Mexico. The endless plains and abundant tall grass made the Kansas prairies seem lush by comparison, at least at this time of year. Vast herds of buffalo that roamed and grazed were a testament to the abundant wildlife that thrived here. This life-giving system also helped to sustain a myriad of Native American peoples competing for the abundance of game, especially bison. The migrating tribes followed the herds in an age-old seasonal rhythm, aggressively protecting their favorite hunting grounds during the peak seasons, but usually sharing the land peacefully if undisturbed. This pattern was now threatened with the coming of the traders, and later

166

with the white settlers, the European cultural tradition of land ownership clashing with the Native American cultural tradition of open use of the land without personal ownership. Charlotte felt sorry for the Indians in a way, but she was well enough schooled in Western civilization to recognize the cultural imperative of European settlers to own their own land, supported and protected by the laws of a sovereign government. The dominant power usually prevailed in these clashes of civilizations, but she hoped for a peaceful resolution and fairness. So much of history had been marked by brute force and bloodshed. The losers had to adapt to survive, and she prayed that the winners would be magnanimous and equitable. Would the promise of this America, this new experiment in freedom and justice, become the place where these ancient longings for peace and fairness might finally take hold? Only time would tell, she thought, only time would tell.

By the 30th of May the small train and soldiers had reached the Cottonwood River, also known as Cottonwood Creek, only a day's travel from Council Grove. They camped overnight on the west bank, as it was almost dusk. The following morning early departure was exciting for all, as Council Grove was the first stop on the way back to civilization for many of the group after spending months or even years in the desert southwest. Jacob and Charlotte and the boys were excited about seeing their new home, looking forward to beginning a new life. Charlotte was dreading the inevitable return of Jacob to New Mexico in the fall, but she had made up her mind to take one thing at a time. There were just so many unknown details to confront in a new place she had never seen before. However, she had been without her husband for many months at a time in New Mexico, and she would find a way to cope. She trusted Jacob to do his best, realizing it was unrealistic to expect him to make it back to eastern Kansas very often. She would trust in the Lord to give her the strength she would need and find a church to help her provide her sons with a moral upbringing. Anyway, who knew what would happen with Jacob and the Army while this insane war with the southern states continued. She didn't believe that he would be sent back east as he was no longer a regular Army soldier. Now that he was only a militia officer, it was doubtful that he would have to leave New Mexico. Most people thought it highly unlikely that the Texans, or any other Confederate troops, would be sent back to invade New Mexico. Jacob had ten years of experience fighting Indians, knew what he was doing, and could take care of himself. While Charlotte was musing over these things, Jacob was concentrating on getting his family settled in this little Kansas town he hoped to be a permanent home. He was anxious about where they would live, and whether he could afford it. He wouldn't have to leave for Santa Fe until the middle of August, to get back on time to join his new company. He would find work in Council Grove for the summer to leave as much money as possible for Charlotte.

The train crossed Six Mile Creek and the group went on Diamond Springs, arriving in mid-afternoon. This famous watering hole on the Santa Fe Trail was a favorite stop for travelers, as it was the location of one of the purest water sources on the trail. It was still nearly fifteen miles to Council Grove, so the party decided to camp at the Springs for the night. The following morning, they moved on past Four Mile creek, arriving at Council Grove in the early afternoon. The soldiers stopped at the Main Street Hotel, formerly the Hays House, for coffee and cakes, before moving across the Neosho ford to the military campground south of the trail. The families went across the street, taking lodgings in Gilkey's Hotel. After getting his wife and three boys settled in two rooms at the hotel, Jacob walked back to the Main Street Hotel to talk to the manager, Mr. Goodson Simcock. Jacob was expecting to see Seth Hays, the proprietor he had met with briefly on previous trips through the town. Mr. Simcock informed Jacob that Hayes had moved to Colorado over a year before, selling his interest in their supply store business to Mr. Simcock. Hayes, however, had maintained ownership of the adjacent hotel and restaurant property. Jacob explained to Simcock his plans to settle his family in Council Grove until he could finish his military obligation in two years. He asked Simcock for his advice on temporary housing for the family, and also discussed his arrangement with the sutler's store at Fort Union. He told Simcock that he had over half a wagon load of buffalo and other animal hides, along with a small collection of turquoise and silver jewelry from New Mexico, to trade for specialty items and wine and liquor from the United States. Simcock seemed to be interested in the trading deal, as his supply store could certainly use the merchandise from New Mexico. He was concerned about how much time Jacob could devote to the enterprise outside of his military duties. Jacob said it would be difficult for him to make the trip to Kansas more than once every four to six months, but he thought Charlotte and the boys would be safer in Kansas, until he

168

could rejoin them here after his service obligation was finished in two years. Simcock was skeptical about how safe Council Grove was going to be, being so close to the border with Missouri. Cantrell's confederate raiders and other groups had caused a lot of problems in the area. The frequent passage of military trains and patrols to and from New Mexico from Westport Landing and Fort Leavenworth were the only protection against these outlaws. There was some movement to forming militias and home guards in Council Grove and Morris County to provide some local protection. Jacob said he was most concerned about a place for his family to live for now, and offered that his wife, Charlotte, was willing to do cooking and laundry for room and board. Jacob said that he also had a couple of hundred dollars saved up to help support his family temporarily. Simcock thought about this situation while he listened to Jacob's story and his experiences in Texas and New Mexico, and he began to develop a liking for this German fellow. Simcock excused himself and stepped out for a few minutes, conferring with the restaurant cook, Maggie, a middle-aged widow. She agreed to have Charlotte and the boys temporarily use two small rooms in the back of the restaurant next to where she lived. She did most of the cooking, and could use some help with cooking, dishwashing, and laundry. Simcock showed Jacob the two rooms and offered to rent the space for five dollars a week. They would have to provide their own furnishings. Jacob said that he had a small bed and a crib in the wagon, and he could make a couple of beds for the two older boys, and a table. Simcock told him that he had four chairs and a small table in his store that he could sell for ten dollars. Jacob expressed his appreciation, and his family could continue to live at the hotel across the street until he had to leave in mid-August, returning to New Mexico. In the meantime, he would try to do some wagon work at the blacksmith shop and would be happy to do any work that Mr. Simcock might have for him. This would give him a little more cash and give him time to get the rooms ready. He agreed to bring Charlotte over in the morning to meet Maggie, to let them work out a plan for work and child-care. The two men agreed and shook hands on the deal. Jacob walked back to the hotel where he met his family for supper.

Charlotte was apprehensive as they sat down to breakfast the next morning at the Hays House. They were served by a pleasant, but quiet young woman who brought them bacon, fried eggs, and stacks of hot cakes with sugar syrup. Mr. Simcock brought milk for the boys and oatmeal porridge for Kit, who was still only a year and a half old. He poured coffee for Charlotte and Jacob and one for himself as he sat down with the family. Charlotte was weary from the past few weeks of traveling. The bath at the hotel the past evening made her feel almost human, relieving some of her muscle aches from riding in a wagon. Her boys were a little cranky, but somehow holding up pretty well overall. No one had come down with any illness on the trip. At least it wasn't winter, and still not into the hottest part of the summer. She was glad that Jacob had gotten along so well with Mr. Simcock. They spent some time talking about their experiences in New Mexico, and about Seth Hays settling in Council Grove, after leaving Missouri and about their long-standing partnership. Simcock told Jacob about the origins of the Santa Fe Trail in central Missouri, and Seth Hays' famous ancestor, Daniel Boone. Boone was already a national folk hero of sorts. He had helped pioneer the opening of the West, and Seth's family had helped push that frontier further into Missouri. Many had even ventured as far as the Rocky Mountains and deep into Texas and New Mexico.

Seth had found his niche on the Santa Fe Trail after living at Westport Landing, where the steamboats brought much of the cargo to be loaded on wagons for New Mexico and the Colorado gold camps. He was one of the first settlers in Council Grove, and over the years became one of its leading citizens. Seth never married and lived alone except for one paid servant, his freed former slave, Sarah Taylor, known to all as Aunt Sally. Simcock received occasional letters from Hayes, not expecting that he would return to Kansas one day.

Charlotte found Maggie to be very pleasant, though not very talkative. She seemed to be a very happy person and was very kind to Charlotte and the children. Maggie seemed to be grateful for the job and a place to live, but she was in her late forties now, and she didn't know how many more years she could work. She had some sisters back in Ohio but didn't think she could ever afford to go back home. Many of her family and friends had been killed in this terrible civil war. If there was any such a chance to return, she was afraid she wouldn't be very happy there. Charlotte told Maggie of her home in Germany and having to leave her family behind and knew how difficult it was to leave home. Later, Maggie showed her the available quarters, a small two-room unit behind the kitchen, each with a small pot-bellied stove, separated from the kitchen by a small garden, where

Maggie grew some herbs and seasonal vegetables. The rooms were small, and Maggie lived across the garden in a similar small room. Mr. Charles Gilkey, the hotel host and clerk, lived on the second floor over the tavern. Mr. Simcock and his family lived in a two-story stone house he had built on Columbia Street, a short walk from Main Street. Charlotte thought she would be able to manage living here for a year of two, at least while the boys were small. She felt safe here, and Jacob was already working on finding or making some furniture. They would be living in the hotel until he had to leave in August, with Charlotte starting to help Maggie in a few days.

After breakfast, Jacob brought the wagon around to the store and unloaded his trade goods. Mr. Simcock was glad to have these items, but they would sell better in the fall, especially the hides, when cooler weather was coming. Some of the buffalo robes and most of the Jewelry would be shipped to Westport and on to St. Louis, where there was a growing market for such western novelties. While there, Simcock showed Jacob a small oak drop leaf table with one insert, and four cane-back chairs. Jacob bought those and two folding camp cots for the boys. Charlotte saw a few things she liked, including a small wardrobe, a dresser, and a wall mirror. She decided to delay purchasing them until Jacob could make a little more money during the summer. The family all got in the wagon, and Jacob took them on a short tour of the little town.

Council Grove in the early 1860s was very small, straddling the Neosho River, and had only a few streets. Main Street followed the Santa Fe Trail, from the east side of the river, bounded by the Kaw Indian Mission to the north. The road crossed the Neosho ford site heading west and ending at the Last Chance Store several blocks later. Parallel to Main Street, one block to the north was Columbia Street with only a few houses. Simcock told them that the population was only about 700, but the town was growing faster every year. The town was growing to meet the needs of westbound travelers. By the beginning of the Civil War, traffic on the Santa Fe Trail had reached nearly 5,000 wagons annually, carrying nearly $40 million worth of trade goods. Jacob felt that he knew the trail well enough to be able to make a living for his family as a freight driver, and possibly, in time, as a guide or wagon master. Council Grove had everything necessary to organize and finish outfitting large trains of wagons, starting them down the next six-hundred miles of the trail to northern New Mexico. Jacob was also very happy that Mr. Simcock was interested in the reciprocal trade goods, which he could bring back from New Mexico on the return trip. Simcock was also pleased at the prospect of Jacob recommending the Hays House and store to eastbound travelers. Overall, it seemed to be a very comfortable arrangement, especially to Jacob, who was very relieved to have a temporary place for his family to have room and board, be reasonably well protected, and a small income for Charlotte.

The family quickly settled into a daily routine, with Charlotte and the boys soon moving into their new quarters behind the Hays House. Jacob found a part-time job repairing wagons at the blacksmith shop at the Kaw Indian Mission. When he wasn't needed there, he would spend his days at the supply store repairing some second- hand furniture for his family's rooms at the Hays House. Meanwhile, he continued to stay at the hotel for a reduced monthly rate. Things settled into a routine, with Jacob spending as much time as possible with his children, especially when Charlotte was busy at the Hays House. On Sunday mornings, Jacob would hitch up his team to the wagon and take short tours of the town and the immediate surroundings. After a picnic lunch along the banks of the Neosho River, they would drive out to see the mission grounds or visit the old camping sites southeast of town where the Osage Indians had lived before their removal to southeastern Kansas. The family loved this country, significantly more wooded than the New Mexico prairies and southwestern deserts they had known in recent years. During this time, there were no hostile Indian raids, and no significant incursions of Confederate sympathizers from Missouri. It seemed to Jacob and Charlotte an ideal place to raise a family. So went the summer, until the middle of August, when Jacob tearfully bid his family goodbye, promising them that he would do his best to return as often as possible. Charlotte was very concerned that Jacob's visits would be few and far between. It was only two years more until his obligation was finished. He was an officer now, a Lieutenant of cavalry in the New Mexico Volunteers. It was very unlikely that he would be called to the east to participate in the horrid conflict between North and South. He was an Indian fighter primarily and had learned how to survive in the southwest over many years. Little did he know that he would rejoin his family for good, much sooner than expected.

On August 15th, Jacob joined an Army column passing through Council Grove headed for Santa Fe, escorting a wagon train of supplies from Fort Leavenworth and Westport Landing. Jacob took only his personal mount and weapons, along with some liquor and perfume and a few other luxury items, which Mr. Simcock had sent with him on consignment. He was able to stash them in an army supply wagon, to be sold to the sutler at Fort Union. He was due to report to Fort Marcy at Santa Fe on September 15th for mustering with a newly authorized unit, Company M, 1st New Mexico Volunteer Cavalry. He assumed that they would be assigned to Fort Union, as much of the regiment was there under the command of Colonel Kit Carson, a man he had greatly admired for some time, especially since Valverde.

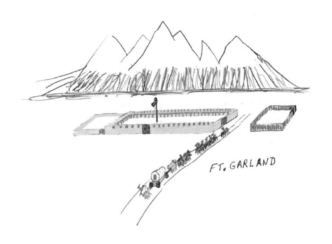

FT. GARLAND

XXV. Fort Garland

Jacob arrived at Fort Garland with his newly mustered in unit, Company M, 1st New Mexico Volunteer Cavalry, at the end of October, 1862. They had been sworn in at Santa Fe, outfitted and armed, and marched northward through Taos and Antonito to Fort Garland, in what was now Colorado Territory. This small cavalry outpost had been built in 1858, replacing Fort Massachusetts a few miles to the north, which had been poorly placed and considered indefensible. A garrison in this area had been needed since the early 1850s to protect settlers in the San Luis valley, then part of the Territory of New Mexico. This was the northern most outpost of the Army's Department of New Mexico, and had been named after Brig. Gen. John Garland, a former commander of the department and a distinguished veteran of many wars, beginning in the War of 1812.

With the withdrawal of the confederate threat from New Mexico after the defeat of Sibley's Texas Brigade at Glorieta Pass, Colonel Canby departed for service in the eastern states. New Mexico then came under the command of Brig. Gen. James Carleton, a veteran of the War with Mexico and the Indian Wars in New Mexico. He gained notoriety for his remarkable march through hostile Indian territory in 1862, defeating Confederate forces in Arizona and acting as a relief force to assure the removal of the Texans from New Mexico. With the end of the confederate threat, and the departure of

174

Canby, Carleton began a much more aggressive campaign against the hostile native tribes, especially the Navajo, Apache, Kiowa, and Comanche. In the San Luis Valley, there was an ongoing threat against the white and Hispanic settlers by the Ute Indians, which was to last for a number of years until they were eventually confined to reservations in southwestern Colorado by 1883. In late 1862, Brig. Gen. Carleton began to orchestrate operations in New Mexico to deal with Indian problems as quickly as possible, in order to secure and expand areas of settlement in the territory. His preferred methods of Indian pacification included relocating the tribes onto reservations, by force if necessary, and leading expeditions against bands refusing to peacefully submit. He decided to use the First New Mexico Volunteers commanded by Colonel Kit Carson to carry out this mission. He was determined to pacify the Navajo and Mescalero Apache first, before turning his attention to the more powerful adversaries in the eastern plains, the Kiowa and Comanche. Dealing with the Ute bands in the northern part of the department, now Colorado Territory, was considered a lesser priority, but none the less important. The Utes had the ability to cause unrest by attacking not only the settlers, but also the Navajo and Apaches, their ancient enemies.

Jacob was just getting his unit settled in at Fort Garland in November and beginning to train the troops of Company M, even though he was only the acting commander in the absence of Captain Charles Deus. Deus had been detailed to recruiting duty in the Colorado mountains at the mining camps. The authorization for this was unclear, and his activity drew sharp criticism from the Colorado governor. Jacob, as the acting commander, was doing the best he could, but did not have the proper background and training to handle all the details of unit administration. He was criticized sharply by the inspector general team that visited Fort Garland at that time. After just two months in the job, Company M received orders from Santa Fe to proceed with two other units, via Fort Union, to Fort Sumner, a new post near the Bosque Redondo, where the Mescalero Apache had been relocated to a reservation. He was told that his company commander, Captain Deus, would meet him at Fort Union to take charge. The contingent was to proceed south to Taos, then east through the mountain gaps to Cimarron. The company camped near the military corrals at Cimarron, then proceeded south to Fort Union, reporting to the post commander. Company M then joined other units heading for the Bosque Redondo.

This temporary relocation center and resettlement reservation had been established to confine and control the Navajo and Apache, which had been attacking American and Hispanic settlements in recent years. Brig. Gen. Carleton, the department commander, was adamant about bringing the Mescalero Apache and the Navajo to heel. He continued reinforcing Colonel Carson's regiment with elements of California Volunteers, and other units from quieter areas of New Mexico. Carleton made a command decision that the Utes in southern Colorado were a lower priority than the Navajo and Mescalero tribes. Jacob's company and several others were being transferred to the newly established Fort Sumner, near the Bosque Redondo, to aid in the pacification effort. This location not only served to relocate and subdue Comanche, Kiowa, Mescalero Apache, and Navajo tribes, but also served as a strong point from which to block any possible, but unlikely, Confederate access to Fort Union via the Pecos Valley. Carleton had visited the southern part of the territory and Fort Bliss in January of 1863 and was convinced that there would be no further Texan invasions, unless the Confederates were able to decisively gain the upper hand in the east. By the summer of 1863, Gettysburg and its aftermath would finally put that concern to rest. The industrial advantage held by the North would finally dictate the outcome of the great national struggle.

Fort Union was a welcome sight to Jacob and many of the soldiers of Company M. The trek through winter weather in the Sangre de Christo Mountains was over, and northeastern New Mexico was milder at this time than the frigid San Luis Valley of the new southern Colorado Territory where the mid-winter temperatures could hover near the zero mark. It was around forty degrees when they arrived in the middle of January. It would be even warmer in the upper Pecos River Valley when they reached Fort Sumner. In the meanwhile, Company M would enjoy a few days rest and outfitting at Fort Union. The food at the commissary was better now than Jacob had remembered. There were temporary improvements in the officers' quarters and the enlisted barracks, while plans for a new depot and storage facilities were underway. Fort Union was in expansion mode, as the main source of supply for the troops in the Department of New Mexico, but also as the supply center for the care of the defeated Indian tribes. The Mescalero tribe was nearly subjugated, and a reservation was being created from them at the Bosque Redondo near Fort Sumner, where Jacob's unit and others were to provide security and policing functions for the Apaches arriving there. Later in the year, Colonel Carson's regiment would begin a campaign to subdue the Navajo nation, relocating large numbers of their people to the Bosque Redondo. By the spring of 1864, more than 8,000 Navajo would be rounded up and placed on the reservation. Jacob had no way of knowing that he would be long gone from the Army by then. His letters to Charlotte were always welcome, but she was very concerned about the treatment of the Indian tribes described by her husband. She understood the need to protect the American and Spanish settlements from Indian raiding parties, but the idea of removing whole villages of native people to internment camps was extremely disturbing. The word "reservation" was too nice a label to give to the places and conditions her husband described in his letters.

Jacob left Fort Union leading Company M near the end of January 1863. They were to follow the military road south into the Pecos River Drainage. The journey to Fort Sumner was uneventful, except for an incident where a Confederate spy named Walker was captured attempting to scout a route from the Pecos Valley for a possible future return of the Texans to try to capture Fort Union. Brig. Gen. Carleton by this time was convinced that, unless the Confederates where to suddenly gain the upper hand in the east, the chance of a second invasion of New Mexico was probably out of the question. The prisoner was taken under guard to Fort Union, and Company M continued on to meet Captain Deus, the unit commander, at Fort Sumner. Deus, a German immigrant himself, had been a resident of Huerfano County, near Trinidad, now part of southern Colorado, for some time. He had come to New Mexico during the Mexican War and had served in actions against the Utes in the 1850s. Barely older than Jacob, Captain Deus was very active and well connected in local politics, obtaining a direct commission at the opening of hostilities against the Texas invaders. He had participated in the Battle of Valverde, commanding a company in the New Mexico Volunteers. Having little or no respect for Jacob, who had come up through the ranks, Deus treated him and his subordinates very poorly by most accounts. This would become a bigger problem at Fort Sumner, ultimately leading to a court-martial for Jacob and resulting in his dismissal from the service.

Over the next month or so, Jacob would have occasion to challenge Captain Deus regarding poor treatment of the some of the troops of Mexican descent in Company M. The unit was detailed as part of a larger cadre of troops of the New Mexico Volunteer Regiment to occupy the newly constructed Fort Sumner, and to help supervise and police the nearby Bosque Redondo, a reservation set up for receiving and containing several hundred Mescalero Apache from areas west of the Pecos River Valley. Brig. Gen. Carleton had ordered Colonel Kit Carson to round up all the Apache members of these tribes, killing any Apache men who resisted, and relocate all the prisoners along with women and children to the new reservation. After the Apache were under control, Carleton would send Colonel Kit Carson to the northwest part of the Department to forcibly relocate the Navajo nation to the Redondo. This would not happen for another year, when the "long walk," the forced march from the northwest area of the department would take place. The suffering of this forced relocation would leave an indelible mark on the history of the Navajo People.

A serious conflict between Jacob and his commander developed in early February, when Captain Deus refused to listen to a Private named Baca, who was being unfairly punished for a minor matter. The soldier was taken by senior sergeants in the company a mile from the post, tied to a tree, and given 25 lashes. Jacob heard the complaint from the injured man about the severe unjustified beating, and that the sergeants had sent another Spanish-speaking soldier to tell Baca that if he complained about it, they would kill him. It sounded as if the punishment was way too severe for the alleged infraction of not speaking English well enough, and there was no reason the soldier should have been threatened with death for reporting this barbaric action. Jacob took the man to Captain Deus, but Deus refused to listen to either the soldier or his executive officer, Lt. Stenger. Captain Deus said to them that he knew all about it, and that Baca deserved what he got. Deus dismissed Jacob and Baca, and this prompted Jacob to write a letter to Brig. Gen. Carleton about the matter in mid-February. In the meantime, Captain Deus began to seriously mistreat Jacob, including making him move into a tent, then taking away his camp stove, and harassing him in various ways. The Spanish-speaking soldiers in the unit were also intimidated and mistreated by the non-commissioned officers.

After a couple of weeks, Jacob went to the post adjutant to inquire about any response to the letter he had sent to Brig. Gen. Garland. The adjutant said that there was no response. Deus continued to disrespect Jacob, preventing him from carrying out his duties, and a few days later, the adjutant's office informed Jacob that he had been court-martialed in a general order received from Santa Fe. He was informed that he would be processed and separated from the Army effective March 25th. Jacob was shocked at first with this news. He was being railroaded out of the service for merely trying to stand up for his soldiers. He had not even been given the courtesy of a trial, or even a hearing, to challenge the grossly unfair decision. That evening he cleaned out his tent and moved to the visiting officers' quarters. The following morning, Jacob filled out a few papers required to complete his separation, including any medical pension claims. He was still having occasional problems with his knee, previously injured during the supply trip to Utah five years earlier. The adjutant told him he might only be eligible for a couple of dollars a month. Jacob replied that he would be happy with that, a small but important reminder of what he had given up for his service to his country. A few days later after regaining his balance, Jacob realized that he was finally free, that it was over, and he could now go back to Council Grove and begin a real life with his beloved Charlotte and his boys. He had served honorably, and whatever he made of his life from here on out didn't depend on the blessing of people like Charles Deus, or even a commanding general. He thought about writing a letter to Charlotte, but calculated that he could beat the mail and just surprise his family. Jacob made arrangements to travel with the mail and an escort of troopers back to Fort Union, where he had temporarily stored his gear. At least he owned his own mount. He would join the next large group of travelers headed for the United States.

Chapter XXVII. Homecoming

Two weeks after leaving Fort Sumner, Jacob had been to Santa Fe to finish his out-processing from the Army, bought a new wagon and team of two, and followed the mail service wagon to Fort Union. After stabling his team and his personal mount, he enjoyed a good meal and a night's rest at the visiting officers' quarters. The next morning, he reported to the post adjutant's office to get permission for travel east with the next military courier and mail dispatch scheduled to leave for Fort Leavenworth. In four days, a group of five officers, being transferred to the East with their families, were scheduled to depart with a company-sized detail of troops being reassigned to duty in the Army of the Potomac. Still hurt and confused over his treatment by the command in New Mexico, Jacob could not wait to be reunited with his family in Council Grove. He wondered if a letter would have reached Charlotte before he arrived. It was likely that she might have already received it, but one never knew for sure. At least there were no reports at Fort Union of attacks on the mail service recently. In any event, Jacob decided to visit the sutler's store, and stock up on whatever trade goods he could carry in his small buckboard wagon. He had saved up about two hundred dollars, and he hoped that Mr. Moore, the post sutler, would be willing to extend him some credit if needed. The next day, Jacob hitched his team up and drove the buckboard to the trading post. Moore was glad to see Jacob, expressing sympathy for his situation and maltreatment by the Army. He liked Jacob, believing him to be an honest man. The two hundred dollars bought a number of buffalo hides, nearly a hundred pounds of silver and turquoise Indian jewelry and trinkets, and some Navajo pottery. Mr. Moore decided, that under the circumstance, Jacob would need some cash for the trip and to get started in his new business as a freight hauler. He gave Jacob half of his money back, along with a list of items from the east, for Jacob to bring back to New Mexico on his next trip. Jacob was overwhelmed by the generosity, promising that he would be back as soon as providence would allow.

Jacob really had no idea when he would be able to keep his promise to return to New Mexico. All he knew was that his wife and children were several hundred miles away, and that he just wanted to be back with them as soon as possible. At least he would be able to travel east with an armed escort. Other than his long-held wish of becoming a freighter on the trail, he was still unsettled mentally and emotionally due to his ordeal with Captain Deus, and what he perceived as a lack of justice from the Army. Hell, he hadn't even had a chance to defend himself! No matter now, he realized. From now on he would be responsible for his own fortune. He would have a few days now to think everything through and make some plans. He thought about his trip across Texas, nearly a decade earlier, and remembered how he had admired the grit and determination of that wagon train commander, Captain Murphy. Someday he thought he could be like that man, strong enough to lead a train of wagons on long trips through hostile country. After all, he knew the Santa Fe Trail pretty well, knew it from Leavenworth to Santa Fe, and back. He had even been through the great mountains, all the way to the Green River Valley. His knee twitched and hurt a little bit with the memory of his fall from his horse and the long wagon ride back to Fort Union. He knew horses and mules and wagons, and how to fix them. He knew how to travel long distances and protect people. Jacob's musings fell away as he reached his temporary quarters at Fort Union with his wagon load of Indian trade goods. He piled the buffalo hides, rugs, and silver and jewelry into his small bachelor quarters, and drove the empty wagon over to the post corral, stabling his team along with his personal mount. After a bowl of stew at the officers' mess, Jacob walked back to his room, thought about his family in Kansas, pulled off his boots, and fell asleep on his cot with his clothes on. It was still a little cold in April in northern New Mexico, and he woke up shivering in the middle of the night, pulled a buffalo hide over himself and didn't wake up until the sunrise poured light through the window.

After shaving, and a breakfast of beans and bacon, biscuits and coffee at the mess, Jacob walked over to the adjutant's office. He was informed that his travel group had a meeting in the small post chapel that afternoon. He met the officers and their families assigned to the convoy, before being briefed on the trip. They all made arrangements for coaches and wagons for their household goods, paying for their subsistence as required under regulations. Meals were to be provided by a quartermaster field mess wagon. Two mail wagons and dispatch couriers were traveling with the group along with a cavalry squadron being transferred back east. The families were grateful to have the protection of the mounted troopers. Even though the group was going by way of the mountain route, due to recent reports of Kiowa and Comanche attacks on the Cimarron route, more escort protection was always welcome. Teams of mules, and horses, if necessary, would be available at Bent's old fort, Fort Larned, and the old camp at Walnut Creek.

It was the 5th of April when the travelers and their mounted escort pulled out of Fort Union. Jacob pulled into line behind the commissioned officers' carriages and wagons, just in front of the commissary and mess wagons. He was happy with the prospect of being close to where the hot coffee was brewed and available most of the time in a steaming caldron at the rear of the mess wagon. Even though he was near the end of the train, about half of the cavalry escort were behind him. As the caravan moved down the road toward Watrous, they passed the nearly completed new house of the Fort Union commander. The Star Fort was the present site of the troop billets and armory, but the new commander's quarters were the start of a major reconstruction of Fort Union. Jacob would return to this site many times in the years to come, always surprised at the growth of the garrison and the depot. The procession turned back to the northeast at Watrous, toward Wagon Mound. Continuing for another 20 miles, the train reached Rayado, a small settlement on a creek of the same name, established by Lucien Maxwell after the War with Mexico. An American military post was established there in 1850, prior to the construction of Fort Union. It was an important watering point, resupply, horse and mule replacement depot on the trail, and became the junction of the Cimarron and Mountain branches of the road to Fort Leavenworth. After a night of rest and nourishment at the military compound, a few horses and mules were replaced, and the group moved out toward Raton Pass to the north. At Cimarron, about 10 miles north, they passed by the ranch and mansion of Lucien Maxwell, the famous mountain man and explorer. Maxwell had married into a wealthy family, which owned one of the largest Spanish land grant properties in the Americas. The estate encompassed much of northeastern New Mexico and nearly two million acres east of the Rocky Mountains. Maxwell was best friends with the likes of Kit Carson and John C. Fremont. He had always been a true patriot and friend of the Army, providing food, livestock, and building materials, including timber.

The caravan moved steadily on to the north. It was still late winter in the Rockies and the convoy commander wanted to get over the pass at Raton before they might encounter a late snow or blizzard. Arriving at Raton on the south side of the pass two days later, they replenished water barrels and checked the wagons and animals and prepared for an early departure next morning toward Trinidad and the Purgatoire River basin. The road over the pass had been constantly improved since the Kearney invasion of New Mexico nearly twenty years earlier, but the train carried extra timbers to bridge any washout, which might be encountered. With any luck they would avoid any serious weather and cross in two days. It was still early in the spring and the snow melt and runoff from the Sangre de Cristo Mountains to the west would not peak until late June or July.

The convoy reached the summit by dusk on the first day and camped quietly without Indian encounters. Jacob had been in similar situations before and was always wary. He stayed up until the sentry patrols changed at midnight, drinking coffee with the guards at the mess wagon, swapping stories with some of the younger troopers. The night was quiet except for a terrifying few minutes around 11 p.m., when a bear wandered into one of the rope corrals. The horses spooked momentarily, but everything settled down after a sentry shot the bear with his carbine, taking at least five shots to finally put the bear down. There was a lively interchange along the train, but everyone finally went back into their wagons or carriages until dawn. The wagons moved out again after breakfast, heading down the steeper northern slopes of the mountain road. Only one wagon broke down during the descent, requiring a wheel change and delaying the train by a little over an hour. As the convoy approached the little settlement of Trinidad at the northern end of the pass, a strong wind picked up, blowing down the front slopes of the mountains to the west. The temperature dropped about twenty degrees, accompanied by flurries of snow blowing from west to east. This lasted for about an hour, but less than an inch of accumulation resulted. The train was moving steadily without further incident, but a few of the mules and horses were showing signs of impending lameness.

Fortunately, Trinidad was a well-established stop on the route with an adequate supply of replacement animals. Since the discovery of coal in the region the previous year, the town was starting to grow rapidly. The convoy commander decided to stay in Trinidad for the night, and the train circled up for the evening. The snow was tapering off, but it was safer to stay put for the night than trying to move down into the river drainages so late in the day, risking a night stream crossing. Most of the families were weary after the jerky, two-day trip across Raton pass. Captain Jones was a savvy veteran with three years of service in the west, and he had made this trip a few times, back and forth to eastern Kansas. He knew the next two days would be fairly easy, and they should reach Bent's Fort in less than two days. He was very happy to be this far along the trail, a couple of days ahead of his conservatively estimated pace of travel. There was no heavy freight on these wagons, which was probably the difference, with no oxen required to pull the lighter military wagons or coaches. Freighters driving the big Conestogas with three or four thousand pounds of cargo would be fortunate to make fifteen to twenty miles a day with large teams of oxen. An Army field wagon or stagecoach with team of four to six horses or mules traveling on easy terrain could make up to forty miles a day on dry flat land.

The group camped at Iron Springs on Timpas Creek the first night, replenishing water supplies and grazing the animals. Bent's Old Fort on the Arkansas River was the next stop, arriving about midday. The trading post for Indians and fur trappers had been abandoned by William Bent in 1849, due to a cholera epidemic. It was blown up and the stores moved northwest along the front range of the Rockies to Bent's other trading post, Fort Saint Vrain, on the South Platte. Bent later moved back to the Arkansas in 1853, a little more than ten miles east of the old fort to an area known as Big Timbers, a better location for trading with the Plains tribes in a traditional native gathering place, and a good location on the Santa Fe Trail. The fur trade faltered, however, and Bent leased his newer sandstone fort to the Army, which named it Fort Fauntleroy, later changing it to Fort Wise, and it was now known as Fort Lyon. The caravan arrived at the site late in the afternoon and decided to stay two nights, for replacement of some of the mules and horses, wagon repairs, and to take advantage of the newly constructed quarters and barracks with bathing facilities.

Captain Jones received the latest scouting reports from Lt. Davis, the post commander. There were no reports of hostile Indian activity as far as Fort Larned, and the mail was on schedule. The weather was steady for early spring with no flooding reported by travelers. Captain Jones was confident because they had already crossed the Arkansas and should have no major trouble with the tributaries with the possible exception of Pawnee Creek and Walnut Creek. Jacob also thought this was a good time to travel, barring any catastrophic storms. He would reserve judgement regarding the Little Arkansas and Cottonwood Creek crossings. Those fords could be unpredictable in his experience. The crossings also turned out to be uneventful. The group encountered nothing except an occasional small Arapahoe hunting party, none of which were interested in taking on a platoon of mounted soldiers. They camped together some nights with the westward bound trains, and shared news, stories, and cautions to be observed on the trail. The days were going faster for Jacob as Council Grove began to occupy more of his thoughts and longings to be reunited with Charlotte and their boys.

Chapter XXVIII. Starting a New Life

Jacob reached Council Grove on May 12th. He had attached himself to one of the many groups of soldiers and families, and other civilians heading back to the United States. His new wagon was full of trade goods, including buffalo robes, hides, Indian rugs, jewelry, pottery, and blankets. His team of two mules had remained healthy, as was his personal mount, following in tow. Goodson Simcock was on the front porch of the hotel as Jacob drove up. Simcock had greeted most of the other military and civilian members of the party, but was shocked to see Jacob, even though Charlotte had told him that Jacob was being released from the Army. They didn't know exactly when he was coming. Jacob hugged the older man, and briefly recounted the rough treatment he had been subjected to, leading to his dismissal. Simcock was visibly angry about the situation, but extremely happy that Charlotte and the boys now had their papa back. Jacob couldn't wait to see his family.

"Where are they, Mr. Simcock?", he asked excitedly.

"They are inside, Jacob. Charlotte is busy helping Maggie with this load of visitors you have suddenly thrust upon us. The two older boys are in the back, in the garden. Kit is in the kitchen, so go ahead, I know you are dying to see them."

Jacob took off on a dead run around the back of the building, looking for the boys. They were playing on a small swinging rope that Simcock had made for them in the garden. Jimmy squealed when he saw Jacob, and he and Will both ran into Jacob's arms as he lifted them up to his chest. They all jumped up and down and danced around, savoring the moment. Charlotte, having been busily attending to the customers in the dining room and tavern, was returning to the kitchen for more bread, soup, and drinks, and heard the commotion out back. She looked out of the window and nearly fainted at the sight of Will and James embracing their father. She quickly scooped up Christian, "Kit" as Jacob preferred to call him, and ran out to embrace Jacob. "Jacob, I didn't hear from you that you were coming."

"I joined a wagon train earlier than I thought, and I wanted to surprise you, Schatze", Jacob exclaimed.

"Was fur ein Uberaschung, what a great surprise, Jacob!" Charlotte answered, and then she smothered his face with kisses, while Kit clung to his father's neck. Suddenly Charlotte remembered that she was waiting on the other customers. Tugging at Jacob's arm, she pulled him and his clinging sons back into the kitchen. She scooped a cup of coffee and a bowl of stew for Jacob and told him to mind the children while she tended to her customers. By mid-afternoon, the weary travelers began moving into rooms at the Hayes House or the Gilkey Hotel across the street. The troopers rode on across the Neosho ford to the military campground to set up tents and prepare for a night's rest. Exhausted, but in great spirits, Charlotte and Maggie finally joined Jacob, Mr. Simcock, and the boys in the kitchen for stew and bread. Maggie poured some fresh milk for the youngsters and passed a plate of oatmeal cookies. Simcock had a lot of questions for Jacob, and they talked for an hour before heading out to take inventory of the trade goods in Jacob's wagon.

The merchant was glad to see Jacob reunited with his family, and he was delighted to have the special items from New Mexico. Jacob kept a few things for the use of his family, selling the rest for a twenty percent profit over the money he owed the sutler at Fort Union. Jacob was greatly relieved, and this transaction increased his confidence that he would be able to provide for his family as a freight hauler and trader. Simcock asked him about where he would like to set up housekeeping now that his family was back together. Jacob had thought about this constantly, planning to rent a house as soon as he could find an adequate family dwelling. Simcock offered that they were welcome to stay in his rooms out back as long as needed. He would keep his eyes open for any available housing that might be suitable for the Stenger family. Jacob expressed his thanks and appreciation, and that he and Charlotte would be talking about finding a place as soon as possible.

Due to all the problems with the Army, Jacob had not been able to make it back to Kansas for Christmas, but those days were over now. The family was back together for good, and it was worth the wait. A couple of days after the Army caravan had departed eastward, Simcock and Maggie put on a special celebration dinner for the Stengers. They served the family and a few local friends the finest meal that Maggie and Charlotte could put together. They had onion soup, roast beef, fried chicken, mashed potatoes, candied sweet potatoes, canned beets, fresh bread and gravy. Maggie made pecan pies, and apple pies from fruit she and Charlotte had canned the previous fall. After dinner, the tired children were settled into bed, and Mr. Simcock broke out a bottle of brandy, which the adults enjoyed with their coffee long into the evening. The guests were

188

entertained by Jacob's accounts of his adventures in Texas and New Mexico. Not to be outdone, Simcock regaled them with legendary tales of Seth Hays from Missouri, and the early days of the Santa Fe Trail, and how Council Grove had become one of the best-known stops on the way west.

Jacob spent most of his time over the next few days with his family, recounting to his wife and children the events of this past several months away from them. He let them know how happy he was to be with them again, and about plans for the future. Jacob reassured them all, that even though he might be absent for a few weeks or a month or two on occasion, due to his new work as a freight hauler. Council Grove would always be that stabile place called home. He would be in control of his time away from them, and no longer had to answer to some brass hat boss, far away, who might not care about his family's needs. The older boys, Will and Jim, were almost old enough to understand, and Charlotte was especially relieved that they were in charge of their lives again. She encouraged Jacob to seek jobs on the shorter end of the trail, from Leavenworth and Westport as much as possible. Jacob promised that he would, but reminded her that New Mexico and Colorado were the places where the freighting money was to be made. At any rate, it would take a while to secure those contracts. In the meantime, he was going to try to get a job as a blacksmith and outfitter, getting wagons ready for the long journey ahead. It was getting pretty busy on the trail these days. If the Union prevailed in this terrible war, he expected an ever-increasing push to expand the nation westward. Freighters should have great opportunities, and wagon masters and guides maybe even more so. Jacob certainly was right about a promising future in the freight and wagon business, but there was no way of knowing at the time, that in only a couple of decades, the railroad would dominate transportation of goods and people, across the whole continent. For the time being, Jacob and his family were finally free to choose their own life, and they were in a good place to take advantage of it. Within a couple of weeks, Jacob was able to get a part time job at the Army blacksmith shop just east side of the Neosho. How much work depended mainly on the amount of wagon traffic moving along the trail. In the early summer months, the traffic was heavy, as people wanted to make it to the southwest or even to California before winter slowed down or stopped the travel. Getting to the west coast, even though the southwest corridor, was very difficult later in the year after the cold weather and snow began to impede wagon traffic. By late September or October, passage through the Rocky Mountains could be nearly impossible. Many people, traveling to the far west from the east or the upper Midwest would already be exhausted or out of provisions by late summer or early fall. Land was cheap and available for homesteading in the prairies and high plains, especially in the later years of the war, and as the Native Americans were increasingly relocated to reservations. These factors caused many migrants to reconsider and settle down east of the Rockies, rather than risk crossing the mountains too late in the year. This phenomenon would lead to opportunities for guides and wagon masters to show the way to safe settlement areas or land grant opportunities. Towns like Council Grove would become "last chance" places to obtain guides, fresh mules and horses, wagon repairs, and supplies for the rest of the journey.

The early summer of 1863 was a blessing for Jacob and his family. He was working steadily at the blacksmith shop helping to outfit and prepare wagons and animals for the trip west. The Army wagon trains moving both east and west were also a major part of the business, with troops increasingly being moved to the eastern theater, and supplies from the Missouri River bases being sent to New Mexico. In June, Jacob had been dispatched to Fort Leavenworth for more iron and livery supplies for the Council Grove shop. Jacob was only gone for nine days, but on the trip to Leavenworth, he heard many concerns and warning about impending Confederate raids into Kansas. There had been several years of border strife and raids across the Kansas-Missouri border by anti-slavery Kansas "Jayhawkers" and pro-slavery "Border Ruffians" from western Missouri. The Kansas-Nebraska Act of 1854 had been the catalyst for the fighting between the "Free-Stater" abolitionists, and the Missouri "Pro-slavery" settlers. There had been small cross border raids by both sides in recent years, with major escalations in 1855 in the Wakusa Valley and the sacking of Lawrence in 1856. The "free staters" under John Brown carried out retaliatory raids on pro-slavery settlements, with notable fighting at Ossawatomie and Palmyra in the Battle of Blackjack. These successful defenses of Kansas settlements led to large retaliation raids by Missourians under General John Reid, a Mexican War veteran and militia leader. John Brown's son, Frederick, was killed, and the Kansans were routed. They later regrouped to help defend Lawrence from another planned attack by a large force of Missouri Border Ruffians. The Kansas governor intervened, brokering a cease fire and amnesty for both sides. This, along with the departure of John Brown and many of his abolitionist supporters, helped to quell most of the major violence along the border before the beginning of the Civil War. During the early years of the war, there was some violence and small raids along the border, but by 1863, Cantrell's Raiders, including the Younger and James brothers, were becoming a growing concern. There had been a few major Union versus Confederate battles in 1861, including the battle of Wilson's Creek near Springfield, Missouri, the first major battle fought west of the Mississippi River. Shortly after that battle, William Quantrill, a Confederate ranger commander, formed a guerilla band near Blue Springs in western Missouri, with plans to raid the Kansas border towns. They began a campaign of cross border raids lasting over a year and a half. Dick Yeager, one of Quantrill's men, had robbed a stagecoach stop at Diamond Springs, west of Council Grove, killing the station master. This was only a week before Jacob arrived from New Mexico. People in eastern Kansas were nervous, and travel in the area was considered risky without an armed escort. On both legs of the Leavenworth trip, Jacob was careful to join a military convoy. There had been no encounters, but he could sense trouble in the air. The return trip was with a large train of wagons bound for the Rocky Mountains and the gold fields of Colorado. Since the major gold discoveries near Pikes Peak and Denver, the gold rush had been steadily growing, limited only by military conscription and increased manpower needs for war production. Traffic was nearly constant on the Santa Fe Trail, and Jacob was thankful for the added security this afforded.

After delivering the wagon load of iron stock and wagon supplies to the blacksmith shop, Jacob headed for the Hays House, where he was met with a joyous greeting from his family. Charlotte fixed a chicken dinner with fresh garden vegetables and biscuits with gravy. It was quickly consumed by all, including Mr. Simcock, who had joined them after closing up the store for the night. Jacob had delivered a shipment of Indian goods for the store while he was at Westport Landing on the way to Leavenworth. He returned to Council Grove with some sundry goods that Simcock had ordered for the store. He paid Jacob twenty dollars for the delivery and pick-up and seemed well pleased with the arrangement. Jacob had also picked up some small wooden toys for the three boys and some calico cloth and a pair of shoes for Charlotte. She was very grateful for the thoughtful gift from her husband, and glad to have him home. Jacob was pleased with the progress he had made in only a couple of months, but realized that his family situation was only temporary, living behind the Hays House. Jacob was making enough money at this point to rent a small place for his family, but the town was still so small that nothing was available. Jacob was grateful for the space Mr. Simcock had let them rent for a few dollars a month, but it was too small for a permanent residence. Jacob decided to ask Mr. Simcock for some help and advice. Over dinner one night at the Hays House, they came up with a plan that would provide adequate living space for the Stenger family for years to come. They would simply remodel the space over the store into a bedroom area. The kitchen and dining area could be built later downstairs behind the store.

The supply store that Simcock had purchased from Seth Hays was slowly becoming a local grocery store, as well as a general supply store for the growing population of Council Grove. The building extended back to a small alley from the storefront, which had far more storage room on the ground floor than was required for the business. This joined the kitchen of the Hays House restaurant at the rear.

Above that area was an attic that had been previously used for livery and blacksmith supplies, but that part of the business had been moved to the new stone blacksmith building in 1860. Simcock believed that the upstairs area could be converted to living quarters with two or more bedrooms. The downstairs area behind the store was big enough for a small kitchen, bathroom, dining room and parlor. There was already a staircase leading from the Main Street entrance to the second floor, and there was a back staircase as well. This space certainly could be adapted to family living, and there was a small barn behind the Hays House where horses could be stabled. Jacob listened to Mr. Simcock carefully as he explained his idea. Although the idea didn't appear to be a permanent solution for his family, Jacob thought it could be a good start for his family at least until he could afford to build his own more private house in a few years. Simcock said that he would be happy to finance the construction if Jacob would agree to rent the place for three years at a decent monthly rate. Jacob said that he would discuss the idea with Charlotte and let him know the following day.

Charlotte was a little disappointed with the idea of living behind or over a store, having already done so for nearly a year. However, there didn't seem to be much else to choose from for the time being. She would at least have a little more privacy and space. Jacob was just getting started as a freighter and used the blacksmith job to fill in the gaps. Charlotte would be able to continue working at the Hays House and the boys would be close to the "Brown Jug," the multi-purpose city hall that for the past five years had been used as a school. Living behind a store wasn't an ideal place for a family, but still was more convenient than trying to build a new house further away from the school. The Stengers agreed that family stability was the main priority for the time being. The next morning, Jacob met with Simcock to iron out the details. Simcock agreed to a general plan for partitioning the space upstairs and down, with priority to building a back staircase from the future living space to the second floor where the bedrooms were to be located. The upstairs had been a frequent town meeting place and had been used as a courtroom, meeting hall, post office/ printing office, and social hall by the city residents. The space had windows and a pot-bellied stove in the rear of the large meeting room. The hardwood flooring was substantial and would require little modification. Construction would begin in two weeks to provide sleeping quarters, with two bedrooms and a bathroom upstairs which could draw water from the cistern on the roof. The family would continue to use the kitchen and other facilities of the hotel and restaurant next to the store until the upstairs was finished, and the downstairs living area and kitchen were complete. Simcock estimated the finished cost to be around $800 to $900, with a monthly rent of $15. Jacob wasn't totally convinced that he could pay that much, but he did have a fairly steady job at the blacksmith shop nearby, which paid $25 per month. If he could get a freighting contract once a month to Westport or Leavenworth, he could probably earn at least $40 to $50 per job. In addition, Mr. Simcock had generously offered Jacob a $5 per day credit for any days he could work on the remodeling project. When they finished putting the boys down for the night, Jacob and Charlotte had a long discussion over pie and coffee, deciding to delay the decision until morning as they were exhausted, thinking about all the ramifications and responsibilities involved.

The couple slept fitfully, mulling over this important time in the life of the family. Charlotte most of all, wanted no more dislocation for her family, and was willing to put down her roots in this place. Even though Council Grove was just a very small way station on the Santa Fe Trail, the town was starting to grow faster even in the short year she had been here. The community felt good, and she was starting to make friends. She really was starting to feel a part of this small place on the edge of a frontier that was drawing people westward, looking for the same stability she wanted, fleeing war, poverty, and oppression. Many people, weary of the decisive war between the states were looking for opportunity and a better life. Jacob wanted the same things. They shared their thoughts and agreed completely that this was the right thing for now, with a future limited only by their hard work and faithfulness, and dedication to serving their family and others. It was a deal then! After a hearty pancake breakfast with the boys, Jacob walked next door to the store, to tell Mr. Simcock he would accept his offer, and he was willing to put as many hours into the remodeling work as possible. Simcock was very happy to help Jacob and his family in this way. He knew that Council Grove was booming, with the freight value on the route to New Mexico projected to reach $40 million by the end of the year.

LAWRENCE MASSACRE

Chapter XXIX. Bleeding Kansas

Remodeling work on the Stengers' new residence began right after the 4th of July holiday. The walls of the two bedrooms were erected behind a small entry hall entered by the external staircase above the front entrance to the supply and grocery store. This upper entrance was only for family use, while a guest entrance was built on the west side of the building above a small, elevated landing. Another rear entrance to the future kitchen area was already in place coming from the alley. From the main entrance on the west side, a staircase was constructed from the small entry hall up to the second floor in the rear. The guest entry hall provided passage into the parlor and dining room areas, which would be built later with passages to the rear of the ground floor and the kitchen. Having the second staircase would allow family access to the upstairs without having to go outside. Work continued through the month of July, completing the bedrooms and bathroom upstairs. Dormer windows were installed for each of the rooms for light and ventilation. Mr. Simcock ordered prefabricated window frames, complete with sliding sashes and glass panes, from St. Louis. These were a new innovation that he had discovered during his last visit back east, and these were some of the first to be used west of Missouri. They arrived just in time for installation after the dormer gables and roof modifications were finished. In addition, full-sized galvanized bathtubs were now available from St. Louis, and he had ordered one for Charlotte. Jacob complained that these fancy items would raise the rent above what he could afford to pay. Simcock countered that these were an investment in the property, and not to worry about paying extra. Jacob put in extra time before and after work at the blacksmith shop, sometimes working until midnight after reading to the boys before bedtime. Mr. Simcock hired two extra hands to help finish the upstairs as soon as possible. He knew that Charlotte's two oldest boys, Will and Jim, would be starting school in September, and he wanted the upstairs finished by then. Jacob was scheduled to be a freight hauler on a supply train trip from Westport and Leavenworth to Fort Larned. He would likely be gone for two to three weeks at that time from mid-August to early September. This was good news for Jacob in terms of making some extra money, but it would put more pressure on finishing the upstairs before he left. Jacob worked many late nights by lantern light during the first two weeks of August, and except for some trim and paint work, finished the upstairs enough to move his family into their new bedrooms before he had to leave on his trip. They moved the beds upstairs from the small rooms behind the restaurant, and Jacob purchased a couple of used chests of drawers for the bedrooms, along with a small vanity with mirror for Charlotte's room.

The bathtub arrived at the end of the first week in August, and Jacob installed a drain and piping running under the floorboards and down the back of the building to a large barrel to collect the wastewater. A pipe and faucet from the roof cistern were installed to bring water to the bathroom the tub. Hot water would have to be brought up from the restaurant kitchen in a copper wash boiler, as no fireplace or hearth was available on the second floor. Charlotte would have liked that luxury, but was still very happy and looking forward to the luxury of a full tub, instead of kitchen bathing in a small wash tub. The bathroom and each bedroom had a large chamber pot so the family would not have to go to the outhouse in the middle of the night. These small luxuries helped the family realize they had a lot to be thankful for. They would eventually have their own private kitchen, but for now, the restaurant kitchen would meet their needs.

Jacob left for Leavenworth with an Army wagon train on August 15th. He rode his own horse with saddle bags filled with Indian jewelry, which he planned to sell during a brief layover at Westport Landing. He was one of a group of fifteen freighters, some of whom he had met in New Mexico in the past. Some had driven

196

their wagons from Santa Fe and Fort Union to Council Grove during the past month with trade goods bound for the United States. Some were scheduled, like himself, to pick up military supplies for the return trip to New Mexico, or to Fort Larned, which was his destination.

A contingent of soldiers numbering more than one hundred was being transferred to the East. Word had just reached eastern Kansas in the past few days about the tremendous battle at Gettysburg fought earlier in July. It looked like a tactical defeat for the South under Gen. Lee, but the casualties were very high on both sides. Union replacement troops were headed east, from wherever they could be spared. No one could have known at this time that the Confederacy had reached its high-water mark and was beginning an inexorable decline into defeat in less than two years, the war continuing to consume the lives and treasure of hundreds of thousands of Americans on both sides. In the meantime, the routine business of maintaining the westward expansion of American civilization would continue its steady and growing course. Other hundreds of thousands of pioneers would finish settling the West, according to the manifest destiny dreams imagined decades earlier.

Jacob had kissed his wife and children goodbye but was excited to be working toward a very good payday when he delivered his cargo to Fort Larned. This kind of trip promised to be less risky and at least much shorter than a full New Mexico round trip. He would be home before the Comanche and Kiowa headed for their winter quarters in the Red River Basins of Texas and the Indian Territories. The freight drivers pulled their rigs into a line, led by a platoon of cavalry troopers and twenty Army wagons, followed by another platoon of troopers. There was a mail wagon and two stagecoaches in the middle with east-bound passengers, including the families of two senior officers headed for Washington. Jacob recognized one of the Colonels from his out-processing visit to Santa Fe earlier in the year, but they had not spoken then, and there was no reason to approach him now. He apparently didn't recognize Jacob. Half an hour later, the train commander, a Captain, gave the order to move out. The wagons jerked into a cantering pace and then established a quick walk. Jacob waved to his family and Mr. Simcock as they passed the Hays House. The train crossed the Neosho at the Main Street ford, having no particular trouble as the stream was less than two feet deep. The weather was dry in mid-August and the train moved steadily eastward, crossing a small feeder creek of the Neosho, and crossed into Lyons County after seven miles. The train crossed other small creeks, passing through Osage County, camping near Switler's Creek outside of Burlingame (formerly Council City). The postmaster there warned the soldiers that there had been reports from Johnson County about "Border Ruffians" seen in small groups along the Kaw River north of Olathe. Captain Jewell, the train commander, decided to send a couple of troopers ahead to Willow Springs early the next morning, to check for any sighting of bushwhackers infiltrating from Missouri. The riders returned by noon, with no word of hostile activity in Douglas County. The decision was made to move on and make camp that night at Willow Springs, a watering stop on the way to Gardner and Olathe, some twenty miles southeast of Lawrence.

Captain James Jewell, a Leavenworth native, had been fighting guerrillas and their sympathizers for years, off and on, ever since the 1856 attack by pro-slavery forces against the newspapers in Lawrence. The newspapers had been agitating for free-state status for Kansas. Pro-slavery advocates and Free-Staters had battled politically for years to achieve President Franklin Pierce's mandate of popular sovereignty, to decide whether Kansas would be free or slave. On many occasions, passions spilled over into violence on both sides. Small scale ambushes were frequent and bloody, often between settlers divided over the slavery issue. After the sacking of Lawrence and destruction of the printing presses in 1856, John Brown, the abolitionist, began his rampage against the pro-slavery communities along the border. Brown continued to foment violence until he left in 1859 to instigate a slave rebellion in the East, but he was hanged after his botched attempt to rob the federal arsenal at Harper's Ferry, Virginia.

Captain Jewell had led many military trains through this part of Kansas to the Santa Fe Trail forts, and also to Fort Scott in the southeastern part of the territory. On this trip, he was a little uneasy, but couldn't put his anxiety in focus. Things had been quiet for most of the past year along the border. The Battle of Independence had been fought over a year earlier, and, after the later success of his daring raid on Olathe, Quantrill had been pursued for weeks but never captured. Maybe the slippery Quantrill was on the prowl again; one always had to be alert for that possibility. Jewell would advance toward the Westport area with caution.

198

Missouri had voted to remain in the Union, although the Confederacy claimed it. Union troops seized St. Louis, Jefferson City, and Kansas City. Rebel politicians formed a few volunteer regiments which lead to some major but indecisive battles in the southwest part of Missouri, which remained only a minor theater in the greater War of the Rebellion. The war would be won in the east and southeastern states. Gettysburg was a bitter reminder that the North held the trump cards in this war. Primarily agricultural, and unable to compete long-term with the more populated and industrialized North, the Confederate forces fought fiercely, defended their own soil to the death, and were led by superior military professionals. The logistics advantage of the Union and the pit-bull determination of a few northern generals eventually decided the issue. Men like Quantrill were never going to accept the inevitable and would continue to harass the Yankees and their communities wherever possible. Guerrilla stealthy movement and a hit-and-run fighting style gave them the advantage of surprise. They could attack quickly and unexpectedly, inflicting severe damage on the target, and escape rapidly if necessary. Captain Jewell learned this firsthand at Olathe a year earlier when his company had been surrounded and overrun. Quantrill's superior force of more than two hundred riders had outflanked his unit. Those who did not surrender were shot where they stood, with sawed-off shotguns and Sharp's repeating carbines. His unit was decimated in less than thirty minutes. They probably would have all been executed except for the arrival of the remainder of his regiment, the Kansas 5th Cavalry. Olathe was looted, but the bushwhackers didn't have time to burn the town. After recovering the survivors of the battle, the regiment pursued Quantrill's men through four counties, recovering stolen weapons and supplies, but did not capture the leader.

Waiting for his scouts to return, Captain Jewell was reliving the fear of that day, and trying to plan his reactions if he should encounter the bushwhackers as he turned north toward the river bases and Fort Leavenworth. The scouts had not seen any suspicious riders and heard no reports of such from farmers or other travelers. Jewell began to feel that if bushwhackers were in the Kaw valley, they weren't bothering the local homesteads or small villages. He remembered the reports of the 1856 raid on Lawrence, of the guerrillas who attacked in force after taking a concealed route along the Kansas River, staying deep in the bushes and trees. Small, separated groups who might be foraging or randomly robbing small farms or villages would probably not be so careful. This could be a big raid, after a big political target. Lawrence would be a likely target. Taking out the printing presses years ago had not caused enough lasting damage to Lawrence. A hotel and a few houses had been burned, but didn't put the troublesome town, now headquarters of the abolitionists, out of commission for very long. If Quantrill wanted to get rid of this troublesome town, he would have to kill as many prominent leaders as possible and burn the place to the ground. This was it! There was going to be another surprise raid into the heart of the enemy's headquarters! The route, starting in the deep wooded areas just south of Westport, followed the Kaw valley for cover and concealment. A night ride would allow an attack on Lawrence just before dawn, before the unsuspecting residents could even get their boots on. Shoot anyone who moves, break into the hotels and houses, find and kill everyone you can find, then burn the whole town. That should set the Free-Staters back a year or two. The shock value to the rest of the country could be enormous, maybe encourage more uncommitted sympathizers to support the southern cause.

Captain Jewell was suddenly terrified that he had been able to think as if he were Quantrill himself. It was downright frightening to know that he could have such evil ideas. Maybe he was wrong, but it could happen. Could he send someone to Lawrence to warn them? It was only a few hours ride. Yes, it was his duty to warn the leaders in Lawrence. He would send two riders to tell the local militia commander at Lawrence that they were possibly in danger. As for the wagon train and the officers and families, he would now need to have a plan to provide for their safety.

The problem for James Jewell was that even though he had divined the probable eminent danger, he didn't have a timeline and he didn't know the direction of attack which the bushwhackers would take. He needed a little more information. In the meantime, he knew that his train was moving into a dangerous area between the Missouri border and Lawrence. He decided to bivouac for a couple of days around the area of Gardner or Olathe. He chose the small town of Gardner believing that it was a little less likely to be on the approach or escape routes of retreating raiders leaving Lawrence. If he could move quickly to Gardner, he could quickly set up at least a minimal defensive position for his wagons in the town. He thought it more likely that the guerilla forces moving across the border would stay north of this area, following the Kaw River Valley, which provided more cover and concealment. He felt that his train would be less vulnerable here than further north.

The convoy moved into Gardner later that afternoon, secured a perimeter within the few buildings, informed the local constable and shop keepers of the perceived threat, and waited for his riders to return from Lawrence. The two riders arrived later in the evening, having alerted the militia in Lawrence of the possible threat. They reported that they were not taken seriously, and Captain Jewell was visibly distressed. Maybe he was wrong, possibly too jumpy about his hunches. Still, he decided to stay put in Gardner for a couple of days. The Colonels traveling with the train were irritated with the delay, but decided it was not worth risking the safety of their families. It was the 19th of August, and their riverboat transportation from Westport to St. Louis was not due for another four days. The next morning, after a quiet night at Gardner, there was only light traffic on the trail. The westbound mail and a dozen escort troopers headed for New Mexico stopped for a late breakfast with Jewell's group. They reported no sightings of large groups of horsemen on their trip from Fort Leavenworth. The ferry at Bonner Springs was operating normally the afternoon before, and they had camped there overnight, following a noon departure from the fort. The small group needed to reach Council Grove by the next evening and departed soon after the meal. Jewell decided to sit tight for a couple of days keeping a couple of scout teams between Gardner and Olathe to provide early warning if any of Quantrill's men decided to move back into Missouri by taking a more southern route than expected. A watch of one third of the escort troops was posted every eight hours through the night, but no intruders were seen except for the coming and going of the scout teams. The next day was quiet with little traffic moving up or down the trail, except for local farmers going to market in Olathe. Then, at just about dusk that evening of August 20th, a local villager returning from a supply trip to Westport Landing was brought into the captain's tent by a sentry on the north end of town. He reported that he had heard of sightings of groups of ten to twenty armed riders moving west along the Kaw north of the Shawnee Mission area. There were no reports of looting or harm to any local residents in the area. This was enough to convince Jewell that he was right about an impending raid on Lawrence itself. Quantrill was using the same old tactic of moving his men in small groups, under cover of darkness, along the partially concealed river route toward a probable early morning rendezvous and attack of Lawrence. Captain Jewell was still seething over the fact that his riders the day before had been laughed at and ignored, and he feared for the worst.

The military train at Gardner was informed of the news, and Captain Jewell's decision to remain in place. They wouldn't move until the outcome of the Lawrence raid was known, and where Quantrill's men would be heading afterward. If Jewell was right about the likely guerrilla retreat route, this was the safest place to stay. All the able-bodied men and officers were ordered to be armed and defend the wagons against any incursions by retreating Confederate raiders, as he called them. The women and children, though few, were taken to a small brick jailhouse in town and protected by armed soldiers.

Meanwhile, soon after dawn, nearly 400 of Quantrill's men rode into Lawrence to begin a daylong assault, marked by total mayhem, as the sleeping town was systematically set ablaze following massive looting and ransacking of homes and stores and the Eldridge Hotel. These buildings were set on fire, and scores of people, including civilians were gunned down in the streets. Many freed black residents were intentionally targeted. The rebels then started looking for the Free-state leaders such as Governor Charles Robinson and Senator James Lane, who were lucky to escape with their lives. Dozens of people escaped into cellars, cornfields, and nearby ravines, or across the Kaw to the north side of the river. By the end of the day, the raiders had killed nearly two hundred people, about 20 percent of the male population, and caused nearly two million dollars in damage. By nightfall, the guerrillas were gone, moving back to western Missouri by roughly the same pathways.

The military convoy holed up in Gardner was spared any involvement with Quantrill's men. As the news of the massacre at Lawrence began to reach them, the travelers were not so much shocked, but reminded of the long and bloody conflict along the Kansas and Missouri border, and the costs of this senseless and devastating war between the states. This tragedy would quickly lead to a general order relocating many western Missouri residents from several counties to flush out guerrillas forces and prevent the local populace from hiding and resupplying them. The same Senator James Lane who barely escaped death at Lawrence had been the commander of the "Jayhawkers," a militia regiment which had, only a couple of

202

years earlier, carried out murderous raids on Confederate sympathizers and their homes farms and farms in western Missouri. After hearing the news of the massacre, both veterans and family members renewed their prayers that this horrible war would soon be over. All wars, especially civil ones, usually end badly for both soldiers and innocent bystanders. The grapes of wrath would not be trampled out for another two years.

XXX. Government Freighter

Reaching Westport Landing two days after the Lawrence Massacre, Captain Jewell delivered the senior officers and their families to the steamboat docks, where they boarded a river steamer bound for Jefferson Barracks in St. Louis. The rest of the train, including contract drivers like Jacob, continued on to Fort Leavenworth, moving west to the military road rather than risk encountering any of Quantrill's men who might be straggling eastward around the Missouri River Road. Jacob had managed, during the brief stop at Westport, to deliver a few trade goods, mostly silver jewelry and a couple of buffalo hides from Mr. Simcock to a local dealer. Jacob was paid in cash and a few gold coins, which he stuffed into his saddle bags. On the way to Leavenworth a few suspicious riders were spotted, but no engagement ensued. These border ruffians had apparently had enough of looting and killing in the last few days, and most were interested only in returning to their homes east of Kansas. Their lairs were not going to provide sanctuary much longer. In fact, the Union Commander in the region issued a special order on the 25th of August, relocating many farmers and their families in four western Missouri counties to Union Army controlled areas around Kansas City. This was meant to inhibit the guerrilla forces from using the Confederate sympathizers living along the Kansas border as refuge and resupply points for their forays into Kansas. More Union supporting militia units were also organized for defense against future attacks from the Missouri side.

Jacob was glad to see Leavenworth again. He had made the trip from New Mexico many times over the years as a soldier, but now he had the opportunity to use that experience to help make a better living for his family. Instead of his private's pay of $10 a month, he would be able to contract for freight hauling of up to $50 or more per wagon load of military supplies to various posts, camps, and stations along the Santa Fe Trail. Even though the schedule for this work was occasional and seasonal it sure beat Army pay. With his other job in Council Grove at the blacksmith works, he felt confident that he would be able to provide a decent living and a more normal life for his beloved Charlotte and his three boys.

After picking up his rig, a medium sized military field wagon from the stables at Leavenworth, with a team of six mules, he hitched his personal mount to the wagon, and drove the wagon over to the quartermaster supply point. It wasn't a big Conestoga, able to carry more than 3,000 pounds of cargo, but it could take nearly a ton of cargo. His load included half a ton of ammunition and armorers' supplies, and nearly half a ton of canned food and medical supplies. His was one of four similar rigs bound for Fort Larned, out of more than twenty wagons headed to points west and eventually to Fort Union. Jacob was thankful that he didn't have to make the whole distance to New Mexico on this trip. He hoped to make the trip to Fort Larned and be headed back to Council Grove within two weeks. The Lawrence raid had delayed the overall trip by four days, but he hoped to be home by mid-October. He was counting on the train making an overnight stop in Council Grove on the way west.

Two companies of cavalry from Fort Leavenworth made the trip west with this supply train. One was primarily an escort cadre, with the troop eventually headed for Fort Union to reinforce the garrison and depot in Northern New Mexico. The second troop left the train south of Olathe, taking the old military road toward Fort Scott, Kansas. They were headed south to reinforce the southeastern Kansas forts around Baxter Springs. Following the Lawrence Massacre, Union spies began to hear rumors of imminent large-scale raids of Confederate forces into Missouri. Things had not been going well for the South along the Mississippi River and throughout Arkansas and Tennessee during 1963. Gettysburg had been a severe blow to southern confidence. The plan involving action along the

Mississippi River was not to open up another theater in the war, but perhaps to bring Missouri more fully into the Confederacy. That was at least a ploy to pull political support away from the Union. Only a month later, a great raid would be conducted by Colonel (later Brig. Gen.) Joseph Shelby and nearly one thousand cavalry from northwestern Arkansas up into western Missouri as far as the town of Marshall, east of Kansas City. Stopped by superior Unions forces at that point, they eventually retreated to Carthage, Missouri, where the secessionists maintained a foothold in the state. They were pursued and eventually returned to Arkansas after a few skirmishes. Participating in these operations was none other than William Quantrill's force of four hundred bushwhackers, who attacked Fort Blair, at Baxter Springs, Kansas, capturing and executing more than one hundred freed black Union soldiers. The raiders were driven off by reinforcements, but Fort Blair was later abandoned and burned to the ground.

Jacob heard this sickening news a month later on his return trip from Fort Larned to Council Grove. After seeing his family for only one day at the end of September, the supply train left again for New Mexico. The early fall weather had been favorable and there had been no delays or hostile Indian encounters during the trip to Fort Larned or on the return. He had left his military cargo at the quartermaster warehouse, drawn his contract teamster wage and spent the evening with a good meal and a hot bath. The drivers were allowed to sleep in the enlisted barracks as the garrison was currently only at half strength. After breakfast the next morning, he saddled his horse, and followed the eastbound mail wagon with a ten-man cavalry escort. The trip would take only four days, Jacob figured, barring any weather delays or hostile encounters. There were in fact no delays, except for a broken wheel on the mail wagon, which Jacob helped repair. This took about five or six hours, requiring replacing spline and hub parts, which fortunately were carried as spares by the mail driver. The fourth night, the group stayed at Diamond Springs, as it was a moonless night. A freighter spending the night there gave Jacob the sad news about the murder of the Union prisoners at Baxter Springs. Jacob was so disgusted and angry over this atrocity, that he considered signing up for active duty again. Only the reality of his family and their needs stopped him from following through. The wagon and escort reached Council Grove about ten o'clock the next day. Jacob bid his fellow travelers good-bye and hurried over to the

Hays House to join his family. Charlotte and boys came running to the front entrance when Mr. Simcock yelled out that Jacob was home. Hugs and cheers were given all around, and the boys hung from his neck, nearly pulling him to the floor. After he hugged and kissed Charlotte for about five minutes, Jacob took his horse to the back of the building, unsaddled and combed her, made sure that water and hay were nearby and left her in the small corral in the alley. Carrying his saddle bags, he came in through the kitchen door, and found Mr. Simcock at a table in the restaurant having a cup of coffee. Simcock had poured a cup for Jacob, and they sat down to recount Jacob's experiences of the past month. Jacob opened the flaps of his saddle bag and pulled out the cash from the sale of the trade goods. He explained that there hadn't been enough time to shop for any luxury items to bring back from Westport, under the stress of the situation. Simcock nodded that it was alright, and there would be many other opportunities. He was just happy that Jacob was safe and hoped he would be able to stay home for a while. Jacob said that he was ready for that. He had work to do at the blacksmith shop, and he needed to help finish the renovation of the new apartment for his family. He also paid the next two months' rent out of his earnings from the trip. It was also nice to have a little extra money to help finish up the renovations.

During the next six weeks, Jacob would try to finish the family living and dining area downstairs, which he managed to complete by the end of November, on his days off from Strieby's blacksmith shop. He then started in on the kitchen, finding a second-hand wood-fired cook stove for only ten dollars from the Gilkey Hotel across the street, left over after the recent renovation of the hotel, originally built in 1856. Jacob also built in some cabinets and a dry sink and rolling board for Charlotte's baking needs. Well water was supplied from the pump behind the Hays House, which Mr. Simcock was happy to share with the Stengers. Even though the family dwelling was still a work in progress, other matters claimed some of Jacob's time in late 1863. He spent at least one or two days a week helping Mr. Simcock in the store, which was primarily now a general store and grocery store. His sons would continue to work there for years to come. Jacob's boys were very important to him, and he tried to spend whatever time he had with them. He and Charlotte read Scripture to them, and the family attended church services as much as possible, finally finding a permanent family place of worship at the Congregational Church. Jacob and Charlotte had been well educated and were literate, and they did a fair amount of home schooling until the boys were able to attend regular classes at a community center known as the "Brown Jug." A formal graded school would not be established until 1868.

In 1863, the people of Morris County were still fearful of Missouri raiders and bushwhackers after the attack at Diamond Springs, and especially after the Lawrence Massacre. A large number of homesteaders, originally from Missouri, were suspected by many of the Free-Staters of having southern sympathies. Morris county, however, had supplied a large percentage of military age men for Union service. Many of those, who had already returned from service by 1863, formed a company of volunteer home guards known as the Morris County Rangers. Four more units were formed, with Jacob serving as a First Lieutenant of the Council Grove Guards. There were no more major raids after this time, but a large Cheyenne raid would come a few years later. The local militias were maintained into the 1870s.

Jacob had an interesting but short friendship shortly after returning to Council Grove in the spring of 1863, with an itinerant Italian priest, Matteo Boccalini. He had reportedly been driven out of Italy after being prevented from becoming a Papal secretary. Jesuit enemies accused him of an illicit love affair. He had to leave and ended up wandering throughout Spain and then South and North America, becoming a reclusive faith healer. Jacob heard of this fellow living up in a partially natural cave built up with stones from an adjacent quarry. The "Hermit's Cave" was located on the side of Belfry Hill near the town quarry. Jacob went to visit him several times, and due to his knowledge of Latin, Spanish, and French, was able to communicate with him fairly well. Unfortunately, the wandering priest left in May of that year, traveling to New Mexico, where he died many years later, apparently at the hands of an assassin. Unfortunately, the murder was never solved.

After a two-week trip to Westport for blacksmith resupply in December, with no border violence this time, Jacob was home for Christmas week for the first time in many years. It was a joyous time, and many presents for the three boys were graciously provided by Mr. Simcock. Charlotte sent Jacob and the boys out to find a suitable tree. Since pines were very scarce in this part of the Great Plains, Jacob had to settle for a well-shaped juniper, which he trimmed into the shape of a pine or fir tree. This was disappointing to Charlotte who, even in New Mexico, had found trees similar to the familiar Tannenbaum, the pine or fir trees of her native land. She made the best of it, making candies and cookies to hang on its branches. Several candles in wax catcher holders were placed on the tree for the brief lighting ceremony on Christmas Eve. She made a star from a piece of yellow cardboard for the top. Apples and nuts, a few small wooden toys, and the gifts from Mr. Simcock were wrapped and placed under the tree, along with a small wooden manger scene and a nutcracker she had carried from Germany and kept all these years in a small trunk. At midnight, the family walked to the Congregational Church for the candlelight service. The few German families led the other attending families in singing "Silent Night" (Stille Nacht), both in German and English. Charlotte and Jacob were very happy that night, and very thankful for their family and their new home in Kansas.

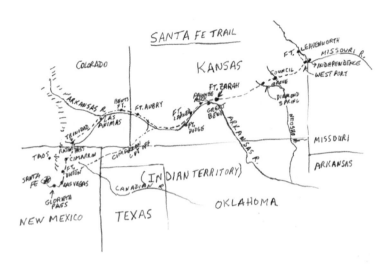

Chapter XXXI. Working the Trail

    The next two years were a very busy time for Jacob and his family. Jacob worked most of his days at the blacksmith shop down the street, when he wasn't on the road to and from Leavenworth and Westport Landing, which people were now calling Kansas City. He made one or more trips for supplies every month, usually timed when military escorts were available. Even though there were no more major raids deep into Kansas, sporadic incidents and a few large-scale cavalry pursuits of confederate and guerrilla forces continued into late 1864 and early 1865, with the threat being greatly diminished after the killing of guerrilla leaders like "Bloody Bill" Anderson in October of 1864, and the pursuit and ambush of William Quantrill in May of 1865.

    Jacob continued to make the "Kansas City" trips with the escorted mail and coach traffic. Mr. Sam Johnson, a old friend of Mr. Simcock became one of his favorite traders in Westport. Johnson had connections with other western artifact collectors and dealers from St. Louis to Cincinnati, and in Pittsburgh. People in the Midwest and East were becoming more interested in possessing artifacts from the West, as tales of western lore became more and more widely read. The most desirable goods ranged from buffalo hides and other animal skins and taxidermy items. Increasingly, there was more demand for Indian artifacts, especially Navajo rugs, pottery, and jewelry. Jacob developed quite a busy side business, helped a great deal by his old sutler friend in New Mexico, Mr. Moore. The extra money was always welcome.

As the war in the East wound down in late 1864, the Union Army began to pay more attention to operations in the Southwest. In New Mexico, Brig. Gen. Carleton was continuing to bring the Navajo and Apache tribes under control, relentlessly pursuing them until they surrendered in large numbers at Fort Defiance in Arizona, and at Fort Wingate and Fort Stanton in New Mexico. He utilized Jacob's former regiment, the 1st New Mexico Volunteers, under the command of Colonel Kit Carson, to force more than 8,000 native Indians, by the summer of 1864, into the newly completed Fort Sumner in east central New Mexico, in the area known as the Bosque Redondo. This worked for a while, breaking their resistance, but by 1868 the experiment was deemed a failure, and abandoned. Gen. Carleton, however, believed that he needed this expedient solution in order to stabilize the situation in New Mexico and Arizona. The far greater threat to the Southwest was, in his opinion, the plains Indians, the Comanche, Kiowa, and their allies operating in the panhandle areas of Texas, northeastern New Mexico, and western (future) Oklahoma. These tribes were a constant threat to settlers in the area and those moving west, especially on the Santa Fe Trail. Carleton was required to provide cavalry escort service on the western half of the trail.

During the summer and fall of 1864, there had been multiple attacks against wagon trains on both the Cimarron and Mountain branches of the trail in southwest Kansas and northeastern New Mexico. Carleton therefore decided to try to end the threat to the trail by sending Colonel Kit Carson and his regiment to engage and punish the Comanche and Kiowa tribes in their winter quarters in the Texas Panhandle. Jacob had been driving wagons for most of 1864 from the Missouri River bases to the Army outposts in western Kansas. He had only been as far as Santa Fe once, in June, with a large supply train to Fort Union and Fort Marcy.

The mountain route was used for that supply mission and most other traffic, due to increased attacks on the Cimarron route by the Kiowa and Comanche and one raid by Texas guerrillas, mostly outlaws, in April. After that time, wagon trains were escorted by mounted troops from Fort Larned in Kansas and handed off to troops from Fort Union. Eastbound trains from New Mexico were handed off near the Arkansas River to troops from Fort Larned. Attacks and raids by

Indians and outlaws still happened, but with less frequency and fewer losses. It was not until the Kiowa and Comanche tribes moved into

Raton Pass

winter quarters in the Texas panhandle that Brig. Gen. Carleton was able to launch an offensive against these Indians. With less pressure to protect the wagon trains, he was able to send Colonel Kit Carson and his New Mexico Volunteer regiment against the Indian villages located east of Fort Bascom on the Texas-New Mexico border. Carleton and Carson felt that winter was the best time to attack as large numbers would be concentrated in those camps.

Colonel Carson left Fort Bascom with a force of more than 400 soldiers, plus Ute and Apache scouts and volunteers, in mid-November. Two weeks later, near an abandoned trading post on the Canadian River, known as Adobe Walls, Carson's force encountered a large Kiowa village of about 150 lodges, routing the Kiowa warriors who fled and regrouped at Adobe Walls. Carson's troops pursued and forced the Indians out with bombardment from two mountain howitzers brought from Fort Union with the expedition. Carson's forces occupied the ruins for defensive cover as the Kiowa and Comanche attacked in force with thousands of warriors. Carson realized that he was surrounded and outnumbered ten to one and made a quick decision to break out with the help of his artillery pieces and was able to get back to his supply trains, destroying the Kiowa village in the process. The expedition was unable to secure sufficient supplies to continue the campaign and returned to Fort Union a few days later. While the campaign was not the crushing blow hoped for by the command, it did help reduce the number intensity of the raids on the Santa Fe Trail for several months. The military settled on regularly scheduled heavy escorts through the danger zones of the Cimarron passage, and, to a lesser extent, on the mountain routes.

Jacob heard the news about his old commander, Colonel Kit Carson and his campaign against the Kiowa and Comanche, a week or so after delivering a load of food and ammunition to Fort Larned. He was proud of the man he had so admired and trusted during his service in New Mexico. He was especially happy that his youngest son had been named after such a valiant soldier. Jacob was scheduled to drive a freight wagon from Westport to Fort Union, in February 1865, as part of a major Army resupply effort to the Department of New Mexico. The war in the East was dramatically winding down at this point, and the War Department was able to divert major resources to the West for the first time in three years. Fifty wagon loads of supplies were scheduled for delivery to the Depot at Fort Union, and since more regular Army troops were now available for frontier service, several hundred mounted troops would be needed to escort large trains to New Mexico to relieve or reinforce the volunteers struggling to control the threat from the plains Indians who were now resurgent, especially on the Cimarron branch of the Santa Fe Trail. Winter travel on the Mountain branch would be more hazardous until late spring or early summer. Large numbers of escort troops were necessary to adequately protect the supply trains. Jacob was greatly reassured by this news. However, his attention was focused on home, where he would spend the holidays with his family in Council Grove for the second year in a row. What else could he ask for? He felt very blessed indeed. The future looked bright as Jacob and many others in his new hometown anticipated an increase in westbound traffic after the war. He could foresee a great surge of pioneers seeking new opportunities in the western prairies, mountains, and even as far as the Pacific. The Homestead Act of 1862 helped enable the fulfillment of the "American Dream," and "Manifest Destiny," offering a chance to own 160 acres to those who built a house and farmed the land.

This idea of individual opportunity and equality was to become a major force driving the development of the western half of the nation. It was delayed in its implementation because of the difficulty of the journey and relatively harsh living conditions and more difficult agricultural challenge. In addition, the railroad interests had bought up most of the easily accessible land. Former slave-owning southern landowners feared loss of their workforce, and government assistance to the poor was practically non-existent. By the end of the Civil War however, the westward expansion was fueled by the idea of free land leading to equal opportunity for homesteads, and ownership of land. The reforms of the Railroad Act began accelerating access to markets and goods for the settlers. The rapid population growth of the eastern states added to the pressure for westward expansion. As exciting as this period of time became for the nation, it came at tremendous cost for the original inhabitants of the land. Native Americans would lose nearly all the land and most of the cultural heritage they had enjoyed for thousands of years. The plains Indian tribes, whose nomadic existence was linked to the seasonal movements of the vast buffalo herds, would see that lifestyle virtually disappear with the coming of the iron horse, the buffalo hunters, and the homesteaders. Even though the railroads would quickly overtake the wagon freighting business, many of the old freight haulers were able to survive by leading large groups of settlers westward into the prairies and beyond. Jacob and many other freight haulers would take advantage of their past trail experience and transition to guiding wagon trains of homesteaders to western Kansas and eastern Colorado.

The railroads threatened to greatly diminish the business of the freighters, and this was widely recognized by the teamsters by September of 1865, when the Missouri Pacific Railroad reached Kansas City. The railhead moved westward in leaps and bounds, pushing the departure point for wagon freight to Junction City by November of 1866. Various competing railroad companies would keep pushing the rails westward, with the Santa Fe railroad reaching Dodge City by September of 1872, and the Colorado border by Christmas of that year. The competition was fierce, and progress made in fits and starts with several bankruptcies and mergers and acquisitions barely slowing the race west. Denver had been reached two years earlier by the Kansas Pacific Railroad, just a year after the Transcontinental Railroad was completed, linking the nation further north. It would be another decade until the final stretches of the rails would link Santa Fe to that network. In the meantime, the wagon freighters hauling from the western terminus of the railroads would still have plenty to carry to Santa Fe until 1880 when the rails finally reached that storied city.

Jacob and his fellow teamsters had to become more flexible. The last large freight wagon caravan left Kansas City in late 1866. The freight contracting would move to from one terminus to another as the rails grew westward, starting or expanding towns like Junction City, Salina, Hutchison, Great Bend, Dodge City, Kit Carson, and eventually reaching Pueblo, Colorado, in 1876. The wagon freighters were able to adapt to the shorter haul contracts as long as the railroads stayed east of the Sangre de Christo mountains of southern Colorado and northern New Mexico. When the demand for freight hauling was periodically slow, the teamsters were able to work as guides or wagon train masters helping to lead the homesteaders to new settlements in western Kansas and the eastern Colorado plains, especially in the Arkansas River Valley. Jacob was able, in the decade following the war, to lead several wagon trains of settlers and homesteaders to these areas. He would often lead trains to Pueblo, the newly founded Colorado Springs, Denver, and occasionally to the mining camps of Cripple Creek, and Central City. His true interests and experience were of course, further south, in New Mexico. Jacob made numerous trips in the late 1860s and early 1870s, guiding both freight and migrant trains over Raton Pass to the junction with the Cimarron branch of the trail. During the years before 1875, the Cimarron passage was still risky. Not until the final surrender of the Comanche nation under Quanah Parker, would the Texas panhandle and northeastern New Mexico be considered safe for civilian traffic. Jacob made numerous trips over Raton Pass, over the toll road built by his old friend, "Uncle Dick" Wooten, a former mountain man and trapper. Wooten had recognized the value of Raton Pass and purchased the right of way in 1866, a year after the railroads reached Kansas City. Uncle Dick had hired a tribe of Ute Indians to build a much better road, following the old wagon trail blazed by William Becknell a half century earlier. Wooten made a small fortune charging tolls for passage over that road in the next decade. As the railroads inched further south, Wooten sold the rights to the Raton Pass roadbed to the Santa Fe railroad. The tracks reached Las Vegas, New Mexico, by 1879, and were completed to Santa Fe the following year.

Chapter XXXII. Legacy

     The Santa Fe Trail was finished as a major wagon road. Jacob
had done well in his chosen occupation, and despite many long
absences away from Council Grove and his family, the road always
ended up at home. He was at home enough to help properly raise his
boys, so that they became strong responsible young men. Will spent a
good deal of time on the trail with his father, especially in the
summers when he was not in school. For Will, formal education
ended after grammar school. He was nearly 15 years old at the time.
The younger boys attended the graded school that opened in 1872 and
finished the higher grades, although short of a high school diploma.
The first four-year high school diplomas would not be granted for
another thirty years. The younger two boys were known at the time as
practical jokers and cut-ups, but were well respected in the
community. Charlotte had helped raise her boys to be kind and
generous. She made sure that they were hard working and ingrained
with strong Christian principals and a good knowledge of the Bible.
The Stengers remained active members of the Congregational Church.
They had joined that denomination while it was still meeting in the
"Brown Jug" community center. Later, a formal church was built in
1872. Will worked with his father, including making many trips with
the wagon trains. By age 18, however, Will became restless, and

decided to strike out on his own. He moved to central Texas and eventually lost contact with his family. Jim and Kit had worked with their mother, Charlotte, at the Hays House. They were later mostly in the grocery and general store business, and their home was still behind the store for several years. After many years of cooking at the restaurant, Charlotte took over the management of the store in 1871. Seth Hays had returned from Colorado in late 1865, and in January of 1866, took over his old restaurant and hotel. Mr. Simcock moved his business across the street. In 1871, Hays built a large stone barn east of the Neosho, which he used to house his large livestock holdings. Charlotte took over the day-to-day operations of the grocery and general store and the hotel. Her younger two boys worked with her, with Jim eventually running the business. He later managed and owned the business for many years. Seth Hays died in 1873 and was buried in Greenwood Cemetery, on the west edge of town, as an honored founder of Council Grove.

When he wasn't on the trail, Jacob worked part time at the Strieby blacksmith shop. He helped keep the grocery store stocked and in good repair, and even tried his hand at cooking at the Hays House. Jacob helped maintain the buildings as well as constantly making improvements to the adjacent dwelling of the Stenger family. Jacob and Charlotte had always intended to build a new house away from the main business street, but they eventually decided it was a lot more convenient to stay where they were, next to the grocery. Charlotte had found her niche serving customers and was loved and trusted by the townspeople. The boys would eventually move into their own houses several blocks away, after they married and started their own families. Will had left for Texas by 1870 and never returned. Jim stayed with the grocery business for the rest of his working life. Christian (Kit), the youngest, finally married at age 26, shortly after Jacob's passing in 1885. Kit built a house nearby on Columbia Street for his bride, the beautiful Sarah Snodgrass, who had recently moved to Kansas from Ohio. Kit had become an apprentice in the jewelry and optometry business, spending more than forty years in partnership with George Methe, his mentor and lifelong friend.

After the Atchison, Topeka, and Santa Fe Railroad finally reached Santa Fe in 1880, Jacob decided that he had worked as a wagon freighter long enough, was 55 years old, and it was time for him to stay home. He had made a decent living over the past 15 years, but the months and years on the trail had taken their toll. He was ready to enjoy the rest of his life with his beloved Charlotte, and the two sons who had stayed in Council Grove. He was beginning to have a little more trouble with his old knee injury incurred during the big horse and cattle drive to Utah. He was also having occasional shortness of breath from residual lung problems subsequent to the same fall from his horse. He was ready for a more sedentary life and could now be with his wonderful wife without weeks and months of separation. Jacob was wise enough to have saved about ten percent of his income over the past ten years or so. He had a couple of thousand dollars in gold coins stashed away for Charlotte. Even though he wanted nothing to do with the Army, Jacob had been encouraged by an old Army friend to apply for a disability pension, for injuries resulting from his military service. He was eventually successful, although receiving his disability payment of four dollars per month took more than two years and required an act of Congress. At least Charlotte would have something to show for the years of sacrifice, which she would enjoy until the end of the century. In any event, he felt a little better about being appreciated for his service, if only a token compensation.

The next few years were too short. Jacob enjoyed his retirement, working at the blacksmith shop and various odd jobs. Seth Hays had specified that he and Charlotte could stay in their present living quarters as long as they wanted. Charlotte had access to all the food they might need at wholesale prices. The Stengers were well respected in town, especially by the longtime residents. Charlotte was active in church affairs, and Jacob was a member of a few civic organizations, including The Oddfellows, and veterans' groups. He was affectionately known to the townspeople as Captain Stenger.

The town was still young and enjoying slow steady growth. In 1880, the population was just over a thousand people. Although the town had survived a couple incidents with Indian raiders, and a prairie fire or two, life was generally peaceful. Council Grove was a wonderful place to retire and reflect on life, and watch your children and grandchildren grow up. Jacob passed on in 1885, from a long illness complicated by problems with old injuries dating back to his military service. Charlotte would live to be 75 years old, able to enjoy several grandchildren from her two youngest boys. Council Grove had been their promised land, this quintessential small town in the heartland of rural mid America. The Stengers had truly found their place of solitude in this young nation, tested by the hardships of

218

westward expansion and war. Council Grove on the Santa Fe Trail would continue to serve as a point of departure for those reaching out to the edges of the frontier and a better life.

Acknowledgements

Internet Sources:
SantaFeTrailResearchSite.com
GenuineKansas.com
Fold3.com
U-S-history.com (New Mexico)
Wikipedia.com (Variety of Sites)
Civilwaronthewesternborder.org

Books:
New Mexico Territory During the Civil War: Inspection Reports of
Wallen and Evans, 1862-63. Univ. of New Mexico Press, 2008.
The Story of Council Grove on the Santa Fe Trail, by Lalla M.
Brigham. New York Public Library, 1921.

Stenger Family Diary

Made in the USA
Las Vegas, NV
18 August 2021

28420914R00125